THE WRITER'S REFERENCE GUIDE TO SPANISH

THE WRITER'S REFERENCE GUIDE TO SPANISH

DAVID WILLIAM FOSTER
DANIEL ALTAMIRANDA
CARMEN DE URIOSTE

UNIVERSITY OF TEXAS PRESS
Austin

First edition, 1999

Requests for permission to reproduce material from this work
should be sent to Permissions, University of Texas Press,
Box 7819, Austin, TX 78713-7819.

∞ The paper used in this book meets the minimum requirements
of ANSI/NISO Z39.48-1992 (R1997) (Permanence of Paper).

LIBRARY OF CONGRESS CATALOGING-IN-PUBLICATION DATA

Foster, David William.
   The writer's reference guide to Spanish / David William Foster,
Daniel Altamiranda, Carmen de Urioste. — 1st ed.
     p. cm.
   Includes bibliographical references (p.) and index.
   ISBN 0-292-72511-6 (alk. paper)
   ISBN 0-292-72512-4 (pbk. : alk. paper)
   1. Spanish language—Style Handbooks, manuals, etc. 2. Span-
ish language—Usage Handbooks, manuals, etc. I. Altamiranda,
Daniel. II. Urioste-Azcorra, Carmen. III. Title.
  PC4410 .F58 1999
  808'.027—dc21
                           99-6172

CONTENTS

PREFACE

This volume was prepared in order to meet the demand for a guide, in English, for writers and editors working in the Spanish language. Although many fine grammars and reference works exist for the study and use of Spanish, none addresses the sorts of issues typically associated with a style manual designed for preparing manuscripts and other text for publication. The style manuals that do exist, such as those of the Modern Language Association and the University of Chicago, attempt to address language-specific issues. However, they are sketchy on some crucial points and in error—at least in terms of prevalent usage—on others. To be sure, Spanish, as an international language, presents a diversity of norms. Not only does it have a monolingual base in approximately twenty countries, but it is extensively used in the United States and in other English-speaking countries. Often usage in the latter cases suffers an interference from English that, rather than maintaining a uniformity of style imposed by English, may result in contradictory and inconsistent practices.

The goal of this manual, then, is to suggest uniformities in such humdrum details as spelling and capitalization, as well as to address important categories of grammatical and stylistic usage where it might be helpful for users to have an international norm or, in some cases, reference to a diversity of norms. Our goal is not to impose any particular brand of Spanish; rather, it is to appeal to the need for consistency of usage and to suggest some practices that may serve to achieve it.

THE WRITER'S REFERENCE GUIDE TO SPANISH

CHAPTER 1

PUNCTUATION

In general, Spanish punctuation follows the same basic principles as English writing to indicate the inflections and pauses of learned talking and to assure the conceptual and organizational clarity of discourse. However, written traditions in the two languages differ in some important details:

1. The comma is used to separate several analogous elements in a series (*lunes, miércoles, viernes*). When the connective words *y, ni,* and *o* are used in a sentence, the Spanish tradition avoids the comma in front of the conjunction (*lunes, miércoles y viernes; ni yo ni tú; Hispanoamérica, Latinoamérica o Iberoamérica*).

2. Suspension marks are always three points, with no spaces between them, even at the end of the paragraph. When used to indicate ellipsis, they may be enclosed by brackets.

Aclaramos que por teatro brechtiano, entendemos una modalidad fundamentalmente didáctica, mediante la cual la obra pretende ilustrar ante y para el público, una circunstancia, un contexto, una crisis sociocultural o política [...] Así, la obra no pretende crear un mundo simbólico, sino que se propone ilustrar ese mundo...[1]

3. Different typographical marks (commas, dashes, parentheses) are used to separate interpolated or parenthetical words and phrases. In general, it is accepted that there is a degree of growing emphasis among them, the comma being the weakest and the parentheses the strongest marks. The dash or *raya* (—) is far more common in Spanish where English would put parentheses.

---

[1] David William Foster, *Estudios sobre teatro mexicano contemporáneo: semiología de la competencia teatral* (New York: Peter Lang, 1984) 71.

Pero en ello, se filtra subrepticiamente un sentido del devenir temporal que subvierte la tesis central que sostiene la novela, ya que la
noción misma de primavera forma parte de una estructura temporal
cíclica—la del tiempo cosmogónico—que se opone al ordenamiento
unilineal de la historia-ciencia y, claro está, de las versiones teleológi-
cas de la historia.[2]

4. In Spanish, the dash is also used to introduce dialogue as direct
speech.

—Carmen . . .
—Qué.
—Pará. ¿A dónde vamos?
—A la despensita.
—Pará un cacho. Dame unos mangos que yo me las pico.[3]

5. The inverted marks (" "), sometimes represented by *comillas es-
pañolas* (« »), enclose quoted passages. The closing mark immediately
follows the last word quoted:

En este contexto, una de las temáticas más abordadas fue el papel que
la ciencia y la tecnología desempeñaban en el desarrollo económico-
social. Se fue conformando así el campo de conocimiento que se ha
dado en llamar "ciencia, tecnología y sociedad."[4]

Note in this example the placement of the footnote reference. Examples can be found of note references preceding ending punctuation, but we recommend the opposite, and more common, practice, as
shown above.

6. Inverted exclamation and question marks (¡/¿) are to be placed at
the beginning of the exclamation or question, and regular ones (!/?) at
the end.

. . . el léxico indigenista de Ercilla no excede de las dos docenas de palabras. ¿Cómo se explica esto tratándose de una obra histórica extensa
inspirada por la guerra contra los araucanos, con referencias a la vida

---

[2] Daniel Altamiranda, "La inscripción en la historia: *La consagración de la primavera* de Alejo Carpentier," *Historia, ficción y metaficción en la novela latinoamericana contemporánea,* ed. Mignon Domínguez (Buenos Aires: Corregidor,
1996) 31.
[3] Héctor Lastra, *Fredi* (Buenos Aires: Sudamericana, 1996) 104.
[4] Hernán Thomas, *Surdesarrollo: Producción de tecnología en países subdesa-
rrollados* (Buenos Aires: Centro Editor de América Latina, 1995) 7.

indígena en los más variados aspectos y además escrita en parte en América, donde el autor residió por siete años y la tradición de utilizar indigenismos en la lengua hablada y escrita era vigorosa?[5]

---

[5] Marcos A. Morínigo, "Los indigenismos de *La Araucana*," *Boletín de humanidades* (Buenos Aires) 1.1 (1972): 52.

CHAPTER 2

SPELLING AND WORD DIVISION

SPELLING RULES AND VARIATIONS

The Spanish language is characterized by an efficient orthographic system that, with few ambiguities and internal contradictions, captures transparently the phonology of the language. Spanish phonology is little affected by regional variation: that is, regional variation is also efficiently represented by the orthography of the language. Indeed, with the exception of homophony in most dialects between the letters *z, s,* and *c* before *e* and *i,* between *b* and *v,* and between *y* and *ll,* there are no other especially remarkable observations to be made.

Moreover, again with only slight variation, spelling conventions between dialects are fairly uniform. Variations of greatest significance involve *mexicano* (universally preferred in Latin America) versus *mejicano* (preferred in Spain, despite the preference by Mexicans for the former); *inscripto* (preferred in Argentina; also affected are all other similar past participles except *escrito*) versus *inscrito* (preferred in general); and *sólo,* in the sense of *solamente* (almost universally used) versus *solo,* also in the sense of *solamente* (as prescribed by the Real Academia Española but used only in a limited fashion, perhaps to avoid giving the impression that the writer does not know very well the difference between *sólo = solamente* and *solo = único,* this *solo* never taking a written accent).

The sort of variation presented by *torcer* versus the nominalization *torsión,* where one would expect **torción*[1] (with the attendant pronunciation difference in most nonsouthern dialects of Spain) is a rarity in Spanish, although there are some limited morphophonemic alternations in the language: *verdura* versus *verdulero, hierro* versus *ferro-, femenino* versus *feminista.* Important examples of spelling

---

[1] Asterisks signify substandard forms.

variation, for segmentals as well as supersegmentals, are given in the Dictionary of Spanish Grammatical and Lexical Doubts in the back matter of this volume.

Because of a history of fluctuating usage, many writers are unsure whether a written accent should be used with verb forms like the infinitive *oír* (it should), the past participle *oído* (it should), or the past participle *constituido* (it should not). In the case of the latter, in combinations of two high vowels (*i, u*—often called "weak" vowels), the second one is understood as stressed, making the written accent superfluous.

Confusion frequently occurs with respect to the letter *h*. Since this letter has no phonological value in Spanish, when it does occur in written use, it is, so to speak, as though not there. Therefore, in a word like *rehúsa*, the *h* does not serve to separate the vowels and, in order to indicate that the *u* receives the tonic stress, a written accent must be used.

Foreign words taken into the language usually preserve their original spelling (see section on word division, below), although there are some notable exceptions: *whisky, sóccer* (sometimes *soccer*), *básquetbol, fútbol*. One should not, however, be surprised to find these words also registered minus the written accent.

ACCENTS

The written accent in Spanish is used in a number of different ways:

1. All words ending in a vowel, *n*, or *s* are assumed to carry the tonic stress on the next-to-the-last syllable. That is, this syllable is pronounced with greater emphasis or loudness: *casa, examen, vives*. Note that combinations of unaccented *i* and *u* in combination with each other or with *a, e*, or *o* are counted as single syllables when determining use of written accent: *cuerda, viuda, tiene*.

2. All words ending in a consonant other than *n* or *s* are assumed to carry the tonic stress on the final syllable: *motor, cariz, sutil*.

3. When the tonic stress falls on any syllable contrary to these two principles, such a fact is indicated by a written accent: *fútil, habló, término*. Such a written accent can thus serve to indicate that *i* or *u* in combination with each other or with *a, e*, or *o* receives tonic stress: *confío, flúor, teníais*.

4. In a very few cases, (e.g., *rió, fió*), the written accent serves to indicate that the word is bisyllabic and that the tonic stress falls on the *ó*, by contrast to *dio*, in which the *io* combination is treated as a single syllable, per above.

5. Additionally, the written accent is used to distinguish between homographs, typically single-syllable ones. In the following pairs, the unaccented first example is a dependent part of speech (a preposition, a possessive pronoun), while the accepted second example is a main part of speech (a verb, an object pronoun): *de/dé, mi/mí, tu/tú*. In the pair *sólo/solo*, the pattern is reversed, the first example being an adverb and the second an adjective. The letter *h* often serves the same purpose, to distinguish between a preposition or a conjunction (first examples) and an interjection or a verb form (second examples): *a/ah* and *ha, e/eh* and *he*.

6. In foreign words, the written accent may be carried over from the host language, and it may or may not be interpreted as indicating tonic stress: *élite*, which is alternatively pronounced as *É-li-te, e-LI-te*, and *e-LIT*. The spelling *elite* is also found.

PREFIXES

Prefixes may be divided into two categories, separable and inseparable; which kind of prefix is involved may affect spelling conventions regarding the use of the hyphen. Separable prefixes are those that can stand alone or be joined to another word: *histórico/histórico-social*. Inseparable prefixes cannot stand alone (unless being cited in an example): *sociohistórico, prenupcial, antisocial*. It is necessary to use a hyphen to separate separable prefixes from the word to which they are affixed. Usage varies as to whether or not a hyphen should be used to separate inseparable prefixes from the words to which they are affixed: *anti-social* versus *antisocial*. Contemporary prevailing practice tends toward *not* using a hyphen in these cases, unless the host word is capitalized: *precolombino*, but *pre-Colón*.

WORD DIVISION

Spanish is basically a CV (consonant vowel) language, and syllabic division is almost strictly along phonetic lines, separating CV clusters:

pa-ra-do-ja	*sa-la-do*	*ma-du-ro*	*ca-mi-sa*

Two vowels are divided unless one of the vowels is a phonetically unaccented *i* or *u*. Accents on other vowels do not affect syllabication:

ve-o	*au-ge*	*con-ti-nú-a*	*re-gión*
ca-o-ba	*re-fu-gio*	*san-grí-a*	*ne-cio*

Contiguous vowels that are combinations of *a, e,* and *o* or combinations of these vowels and *i* and *u* that are phonetically accented, as reflected by a written accent, form separate syllables, although many users of the language prefer not to separate them, especially when short words are involved:

cre-er	*le-al*	*ba-úl*	*crí-o*	*re-ír*

Combinations of two vowels in which one is an unaccented *i* or *u,* including combinations of these two vowels, are not separated:

so-sie-go	*viu-da*	*guan-te*

Two consonants are divided. Note that the consonants *ch, ll,* and *rr* have traditionally been considered single letters and are, therefore, never divided. The Spanish Academy recently ruled that these were now to be considered not single but double letter combinations, at least for alphabetizing purposes, and thus they will no longer have their own sections in the dictionary. For purposes of syllabication and word division, though, *ch, ll,* and *rr* are still kept together. Double *c* and double *n* are, however, separated:

fan-tas-ma	*sal-va-jis-mo*	*he-chi-zo*	*an-dan-za*
lec-ción	*ve-llu-do*	*ca-rro*	*in-no-va-ción*

Two separate consonants standing between vowels are divided:

pac-tar	*puer-ta*	*bar-ba*	*pren-der*

The consonants *l* and *r* are never separated from a preceding consonant, except for *s:*

gran-de	*pre-coz*	*cu-brir*	*drás-ti-co*
co-pla	*ais-la-do*	*re-gla*	*bu-cle*
is-ra-e-li-ta			

Combinations of three and four consonants are divided following the rules above; *s* goes with the preceding syllable:

es-tro-pe-ar	*con-ver-tir*	*ex-tra-ño*
obs-tan-te	*cons-tan-te*	*es-drú-ju-la*
cons-tan-te-men-te	*ins-truc-tor*	*em-ble-má-ti-co*
trans-por-te		

Prepositional prefixes form separate syllables:

ab-ne-gar	*ex-pri-mir*	*des-pin-tar*	*con-ce-bir*

However, when the prefix comes before *s* followed by a consonant, the *s* is joined to the prefix:

abs-tra-er	*cons-ta-tar*	*ins-crip-ción*
pers-pec-ti-va	*ab-sor-ber*	*con-subs-tan-cial*
in-sin-ce-ri-dad	*per-sis-tir*	

When a syllable consists of a single vowel (e.g., *o-cupar*, *a-rre-o*), it customarily does not stand alone at the end or beginning of a line.

Forms like *nosotros* (morphologically *nos* + *otros*) appear as either *nos-otros* or as *no-so-tros* (*nos-o-tros* is definitely avoided), with the former being preferred.

Foreign words and names (or words and names incorporated into the language, in the sense that they appear in standard dictionaries of the language) are treated as best as possible, although not always elegantly, in conformance with the syllabication rules of words considered native to the language:

stan-ding	*li-ving*	*Wa-shing-ton*
Ja-net	*whis-ky*	*Ca-rring-ton*
Hur-ling-ham	*ca-me-ra-man*	

CHAPTER 3

GENDER AND NUMBER FORMS

GENDER

Spanish nouns are either masculine or feminine, except for some nouns of undecided gender. The gender of Spanish nouns is essentially arbitrary, although a number of "rules" can be given, as follows.

MASCULINE GENDER

Nouns ending in -o, -e, a consonant, or a stressed vowel are usually masculine:

el abuelo: grandfather
el almacén: warehouse
el amigo: male friend
el amor: love
el anfitrión: host
el bailarín: dancer
el calambre: cramp
el doctor: doctor
el equipaje: luggage
el perro: dog (male)
el refrán: proverb
el rubí: ruby

Masculine gender includes nouns referring to male human beings and animals:

el hombre: man
el león: lion
el padre: father

Names of countries, provinces, towns, cities, and regions are masculine unless they end in unstressed -*a:*

el viejo Perú: the old Peru
la España nocturna: the nocturnal Spain
el frío Canadá: the cold Canada
el Chubut: the Chubut
la Pampa verde: the green Pampas
el Ampurdán: the Ampurdan
el Gran Buenos Aires: the Buenos Aires metropolitan area (or Greater
    Buenos Aires)
la Barcelona revolucionaria: revolutionary Barcelona

However, a "masculine" town may be treated as feminine when the idea of *ciudad* is in the speaker's mind: *la gran Toledo* (the great Toledo), *la fantástica Buenos Aires* (the marvelous Buenos Aires). The cities of Corinto and Sagunto are feminine, following the Latin tradition, in which cities have the feminine gender: *La antigua Cartago* (the ancient Cartago). Conversely, "feminine" towns or countries are treated as masculine when preceded by *todo, medio, un, propio,* or *mismo:*

todo Barcelona: all Barcelona
medio Colombia: half Colombia

This concept of a connoted word is called metonymic gender. Some nouns take the gender of an implied word, such as *el río* (river), *el monte* (mountain), *el volcán* (volcano), *el vino* (wine), *el número* (number). Masculine by meaning are:

A. NAMES OF MOST RIVERS, MOUNTAINS, OCEANS, SEAS, LAKES, VOLCANOES, AND MOUNTAIN RANGES

el Amazonas: the Amazon
el Everest: the Everest
el Pacífico: the Pacific
el Mediterráneo: the Mediterranean
el Erie: the Erie
el Popocatépetl: the Popocatepetl
los Andes: the Andes

But a name that includes a feminine noun—for example, *sierra* (mountain range)—is feminine in its entirety:

la Sierra Madre: the Sierra Madre

B. MONTHS AND DAYS OF THE WEEK

el sábado pasado: last Saturday
Fue un buen enero: It was a good January

C. CARDINAL POINTS OF THE COMPASS

el sur de Chile: the south of Chile

D. COLORS

el amarillo: the color yellow
la rosa: rose
el rosa: pink (*el color rosa*)

Note that feminine color nouns ending in -*a* take the gender of an implied word. Wines (below) follow the same rule.

E. WINES

el cava: sparkling wine
la Champaña: Champagne (region)
el champaña or *el champán:*[1] champagne (*el vino champaña*)
el chartreuse: Chartreuse
el coñac: cognac, brandy
la Rioja: Rioja (region)
el rioja: Rioja wine (*el vino Rioja*)
el tinto: red wine

F. MUSICAL NOTES

el la: the la

G. NAMES OF CARS, SHIPS, AND AIRCRAFT [2]

un BMW:[3] a BMW
el Mayflower: the Mayflower
un 747: a 747

---

[1] In popular speech, it is possible to find *champaña* as feminine: *Está fría la champaña.*

[2] Names of ships are considered masculine, even when they are feminine nouns or carry a woman's name: *el Queen Elizabeth.* Light aircraft are commonly feminine because of the implied noun *la avioneta.*

[3] In some Latin American countries, certain car names are feminine: *una Masseratti, una Ferrari.*

el Picasso: the Picasso
el Botero: the Botero
el Rivera: the Rivera

el Real Madrid: Real Madrid soccer club
el Guadalajara: Guadalajara soccer club

But in the Río de la Plata region, soccer clubs do not carry the article:

Boca Juniors: Boca Juniors soccer club
Peñarol: Peñarol soccer club

el nueve por ciento: nine per cent

mañana: tomorrow
el mañana: the future
algo: something
un algo: a something (a special characteristic)
pero: but
el pero: objection
fumar: to smoke
el fumar: the smoking habit

Exception: *la nada* (nothingness).

FEMININE GENDER

Nouns referring to female human beings and animals are feminine in gender:

la madre: mother
la mujer: woman, wife
la vaca: cow

The noun *marimacho* "mannish woman, lesbian" is generally masculine (*un marimacho*), although there is some variation with *marimacha*. The use of this word is pejorative.

Nouns ending in -*a*, -*ción*, -*d*, -*ez*, -*eza*, -*icie*, -*(i)dad*, -*ie(s)*, -*ión*, -*itis*, -*nza*, -*sión*, -*sis*, -*tad*, -*tud*, -*triz*, -*umbre*, -*z*, and -*zón* are feminine:

la acción: action
el alma (f): [4] soul
el asma (f): [5] asthma
la bondad: goodness
la cabeza: head
la calvicie: baldness
la caridad: charity
la caries: caries
la casa: house
la cicatriz: scar
la crisis: crisis
la diadema: diadem
la diálisis: dialysis
la esperanza: hope
la estasis: stasis
la estratagema: stratagem
la estupidez: stupidity
la flema: phlegm
la lealtad: loyalty
la longitud: length
la maleta: suitcase
la muchedumbre: crowd, multitude
la nación: nation
la opinión: opinion
la otitis: otitis
la pared: wall
la paz: peace
la pereza: laziness
la profesión: profession
la razón: reason
la región: region
la rima: rhyme

---

[4] The feminine article *el* is used when the word begins with a stressed *a-* or with the stressed syllable *ha-*: *el alma* (the soul), *el área* (the area), *el habla* (the language), and *el harpa* (the harp). Exceptions are feminine first names, last names referring to women, and letters of the alphabet: *la Ana, la Álvarez, la a*, and *la hache*.

[5] However, in the scientific language this word is sometimes used as masculine.

la serie: series
la soledad: loneliness
la superficie: surface
la tesis: thesis
la verdad: truth
la virtud: virtue

However, some masculine nouns can be found:

el análisis: analysis
el apocalipsis: apocalypse
el césped: lawn
el corazón: heart
el énfasis: emphasis
el éxtasis: ecstasy
el gorrión: sparrow
el paréntesis: parenthesis
el pez: fish

By metonymic gender, some nouns take the gender of an implied word, such as *la letra* (letter of the alphabet), *la(s) isla(s)* (island), and *la carretera* (road).

A. LETTERS OF THE ALPHABET

la a: a
la m: m
la epsilon: epsilon

B. ISLANDS

las Antillas: the West Indies
las Malvinas: the Falkland Islands

C. ROADS

la 60: route 60
la M30: the M30 beltway

Formation of the Feminine Gender

The majority of masculine nouns make the feminine in *-a:*

el alemán/la alemana: German
el amigo/la amiga: friend

el autodidacto/la autodidacta:[6] self-taught person
el bailarín/la bailarina: dancer
el burgués/la burguesa: middle-class man/woman
el campeón/la campeona: champion
el cliente/la clienta: customer
el comediante/la comedianta: actor/actress
el conductor/la conductora: driver
el danzante/la danzanta: dancer
el danzarín/la danzarina: dancer
el dependiente/la dependienta: shop assistant
el español/la española: Spaniard
el estratego/la estratega: strategist
el feligrés/la feligresa: parishioner
el gato/la gata: cat
el hereje/la hereja: heretic
el hermano/la hermana: brother/sister
el huésped/la huéspeda: host/hostess
el infante/la infanta: royal prince/princess
el lagarto/la lagarta: lizard
el león/la leona: lion/lioness
el lobo/la loba: wolf
el novio/la novia: boyfriend/girlfriend
el patrón/la patrona: landlord/landlady
el perro/la perra: dog
el principiante/la principianta: beginner
el sirviente/la sirvienta: servant
el zorro/la zorra:[7] fox

However, some nouns have different forms for male and female:

el abad/la abadesa: abbot/abbess
el actor/la actriz: actor/actress
el alcalde/la alcaldesa: mayor/mayoress
el alguacil/la alguacilesa: alguacil, sheriff (male and female)
el barón/la baronesa: baron/baroness
el caballo/la yegua: stallion/mare
el carnero/la oveja: ram/ewe

---

[6] In practice, the form *autodidacta* is applied to both masculine and feminine nouns.

[7] Some words have pejorative meaning when applying to women: *lagarta* (sly minx), *zorra* (whore).

el conde/la condesa: count/countess
el cónsul/la consulesa or *cónsula:*[8] consul
el diablo/la diablesa or *diabla:* devil/she-devil
el diácono/la diaconisa: deacon/deaconess
el duque/la duquesa: duke/duchess
el emperador/la emperatriz: emperor/empress
el gachó/la gachí: bloke/chick
el gallo/la gallina: cockerel/hen
el guarda/la guardesa: custodian/custodian's wife
el héroe/la heroína: hero/heroine
el histrión/la histrionisa: actor/actress
el hombre/la mujer: man/woman
el jabalí/la jabalina: wild boar/wild sow
el juglar/la juglaresa: minstrel
el marido/la mujer: husband/wife
el padre/la madre: father/mother
el poeta/la poetisa: poet/poetess (but *la poeta* currently tends to be
   preferred)
el príncipe/la princesa: prince/princess
el profeta/la profetisa: prophet/prophetess
el rey/la reina: king/queen
el sacerdote/la sacerdotisa: priest/priestess
el toro/la vaca: bull/cow
el varón/la hembra: male/female
el yerno/la nuera: son-/daughter-in-law
el zar/la zarina: Czar/Czarina

Some nouns have no distinctive ending for gender:

el/la adolescente: adolescent
el/la agente: police officer
el/la aguafiestas: wet blanket
el/la alférez: subaltern
el/la amante: lover
el/la artista: artist
el/la asceta: ascetic
el/la astronauta: astronaut
el/la atleta: athlete
el/la automovilista: motorist
el/la camarada: comrade

---

[8] This word also has common gender: *el/la cónsul.*

el/la cantante: singer
el/la colega: workmate
el/la conferenciante: speaker
el/la consorte: spouse
el/la cónyuge: spouse
el/la creyente: believer
el/la debutante:[9] newcomer
el/la descendiente: descendant
el/la enlace: union representative
el/la escribiente: clerk
el/la espía: spy
el/la estudiante: student
el/la guía: guide
el/la imbécil: imbecile
el/la intérprete: interpreter
el/la joven: young man/woman
el/la líder: leader
el/la mártir: martyr
el/la mecenas: Maecenas, patron
el/la médium: medium
el/la penitente: penitent
el/la pianista: pianist
el/la pívot: pivot
el/la practicante:[10] practitioner
el/la rehén: hostage
el/la representante: representative
el/la testigo: witness

Until recently, the feminine forms of professions had a pejorative meaning or the meaning "wife of":

el bachiller: holder of a high school diploma,[11] but also chatterbox
la bachillera: bluestocking, chatterbox
el embajador: ambassador
la embajadora: ambassador's wife
el general: general

---

[9] But as a feminine word it also has the meaning of "debutante" (young woman making a debut into society).

[10] In popular speech, *el practicante/la practicanta* carries the meaning of "nurse" or "assistant chemist."

[11] At the present time, with this meaning the word has a common form for both genders: *el/la bachiller.*

la generala: general's wife
el sargento: sergeant
la sargenta: sergeant's wife (but also, tyrant)

Nowadays, in most of Latin America and parts of Spain, feminine forms of the professions are common:

el abogado/la abogada: lawyer
el académico/la académica: academician, member of an academy
el alcalde/la alcaldesa: mayor
el árbitro/la árbitra: referee
el catedrático/la catedrática: professor
el cirujano/la cirujana: surgeon
el comisario/la comisaria: police inspector
el concejal/la concejala: town councillor
el crítico/la crítica: critic
el edil/la edila: municipal official
el embajador/la embajadora: ambassador/ambassadress
el ingeniero/la ingeniera: engineer
el juez/la jueza: judge
el manicuro/la manicura: manicurist
el médico/la médica: doctor
el ministro/la ministra: minister
el presidente/la presidenta: president
el procurador/la procuradora: procurator, lawyer
el sacristán/la sacristana: sacristan

But in Spain there still is a good deal of variation in usage:

el/la arquitecto: arquitect
el/la filósofo: philosopher
el/la fiscal: public prosecutor
el/la jefe: boss
el/la juez: judge
el/la médico: doctor
el/la miembro: member
el/la socio:[12] partner

In Latin America the *-a* ending is utilized more freely than on the Peninsula, especially in popular speech. It can be found in words like *una criminala* for *una criminal* (criminal), *una intelectuala* for *una intelectual* (an intellectual), and *una individua* and *una tipa* as femi-

---

[12] In Spain *socia* means "trollop."

nine variants of *un individuo* (an individual) and *un tipo* (a character). Note, however, that not all of these forms are uniformly accepted in all Latin American countries.

Some words expressing professions are invariable:

el/la modelo: model
el/la piloto: pilot
el/la soldado:[13] soldier
el/la soprano: soprano

COMMON GENDER

Some nouns have an invariable gender applied to either sex. Usually, these nouns are names of animals:

el águila (f): eagle
la araña: spider
la ardilla: squirrel
la ballena: whale
el cangrejo: crab
el canguro: kangaroo
el castor: beaver
la jirafa: giraffe
la llama: llama
la nutria: otter
el puma: puma
la rana: frog
la rata: rat
el sapo: toad
el tiburón: shark

The only way of stressing the sex of such animals is to use the noun *macho* "male" or *hembra* "female" after the noun: the gender of the noun remains unchanged and *macho* and *hembra* are invariable: *Los cangrejos hembra están muertos* (The female crabs are dead), or *La hembra de la araña se come al macho* (The female spider eats the male spider).

Also, nouns which apply to human beings may have common gender:

el ángel: angel
la celebridad: celebrity

---

[13] *Soldadera* also may be found, with the meaning of the woman of a soldier, but she carries arms and fights in the conflict.

el genio: genius
la persona: person
el personaje: character
la víctima: victim

EXCEPTIONS

There is a large number of masculine nouns ending in -*a,* including some very commonly used words and the learned words ending in -*ma.* Words followed by an asterisk (*) in the following list may be treated as feminine in everyday speech.

el aleluya: halleluya
el anagrama: anagram
el anatema: anathema
el aroma: aroma
el caza: fighter plane
el cisma: schism
el clima: climate
el crisma: holy oil
el crucigrama: crossword puzzle
el día/el mediodía: day/midday
el diagrama: diagram
el dilema: dilemma
el diploma: diploma
el dogma: dogma
el drama: drama
el eccema/eczema:* eczema
el emblema: emblem
el enema:* enema
el enigma: enigma
el esquema: scheme
el estigma: stigma
el fantasma:* ghost
el fonema: phoneme
el guardarropa: wardrobe
el holograma: hologram
el insecticida: insecticide
el lema: slogan
el magma: magma
el mapa: map
el miasma:* miasma
el panorama: panorama

el pijama: pajamas
el planeta: planet
   (but also *la piyama/pijama* in some Latin American countries)
el plasma: plasma
el poema: poem
el prisma: prism
el problema: problem
el radiograma: radiogram
el reúma*: rheumatism
el síntoma: symptom
el sistema: system
el telegrama: telegram
el tema: theme, topic
el tequila: tequila
el tranvía: tram
el trauma: trauma
el yoga: yoga

Also, nouns ending in -*a* but denoting males are normally masculine:

el bestia: beast (feminine when used nonfiguratively)
el cabecilla or *el cabeza:* hothead, leader
el cabecita negra: person of color (pejorative)
el cámara: cameraman
el cura: priest
el dentista: dentist
el granuja: rascal, urchin
el impresionista: impressionist
el mierda: shit (feminine when used nonfiguratively)
el piel roja: redskin, Red Indian
el poeta: poet
el recluta: recruit (male)
el sinvergüenza: scoundrel, cheeky person

WORDS WITH TWO GENDERS AND TWO MEANINGS

Many words have different meanings according to their gender. Some examples are:

el canal: canal
la canal: carcass
el capital: capital (money)
la capital: capital (city)

el cólera: cholera
la cólera: anger
el coma: coma
la coma: comma
el cometa: comet
la cometa: kite, bribe
el corte: cut
la corte: court, capital (city)
el cura: priest
la cura: cure
el delta: river delta
la delta: delta (letter)
el doblez: fold
la doblez: two-facedness
el editorial: leading article
la editorial: publishing house
el frente: front (part); political or military front
la frente: forehead
el Génesis: Genesis (book of the Bible)
la/las génesis: genesis (origin)
el/la guarda: guard, custodian (for male and female profession)
la guarda: custody, protection
el guardia: policeman
la guardia: guard; also, policewoman
el lente: spectacles/glasses
la lente: refractive lens
el margen: margin (paper)
la margen: margin (river, road)
el moral: mulberry tree
la moral: morals, morale
el orden: order (in sense of series, or good behavior);
    and note *el orden del día:* dispatches
la orden: order (in sense of command); also, religious order, as in *la orden de los jesuitas:* the Jesuit order
el ordenanza: orderly
la ordenanza: ordinance
el parte: report
la parte: part
el pendiente: earring, pendant
la pendiente: slope
el pez: fish
la pez: pitch, tar
el policía: policeman

la policía: police force; also, policewoman
el radio: radius
el/la radio: radio
el terminal: terminal (electrical or electronic)
la terminal: terminus, terminal in transportation
el/la vocal: member of a board
la vocal: vowel

Sometimes the masculine and feminine genders indicate respectively a tree and its fruit:

el almendro: almond tree
la almendra: almond
el avellano: hazel tree
la avellana: hazelnut
el banano:[14] banana tree
la banana: banana
el castaño: chestnut tree
la castaña: chestnut
el cerezo: cherry tree
la cereza: cherry
el ciruelo: plum tree
la ciruela: plum
el manzano: apple tree
la manzana: apple
el naranjo:[15] orange tree
la naranja: orange

In some words, the feminine gender indicates a larger or broader object or concept than the masculine (*género dimensional*):

la anilla: ring (gym, courtain)
el anillo: ring (wedding)
la banca: banking (system)
el banco: bank
la barranca: ravine
el barranco: cliff
la bolsa: bag (sack)

---

[14] But there are variations in these two words. In Colombia and most of Central America, *el banano* refers also to the fruit. On the other hand, in Argentina and Uruguay *la banana* is used to name the fruit and the tree as well. Other masculine words for the banana tree are *el bananero, el plátano,* and *el platanero.* And other masculine words for the fruit are *el guineo* (San Salvador) and *el plátano* (Spain).

[15] *Manzanero* and *naranjero* may be found in popular speech.

el bolso: handbag (generally used by women)
la caldera: boiler
el caldero: cauldron
la caracola: conch
el caracol: snail; seashell
la cuba: tub, barrel
el cubo: bucket
la farola: streetlight
el farol: lantern/light
la huerta: large kitchen garden
el huerto: smaller kitchen garden; orchard
la jarra: pitcher, churn
el jarro: jar, stein
la leña: firewood
el leño: log
la madera: wood
el madero: piece of wood
la manta: blanket
el manto: cloak, mantle
la ría: river mouth
el río: river
la saca: big sack, mailbag
el saco: sack, bag

But the opposite situation can also be found, namely that the feminine word is the smaller of the pair:

el cesto: basket (large or small)
la cesta: basket (generally smaller)
el barco: ship
la barca: fishing boat
el ruedo: bullring, hem
la rueda: wheel

Sometimes the feminine noun indicates the instrument and the masculine the person[16] who uses it.

el cámara (also, *cameráman*): cameraman
la cámara: camera

---

[16]Until recently the person was a man, but now gender alternation may be found in the words expressing the profession. In these cases, the meaning depends on the context. Also, it is possible to create new words: *la cámara/la camarógrafa trabaja en televisión* (the camerawoman works in television); *la espada mató el toro* (the swordswoman killed the bull). For the trumpeter, Spanish has the word *el/la trompetista* (the [male or female] trumpeter).

el espada: swordsman
la espada: sword
el trompeta: trumpeter
la trompeta: trumpet

Other times, one of the genders indicates the place or the instrument while the other designates the person's occupation:

el cochero: coachman
la cochera: carriage
el costurero: sewing case, sewing room
la costurera: seamstress
el encuadernador: bookbinder
la encuadernadora: bookbinder machine
el planchador: ironer
la planchadora: ironing machine, but also female ironer
el segador: harvester
la segadora: mowing machine, lawnmower, but also female harvester
el verdulero: place for the greens (in the refrigerator)
la verdulera: female greengrocer, but also fishwife

With names of machines, the feminine often indicates the larger or more complex type: *el aspirador/la aspiradora* (aspirator/vacuum cleaner); *el secador/la secadora* (hairdryer/tumble dryer).

WORDS WITH TWO GENDERS AND THE SAME MEANING

These words belong to a *género ambiguo,* "ambiguous gender." However, in modern Spanish, a priority is given to the gender listed first in the list below. Words followed by an asterisk (*) are feminine only in popular speech and considered substandard.

el/la ábside: apsis
el/la anatema: anathema
el/la aneurisma: aneurysm
el/la apóstrofe: apostrophe
el/la azúcar: sugar
    (but often found with a feminine adjective, e.g., *el azúcar morena:* brown sugar)
la/el azumbre: half a gallon
la babel/el babel: bedlam
el/la calor*: heat
el cobaya/la cobaya: guinea pig
el/la color*: color
la/el dote: dowry
la/el duermevela: light sleep
la/el enzima: enzyme

el/la esperma: sperm
el/la estambre: worsted yarn, worsted
el fueraborda/la fueraborda: outboard
el/los herpes/la/las herpes:[17] herpes
el/la hojaldre: puff pastry
el/la interrogante: question
la/el interviú: interview
el/la lavaplatos: dishwasher
el/la lente: lens
la/el linde: boundary
el/la mimbre: wicker
el/la pelambre: thick hair
la/el pringue: grease

Some nouns have opposite genders in Peninsular (first word in the list) and Latin American Spanish:

el bikini for *la bikini:* bikini
una llamada for *un llamado:* call
el pijama for *la pijama:* pajamas
la radio for *el radio:* radio (*el radio* is also "radius")
la sartén for *el sartén:* frying pan
la vuelta for *el vuelto:* change

Arte

Arte can be either masculine or feminine in the singular, but in the plural it is almost always feminine:

el arte gótico: Gothic art

but

el arte (f) *poética:* poetic art
las bellas artes: the fine arts

but

los artes de pesca: fishing tackle

Mar

The noun *mar* is masculine:

el mar Mediterráneo: the Mediterranean Sea
los mares del mundo: the world seas

---

[17] *El/la herpe* may be found.

However, in poetry and in the speech of sailors and people who live by the sea, this word is feminine. In nautical terms and in weather forecasts, *mar* is always feminine:

la bajamar: low tide
la pleamar: high tide
en alta mar: on the high seas
las mares gruesas: heavy seas
hacerse a la mar: to put (out) to sea
la mar llana: smooth sea
la mar picada: choppy sea

The word *mar* is feminine in the colloquial expression *la mar (de)* (a lot [of]).

la mar de gente: full of people

GENDER OF THE COMPOUND NOUNS

Compound nouns usually follow the gender of the noun included (noun + adjective, adjective + noun, preposition + noun). Exceptions are:

el aguafuerte (masculine and feminine word): etching (masculine) / nitric acid (feminine)
el aguardiente: liquor, eau-de-vie
el altavoz: loudspeaker
el antifaz: mask
el contraluz: back lighting
el trasluz: diffused light

When the compound contains two nouns, it takes the gender of the last one. Exceptions are:

el aguamanos: water jug
el capicúa: palindrome

Compound nouns consisting of a verb + a noun or a verb + a verb are masculine:

el abrelatas: can opener
el correveidile: gossiper
el lanzallamas: flamethrower
el paracaídas: parachute
el paraguas: umbrella

el tentempié: bite to eat, snack
el vaivén: swaying

GENDER OF FOREIGN WORDS

Words that allude to human beings will be feminine or masculine according to the gender of the person referred to:

el/la aberzale: follower of the Basque party
el/la baby sitter
la beautiful people
la drag queen (according to the represented gender)
el/la fan
el gay
el/la grunge
el/la heavy
el/la hippy or *hippie*
el homo sapiens
el/la hooligan
la jet-set
el lehendakari or *lendakari*
el maître
la majorette
el/la manager
la mezzosoprano
el/la mod
el ombudsman
el/la outsider
el/la partenaire
el playboy
la prima donna
el recordman
el/la skin-head
el/la wasp

Inanimate foreign words may be feminine if they closely resemble a common feminine Spanish word in form or meaning or because they are feminine in the vernacular language:

la birra: beer
la fast food
la kasbah
la limousine or *limusín* or *limusina*
la matrioska

la mountain bike
la mozarella
la nouvelle vague: new wave
la nova cançó: innovative song
la opera prima
la perestroika
la performance
la ratio

Otherwise, they are masculine and the great majority of foreign-looking words have this gender, although some of them are feminine in their original language:

el aerobic or *aeróbic*
el affaire
el after-shave
el airbag
el bafle
el best-seller
el Big Bang
el bloc
el blue-jean
el boom
el brasier
el break
el burger
el bypass
el christmas
el copyright
el disc-jockey
el dry-cleaning
el fax
el flirt
el footing
el freezer
el happy end
el hardware
el hit-parade
el hobby
el hockey
el jacuzzi
el jazz
el karaoke
el karma

el kerosén or *kerosene*
el ketchup
el kilim
el kilobyte
el kínder
el kleenex
los legging
el leitmotiv
el lifting
el loden
el loft
el long play
el mailing
el marketing
el marron glacé
los mass media
el master
el match
el modem
el new look
el nouveau roman
el off
el opus
el panzer
el petit point
el picnic
el pin
el pizzicato
el plotter
el politburó
el pub
el rafting
el ragtime
el rap
el scherzo
el score
el script
el software
el topless
el walkie-talkie
el western
el windsurf or *windsurfing*
el yiddish
el zapping

GENDER OF ABBREVIATIONS AND ACRONYMS

This is determined by the gender of the main noun:

el BASIC: Beginner's All-Purpose Symbolic Instruction Code
la BBC: British Broadcasting Corporation
el BMW: Bayerische Motorenwerke
la CBS: Columbia Broadcasting System
el CD-ROM: compact disc–read only memory
la CEE: European Economic Community
el DNA/ADN: deoxyribonucleic acid
(la) ETA (Euzkadi ta Azkatasuna): Euzkadi and Freedom
el FBI: Federal Bureau of Investigation
el IQ/el CI (coeficiente intelectual): intelligence quotient
la ONU: United Nations Organization
la OTAN: NATO (North Atlantic Treaty Organization)
el ovni (objeto volador no identificado): UFO (unidentified flying
    object)
el sida: AIDS (acquired immunodeficiency syndrome)
la TWA: Trans World Airlines
el Unicef:[18] United Nations International Children's Emergency Fund
la UVI (unidad de vigilancia intensiva): ICU (intensive care unit)

NUMBER

GENERAL RULES FOR PLURAL FORMATION

Polysyllabic nouns ending in unstressed vowel + *-s* or *-x* remain unchanged in the plural:

el/los análisis: analysis
el/los ántrax: anthrax
el/los atlas: atlas
el/los bíceps: biceps
la/las caries: caries
el/los chotis: schottische
el/los clímax: climax
el/los corpus: corpus
el/los coxis: coccyx
la/las crisis: crisis
el/los énfasis: emphasis
el/los detritus: detritus

---

[18] Very often this word appears as feminine (*la Unicef*) due to the assimilation
to *la (organización Unicef)* (the Unicef organization).

el/los fénix: phoenix
el/los forceps: forceps
la/las laringitis: laryngitis
el/los látex: latex
el/los lunes: Monday
el/los/la/las mecenas: Maecenas, patron
el/los ómnibus: omnibus
el/los pesquis: insight
el/los relax: relax
el/los sílex: silex
el/los siux: Sioux
el/los télex: telex
el/los tórax: thorax
el/los virus: virus

Nouns that end in a consonant other than -*s*,[19] a stressed -*a*, -*i*, or -*u*, a stressed vowel + -*s*, or -*y*,[20] and all words of one syllable not ending in -*e* require that -*es* be added:

el adiós/los adioses: farewell
el ají/los ajíes: chili
el álbum/los álbumes: album
el alhelí/los alhelíes: wallflower
el anís/los anises: anisette
el asquenazí/los asquenazíes: Ashkenazi
el autobús/los autobuses: bus
el bambú/los bambúes: bamboo
el bantú/los bantúes: Bantus
el berbiquí/los berbiquíes: brace
el bisturí/los bisturíes or *los bisturís:* scalpel
el búnker/los búnkeres: bunker
el carcaj/los carcajes: quiver
el carey/los careyes: tortoiseshell, sea turtle
el club/los clubes: club
el colibrí/los colibríes: hummingbird
el compás/los compases: compass

---

[19] Exceptions are: *el baobab/los baobabs* (baobab), *el cheviot/los cheviots* (cheviot), *el cómic/los cómics* (comics), *el crónlech/los crónlechs* (cromlech), *el entrecot/los entrecots* (sirloin), *el hábitat/los hábitats* (habitat), *el robot/los robots* (robot), *el soviet/los soviets* (Soviet), *el test/los tests* (test), *el vermut* or *vermú / los vermuts* or *vermús* (vermouth).

[20] Exceptions are: *el guirigay/los guirigáis* (hubbub) (*guirigayes* and *guirigays* are incorrect), *el paipay/los paipáis* (fan), *el póney* or *poni / los poneis* or *ponis* (pony), *el sumuray/los samuráis* (samurai).

el diesel/los dieseles: diesel
el frac/los fraques or *los fracs:* dress coat
el frenesí/los frenesíes: frenzy
el frufú/los frufúes: froufrou
el géiser/los géiseres: geyser
el glugú/los glugúes: gurgle
el hogar/los hogares: home
el hotel/los hoteles: hotel
la hurí/las huríes: houri
el iglú/los iglúes: igloo
el jabalí/los jabalíes: wild boar
el jacarandá/los jacarandaes: jacaranda
el láser/los láseres: laser
el maní/los maníes:[21] peanut
el maniquí/los maniquíes: mannequin
el maravedí/los maravedíes, los maravedises, los maravedís: maravedi (Spanish coin)
el marqués/los marqueses: marquis
el mes/los meses: month
el non/los nones: odd
el ñu/los ñúes: gnu
el ombú/los ombúes or *ombús:* ombu (tree)
el país/los países: country
la pared/las paredes: wall
el pirulí/los pirulíes or *pirulís:* lollipop
el pis/los pises: wee-wee
el plan/los planes: plan
el poliéster/los poliésteres: polyester
el rajá/los rajaes or *rajás:* rajah
el reloj/los relojes: clock
el rey/los reyes: king
el rubí/los rubíes:[22] ruby
el tabú/los tabúes: taboo
el tárgum/los tárgumes: Targum
la tos/las toses: cough
el vals/los valses: waltz
el yo/los yoes: the I

---

[21] In Latin America *los ajises* and *los manises* in popular speech. Also the word *gurí* (child, youth) makes its plural *gurises*, and its feminine is *gurisa(s)*.

[22] Colloquially plurals as *alhelís, ajís, bambús, bantús, berbiquís, caréis, colibrís, frenesís, frufús, hurís, iglús, jabalís, maniquís, ñus, rubís,* and *tabús* may be found.

Note that words such as *baúl/baúles* (trunk), *país/países* (country), *raíz/raíces* (root), and *raíl/raíles*[23] (rail) maintain their accent in the plural.

Some nouns ending in stressed vowels do not follow the general rule, but simply add *-s* in the plural (instead of *-es*):

el ambigú/ambigús: buffet
el benjuí/los benjuís: benzoin
el bigudí/los bigudís:[24] curler
el canesú/los canesús: bodice, yoke
el champú/los champús: shampoo
el esquí/los esquís: ski
la gachí/las gachís:[25] chick
la/el interviú/las/los interviús: interview
el menú/los menús: menu
el papá/los papás: daddy
el sofá/los sofás: sofa
el tisú/los tisús: lamé

The musical notes do not follow the above rule:

el do/los dos: do
el mi/los mis: mi
el si/los sis: si

When the noun ends in an unstressed vowel or in a stressed *-o* or *-e* (including words of one syllable ending in *-e*), *-s* is added:

el bonsái/los bonsáis: bonsai
el café/los cafés:[26] coffee
el canapé/los canapés: sofa, canapé
el caqui/los caquis: persimmon
el cui or *cuy* or *cuye / los cuis* or *cuises:* guinea pig
el dominó/los dominós: domino
el espíritu/los espíritus: spirit
la fe/las fes:[27] faith
la fruta/las frutas: fruit
el gachó/los gachós: guy, fellow
el grano/los granos: grain

---

[23] But also: *raíl/raíles*.
[24] But *bigudíes* may be formed.
[25] *Gachises* is incorrect.
[26] *Cafeses* is incorrect.
[27] *Feses* is incorrect.

el hombre/los hombres: man
el pie/los pies:[28] foot
el safari/los safaris: safari
el té/los tés: tea

The *-z* of a singular form becomes *-c-* before *-es* in the plural, and the *-c* becomes *-qu- + -es:*[29]

el avestruz/los avestruces: ostrich
la faz/las faces: face
el pez/los peces: fish
la sobrepelliz/las sobrepellices: surplice
el tapiz/los tapices: tapestry
el tictac/los tictaques: ticktock
el vivac or *vivaque / los vivaques:* bivouac

Plural formation customarily causes no variation in stress. Therefore, a written accent must sometimes be added or dropped in the plural:

el aborigen/los aborígenes: native
el alemán/los alemanes: German
el canon/los cánones: canon
el examen /los exámenes: examen
el interés/los intereses: interest
el joven/los jóvenes: young man
el liquen/los líquenes: lichen
la oración/las oraciones: sentence

Exceptions are:

el carácter/los caracteres: character
el espécimen/los especímenes: specimen
el régimen/los regímenes: regime, diet

PLURAL OF COMPOUND NOUNS

Usually, only the last part of a compound noun carries the plural ending:

el altavoz/los altavoces: loudspeaker
el ferrocarril/los ferrocarriles: railway

---

[28] The plural *los pieses* is used in popular speech.
[29] However, in one irregular case, the *c* disappears in the plural: *el zinc* or *cinc / los zines* or *cines* (zinc).

el librepensador/los librepensadores: freethinker
el marcapaso/los marcapasos:[31] pacemaker
la medialuna/las medialunas:[30] croissant
el padrenuestro/los padrenuestros:[32] paternoster
el todoterreno/los todoterrenos: jeep, land rover

Compound nouns remain unchanged when the second element is already plural:

el/los abrelatas: can opener
el/los paracaídas: parachute
el/los paraguas: umbrella

There are only very few, relatively scarcely used, combinations in which both components take the plural ending:

el gentilhombre/los gentileshombres: gentleman
la ricadueña/las ricasdueñas: noblewoman

In compound words including two juxtaposed nouns written as separate units, only the first noun is pluralized:

el hombre masa/los hombres masa: the average man
el hombre rana/los hombres rana: frogman
la hora pico/las horas pico: rush hour
la hora punta/las horas punta: rush hour
el perro policía/los perros policía: police dog
el sofá cama/los sofás cama: sofa bed

However: *el puerco espín/los puercos espinos* (porcupine), *el pura sangre/los puras sangres* (thoroughbred), *la redactora jefa/las redactoras jefas* (female editor in chief).
Some compound nouns are invariable in the plural. They are always forms involving verbs or invariable words:

el sabelotodo/los sabelotodo: know-it-all

A few compound forms of this type have become so common that they are apparently considered as simple nouns, and their plural forms follow the general rules:

el ir y venir/los ires y venires: back-and-forth motion
el pésame/los pésames: expression of condolence
el vaivén/los vaivenes: seesaw

---

[30] But also *la media luna*, plural *las medias lunas*.
[31] But this word is commonly used only in the plural: *el/los marcapasos*.
[32] Also *el padre nuestro/los padres nuestros*.

PLURAL OF SURNAMES

Surnames ending in a vowel tend to take the *-s* of the plural:

los Azcorras: the Azcorra family
los Ruilopes: the Ruilope family

Surnames ending in a consonant and foreign surnames remain invariable:

los Cortés: the Cortés family
los Cosmen: the Cosmen family
los Menéndez: the Menéndez family
los Page: the Page family
los Solís: the Solís family

PLURAL OF FOREIGN WORDS

For some Latin and Greek words, the Real Academia Española has Hispanicized the ending to *-o*, making plurals in *-os:*

el armónium > el armonio/los armonios (but also *los armóniums*)
el auditórium > el auditorio/los auditorios
el currículum > el currículo/los currículos
el detritus > el detrito/los detritos (but also *los detritus*)
el memorándum > el memorando/los memorandos (but also *los memorándum[s]*)
quantum-quanta > cuanto-cuantos
el sympósium > el simposio/los simposios
el referéndum > el referendo/los referendos (but also *los referéndum[s]*)
el ultimátum > el ultimato/los ultimatos (but also *los ultimátum[s]*)

Other Latin words take the Latin plural:

el addéndum/los addenda
el currículum vitae/los currícula vitae (but also *los currículum vitae*)
el desiderátum/los desiderata (but also *los desiderátum*)
el pandemónium/los pandemonia (but also *los pandemónium*)

Some foreign words remain invariable:

el/los accésit: accessit, second prize, consolation prize
el/los chárter (but also *chárteres*): charter
el/los déficit: deficit
el/los escáner: scanner
el/los exequátor: exequatur, permission

el/los éxplicit: last words in a book or form
el/los plácet: placet, permission, authorization
el/los quórum: quorum
el/los réquiem: requiem
el/los superávit: surplus/surpluses
el/los tándem(s) or *los tándemes:* tandem
el/los tedéum: Te Deum

Note that plurals for *el hipérbaton* (hyperbaton), *el lied* (lied), and *el lord* (lord) are *los hipérbatos, los lieder,* and *los lores,* respectively.

Usually, foreign words take the plural in *-s,* unless they end in *-s, -sh,* or the sound /ch/:

el amateur/los amateurs
el anorak/los anoraks
el argot/los argots: jargon
el ballet/los ballets
el barman/los barmans (but also *los barmen*)
el bestseller/los bestsellers (but also *el best-seller/los best-sellers*)
el boicot/los boicots: boycott
la boutique/las boutiques
el brandy/los brandis
el chip/los chips
el clóset/los clósets
el coñac/los coñacs (but also *el coñá/los coñás*)
el debut/los debuts
el esnob/los esnobs
el gángster/los gángsters (but also *gángsteres*)
el gong or *gongo* / *los gongs* or *gongos*
el hámster/los hámsters (but also *los hámsteres*)
el hándicap/los hándicaps
el hobby/los hobbys (but also *los hobbies*)
el iceberg/los icebergs
el penalty/los penaltys (but also *el penalti/los penaltis*)
el piolet/los piolets

Hispanicized foreign words:

beefsteak > *el bisté* or *el bistec* or *el bife* / *los bistés* or *los bistecs* or
     los bifes
beige > *el beis/los beis*
bidet > *el bidé/los bidés*
boomerang > *el bumerán/los bumeranes*
buffet > *el bufé/los bufés*
bungalow > *el bungaló/los bungalós*

cabaret > *el cabaré/los cabarés*
capot > *el capó/los capós* (also *la capota*)
carnet > *el carné/los carnés*
cassette > *la casete/las casetes* (but also *el casete/los casetes*)
chalet > *el chalé/los chalés*
chandail > *el chándal/los chándales* (but also *los chándals*)
chauffeur > *el chofer* or *chófer/los choferes* or *los chóferes*
claxon > *el claxon/los cláxones*
cocktail > *el cóctel/los cócteles* (but also *el coctel/los cocteles*)
complot > *el compló/los complós* (but also *complots*)
confetti > *el confeti/los confetis* (but also *los confeti:* collection of confetti)
dandy > *el dandi/los dandis*
derby > *el derbi/los derbis*
graffiti > *el grafito/los grafitos* [33]
interview > *la interviú/las interviús* [34]
jersey > *el jersey/los jerséis*
koljoz > *el koljós/los koljoses*
leader > *el líder/los líderes*
nylon > *el nilón/los nilones*
pedigree > *el pedigrí/los pedigríes*
record > *el récord/los récords*
sandwich > *el sándwich/los sándwiches*
slalom > *el eslalon/los eslálones*
slogan > *el eslogan/los eslóganes*
smoking > *el esmoquin/los esmóquines*
spaghetti > *el espagueti/los espaguetis*
standard > *el estándar/los estándares*
stress > *el estrés/los estreses*
sweater > *el suéter/los suéteres*
tabloid > *el tabloide/los tabloides*
totem > *el tótem/los tótems*
yoghurt > *el yogur/los yogures*

COLLECTIVE NOUNS

Nouns that refer to groups of people or things are singular:

la agrupación: society
la arboleda: wood

---

[33] It is possible to find *el/los graffiti*, but *graffiti* is the Italian plural of the word *graffito*. Another possible combination is *el grafito* (Spanish singular) / *los graffiti* (Italian plural).

[34] But also *el interviú/los interviús*.

la asamblea: assembly
el auditorio: audience
el cabildo: chapter, town council
la canalla: mob
el conjunto: collection
el coro: chorus
el ejército: army
la gente:[35] people
el gentío: crowd
la loza: pottery
el matrimonio: marriage
la muchedumbre: crowd
la multitud: multitude
la plata: silver, money
la porcelana: china
el público: public
la serie: series
el trío: trio
la turba: crowd

Some masculine plural nouns denoting family relationships or an office carry the idea of male(s) and female(s) as well as being the standard plural of the masculine singular:

los duques: dukes; duke and duchess
los hermanos: brothers; brother(s) and sister(s)
los hijos: sons; children
los padres: fathers; mother and father; parents
los reyes: kings; king and queen; monarchs
los suegros: fathers-in-law; mother- and father-in-law

NOUNS OF UNIQUE ENTITIES

A number of nouns in Spanish are found only in the singular, for example, names of virtues, ideological tendencies, historical periods, and topics of study:

la avaricia: avarice
la bondad: goodness
la canícula: dog days
el caos: chaos

---

[35] In Latin America, *gente* may also mean *persona* (person), in which case it can be used in the plural and the singular.

la caridad: charity
el cariz: look
el cenit: zenith
el ecuador: equator
la envidia: envy
la esperanza: hope
el este: east
la fe: faith
la grima: annoyance
el norte: north
el oeste: west
la pereza: laziness
la salud: health
la sed: thirst
el sur: south
la tez: complexion
el zodíaco: zodiac

NONINFORMATIVE PLURAL

Conversely, other words are found almost always in the plural form:

las afueras: outskirts
las albricias: reward
los aledaños: adjacent
la/las alforja(s): saddlebags, knapsack
los alrededores: surroundings
los anales: annals
las andadas: habits
las andas: stretcher
los andurriales: out-of-the-way place
las angarillas: stretcher
el/los bofe(s): lungs
las calendas: calends
el/los calzoncillo(s): shorts
el/los calzón(es): trousers, panties
los comestibles: food
las completas: compline
las cosquillas: tickling
los enseres: equipment
las entendederas: brains
las exequias: funeral rites
las fauces: fauces
las gafas: glasses, spectacles

la(s) gana(s): appetite
las gárgaras: gargle
los grillos: shackles
las Horas: Hours (in the liturgical sense)
los impertinentes: lorgnette
las laudes: lauds
los maitines: matins
las medias: stockings
los modales: manners
las nonas: nones (from the Roman calendar)
el/los parabrisas: windshield
los prismáticos: binoculars
la/las tenaza(s): pliers
la/las tijera(s): scissors
las tinieblas: darkness
las trizas: pieces
los ultramarinos: groceries
las vacaciones: holidays
las vinajeras: altar cruet
las vituallas: provisions
los víveres: supplies, provisions

Some of these words appear in the singular, but with a different meaning:

el auricular: auricular (phone)
los auriculares: earphones
el celo: zeal, heat
los celos: jealousy
la esposa: wife; spouse
las esposas: handcuffs
el gemelo: twin
los gemelos: binoculars; cuff links
la víspera: eve of the day before
las vísperas:[36] vespers

Plurals are also found in a number of prepositional and verbal expressions:

a ciegas: blindly
a duras penas: with great difficulty
a escondidas: secretly, on the sly

---

[36] But *en vísperas de* means "the day before."

a escondidas de: without the knowledge of
a espaldas (de alguien): behind (someone's) back
a estas alturas: at this point or juncture
a gatas: on all fours
a instancias de: at the request of
a horcajadas: astride
a las claras: clearly, openly
a las mil maravillas: beautifully
a los cuatro vientos: in all directions
a medias: partially
a montones: in abundance
a ojos cerrados: blindfolded
a ojos vistas: visibly
a oscuras: in the dark
a pie juntillas, a pie juntillo, a pies juntillas: firmly, unquestionably
a pocos pasos: at a short distance
a puros gritos: by just shouting
a rastras: dragging
a ratos: from time to time, at times
a ratos perdidos: in odd or spare moments
a sabiendas: consciously
a secas: plain, simply
a solas: alone
(estar) a sus anchas: (to be) at one's ease
a tientas: gropingly
a todas luces: by all means, any way you look at it
a tontas y a locas: haphazardly
a trancas y barrancas: in spite of all the obstacles
con creces: amply
de bruces: face downward
de buenas a primeras: all of a sudden, unexpectedly
de espaldas (a alguien): with one's back toward (someone)
de mentiras: as a joke
de mentirijillas/mentirillas: for fun
de oídas: by ear
de puntillas: on tiptoe
de rodillas: on one's knees
de todas maneras: anyway, at any rate
de todos modos: in any case, by all means
de veras: seriously
echar flores: to compliment
en cueros: naked
en las últimas: at death's door, down to one's last penny
en sus cabales: in one's right mind

en volandas: off the ground, in the air
entre bastidores: behind the scenes, offstage
hacer gestos: to make faces at
hacer las paces: to make up after a quarrel
hacer pedazos: to break into pieces
hacer trizas: to smash to pieces, to tear to shreads
hacerse ilusiones: to fool oneself
para sus adentros: to one self
por las buenas: willingly
por las buenas o por las malas: whether ones likes it or not
por las malas: by force
por las nubes: sky-high
repetidas veces: over and over again
volver a las andadas: to fall back into old habits

In Latin America, plurals are often used with nouns which in the Peninsula would tend to be singular:

los altos: the upper floor
los bajos: the ground floor
mis entusiasmos: my enthusiasm
no me eches las culpas: don't blame me
sin miedos: unafraid

The word *hora* in Latin America is used in the plural in expressions like *¿Qué horas son?* (What time is it?) and *¿A qué horas nos vamos?* (What time do we leave?),[37] whereas in Spain one would say *¿Qué hora es?, ¿A qué hora nos vamos?*

The words *día, tarde,* and *noche* are almost always in the plural when part of greetings: *¡Buenos días!* (Good morning!), *¡Buenas tardes!* (Good afternoon/evening!), *¡Buenas noches!* (Good evening/ night!). The form *buen día* also can be found.

In some instances singular and plural can be used more or less interchangeably:

el bigote/los bigotes: mustache
el cimiento/los cimientos: foundations
la escalera/las escaleras: stairs
la nariz/las narices: nose
el pantalón/los pantalones: trousers

---

[37] However some variation may be found: *¿Me presta su hora?* (What time is it?) or *¿Me dice la hora?* (Would you tell me the time?).

ACRONYMS (*SIGLAS*)

One peculiarity of Spanish acronyms is that the plural is often expressed by doubling of letters:

AAEE (Asuntos Exteriores): State Department
CC.OO. (Comisiones Obreras): Communist Trades Union in Spain
EE.UU. (Estados Unidos): United States
FC (*ferrocarril*) / FF.CC. (*ferrocarriles*): railway/railroad network
FFAA (Fuerzas Armadas): Armed Forces

CHAPTER 4

WORD FORMATION

AFFECTIVE SUFFIXES AND SPELLING CHANGES

Affective suffixes are frequent in Spanish and have a wide range of expressive meanings: affection, irony, repugnance, revulsion, and others. They may sound artificial, but they do follow a few basic rules:

1. The addition of an affective suffix to a noun stem usually does not change the noun gender: *platito* < *plato, casita* < *casa, arbolito* < *árbol.*

2. The augmentative *-ón* may make a feminine noun masculine: *botellón* < *botella, cabezón* < *cabeza.*

3. The addition of a suffix sometimes necessitates a change of spelling: *hamaquita* < *hamaca, cervecita* < *cerveza.*

4. Sometimes the addition of a suffix to the stem word requires vowels to be dropped, or supporting vowels and consonants may be added: *cas + ita* < *casa, mach + ito* < *macho, hombr + ón* < *hombre, leche + c + ita* < *leche,*[1] *examen + c + ito* < *examen, mujer + c + ita* < *mujer.*

5. With the addition of a suffix, words ending in an unaccented vowel or diphthong lose their final vowel, but if the vowel is accented it may be maintained and the *i* of the suffix carries the accent:

familia	family	*familita*
frío	cold	*friíto*
mamá	mummy	*mamaíta* or *mamita*[2]
mesa	table	*mesita*
papá	daddy	*papaíto* or *papito*

6. Words of one syllable often take forms in *-ec-* + suffix. However, some variations in *-c-* + suffix can appear based on dialectic preferences:

---

[1] But also *lechita.*
[2] But also *mamacita.*

flor	flower	*florecita/florcita*
pan	bread	*panecillo* (bread roll)/*pancillo/pancito*
pez	fish	*pececito/pececillo*
pie	foot	*piececito/piececillo*
pis	wee-wee	*pisecito*
sol	sun	*solecito/solcito/solito*
té	tea	*tecito*
tos	cough	*tosecita/tosecilla*
tren	train	*trenecito/trencito*
voz	voice	*vocecita*

7. Suffixes can be added to all grammatical categories with the exception of articles, prepositions, and conjunctions: *sombrajo* < *sombra* (noun), *ricacho* < *rico* (adjective), *primerita* < *primera* (ordinal number), *dosito* < *dos* (cardinal number), *ahorita* < *ahora* (adverb), *bailotear* < *bailar* (verb), *cuantísimo* < *cuanto* (pronoun), ¡*clarito, clarito!* < *claro* (interjection).

COMPOUND WORDS

In Spanish, compound words are formed in several ways:

1. By word juxtaposition, with or without hyphen: *político-social, hombre rana.*

2. By joining two or more words (sometimes the first word is modified) which become a single word: *entrepierna, cuellicorto, vaivén, correveidile.*

3. By adding a Latin or Greek prefix to a Spanish word: *equidistancia, homoerótico.*

4. By adding a Latin or Greek suffix to a Spanish word: *socialismo, electrólito.*

5. By joining Latin or Greek prefixes or suffixes: *egolatría, epidermis.*

PREFIXES AND SUFFIXES

PREFIX OR SUFFIX	MEANING OR USE	EXAMPLES
a-	lack	*amoral*
	negation	*ateo*

PREFIX OR SUFFIX	MEANING OR USE	EXAMPLES
	epenthetic (forming verbs from nouns and adjectives)	*agrupar*
	before vowels, *an-*	*analfabeto*
ab-	separation	*ablación*
	origin	*aborigen*
	character or nature	*abominable*
-áceo, -ácea	having the nature or form	*concháceo*
	relating to	*herbáceo*
	formation of names of zoological classes	*Crustáceo*
aceti-, aceto-	acetic acid	*acetímetro, acetoso*
-acho, -acha	pejorative	*populacho, ricacha*
-aco, -aca	pejorative	*pajarraco*
	one that is of or belonging to	*austriaco*
	relation	*afrodisiaco*
acro-	top, peak, summit	*acrofobia*
actino-, -actinio	ray, radiation, having raylike structures	*actinología, radiactinio*
acu-	water	*acuatizar*
acut-, acuti-	sharp	*acutángulo, acutipenne*
ad-	adjacent to	*adjunto*
	direction	*adentrarse*
	insistence	*admirar*
	before some consonants, *a-*	*anexo*
-ada	group	*estacada*
	action	*alcaldada*
	abundance	*tomatada*
	blow	*patada*
	product	*naranjada*
	content	*palada*
	duration	*otoñada*
adelfo-, -adelfo	having stamens growing together in bundles	*adelfogamia, filadelfo*
adelo-, -adelo	quality of invisible	*adelópodo, carpadelo*
aden-, adeno-	gland	*adenalgia, adenoma*
adip-, adipo-	of or relating to animal fat	*adiposis*
-ado	time	*papado*

PREFIX OR SUFFIX	MEANING OR USE	EXAMPLES
	possession	*barbado*
	similarity	*azulado*
	employment or dignity	*doctorado*
	jurisdiction	*obispado*
	location	*condado*
	group	*alcantarillado*
aer-, aero-	air	*aerícola, aeródromo*
-agogia, -agogía	direction, guidance	*demagogia*
-agogo	leader, bringer	*pedagogo*
agri-	(from Latin) relative to the countryside	*agrimensor*
agro-	(from Greek) relative to the countryside	*agrónomo*
-aico, -aica	one that is of or belonging to	*hebraico, incaico*
	condition	*algebraico*
	similarity	*pirenaico*
-aina	pejorative	*tontaina*
	group	*azotaina*
-aja	pejorative diminutive	*migaja*
-aje	with verbs: action	*aterrizaje*
	location	*hospedaje*
	result	*viraje*
	with nouns: group	*andamiaje*
	time	*aprendizaje*
	fees	*pupilaje*
-ajo, -aja	pejorative diminutive	*colgajo, migaja*
-al	with adjectives: relation to or belonging to	*ficcional*
	with nouns: abundance, place	*peñascal, arenal*
alcoho-	alcohol	*alcoholímetro*
-ales	humoral	*frescales*
-algia, -álgico	pain	*neuralgia, cefalálgico*
-alla	pejorative for groups	*canalla, clerigalla*
alo-	difference, different origin	*alófono*
ambi-	with two qualities or possibilities	*ambivalente, ambidextro*
-ambre	group	*pelambre*
-amen	group	*velamen*

PREFIX OR SUFFIX	MEANING OR USE	EXAMPLES
-án, -ana	one that is of or belonging to	*catalán*
ana-	upward	*anábasis*
	opposition	*anacrónico*
	backward	*anagrama*
	repetition	*anadiplosis*
	conformity	*analogía*
-ancia	result of an action	*fragancia*
-anco, -anca	pejorative	*potranca*
andro-, -andro	relative to man or male	*andropausia, poliandro*
anemo-	relative to the wind	*anemoscopio*
-áneo, -ánea	belonging to	*coetáneo*
anfi-	on both sides, of both kinds	*anfibio*
	around	*anfiteatro*
anglo-	relative to English	*anglohablante*
-ango	pejorative	*caballerango*
-ano, -ana	one that is of or belonging to	*italiano, luterano*
	relation to	*ciudadano*
	advocate	*maltusiano*
anta-, anti-, anto-	opposed to	*antagonista, antípoda, Anticristo*
	substitution	*antonomasia*
	hostile to in opinion	*antisemita*
	opposing in effect	*antiácido*
	serving to prevent or cure	*antioxidante*
-ante	profession	*comerciante*
ante-	temporal priority	*anteayer*
	space priority	*antecámara*
antra-, antrac-, antraco-	carbon	*antracita, antracosis, antracotipia*
antropo-, -ántropo, -antropía	human being	*antropocentrismo, filántropo, filantropía*
-anza	action and effect	*enseñanza*
	person/object that executes an action	*ordenanza, libranza*

PREFIX OR SUFFIX	MEANING OR USE	EXAMPLES
apne-, apneo-	lack of respiration	*apneumia, apneología*
apo-	away from	*apofonía*
-ar	group	*melonar*
	relative to or belonging to	*muscular*
-arca, arce-, arci-, archi-, arqui-, -arquía, arz-	eminent above or before others	*jerarca, arcediano, arcipreste, archiduque, arquitecto, monarquía, arzobispo*
	abundance	*archipiélago*
	extreme (familiar)	*archiconocido*
-ardo	pejorative	*goliardo*
argiri-, argirio-, argiro-	silver	*argirismo*
-ari	profession	*pelotari*
-ario, -aria	group	*vocabulario*
	profession	*funcionario*
	location	*santuario, ovario*
	order	*terciario*
aristo-	excellence, the best	*aristocracia*
aritm-, aritmo-, -aritmo	number	*aritmética, aritmómetro, logaritmo*
arque-, arqueo-, arqui-	primitive, ancient	*arqueología*
	points of origin	*arquiplasma*
-arraco, -arraca	pejorative augmentative	*bicharraco*
-arria	pejorative	*fanfarria*
-arro, -arra	pejorative	*buharro*
-arrón, -arrona	augmentative of *-arro*	*vozarrón*
arterio-, artero-, arteri-	artery	*arteriosclerosis, arteriectopatia*
artri-, artro-	joint	*artritis, artropatía*
-asco, -asca	augmentative	*peñasco*
-asta	profession	*cineasta*
-astenia	weakness	*neurastenia*
aster-, astro-	relative to or similar to stars	*asteroide, astrofísico, astronauta*

PREFIX OR SUFFIX	MEANING OR USE	EXAMPLES
-astro, -astra	pejorative	poetastro, camastro
-ático, -ática	belonging to	lunático, catedrático
atmos-	air	atmósfera
-ato, -ata	dignity or rank	decanato, bachillerato
	action (in feminine)	cabalgata
	jurisdiction	virreinato
	character or nature	pazguato, sensato
auto-	self-acting, self-regulating	automóvil, autodidacta
-avo, -ava	number of parts of the unity	doceavo
-az	character or nature	voraz
-azgo	status	noviazgo
	action	hallazgo
-azo, -aza	augmentative	muchachaza
	result of an action	martillazo
	origin	linaza
bacili-	rod-shaped	baciliforme
bacteri-, bacterio-	bacteria	bactericida, bacteriófago
bari-, baro-	relative to the weight or pressure	baricentro, barómetro
ben-, bene-	virtuous or righteous	bendición, beneficencia
bi-, bis-, biz-	repetition	bicolor, bisojo, biznieto
biblio-	book	biblioteca
bio-, -bio	life	biología, microbio
blasto-, -blasto	germ	blastogénesis, espongioblasto
-ble	with the capacity of	adaptable, temible
bleno-	mucus	blenorragia
-blepsia	vision	monoblepsia
-bola, -bole	direction	parábola, hipérbole
botan-, botano-	plant	botánica, botanomancia
bradi-	relative to slow organic processes	bradicardia

PREFIX OR SUFFIX	MEANING OR USE	EXAMPLES
branqui-, *-branquio*	relative to or similar to branchiae	*branquífero,* *lamelobranquio*
braqui-	short	*braquicéfalo*
brio-	moss	*briófago*
broma-, *bromato-,* *bromo-*	aliment	*bromatología,* *bromotológico*
bronco-	bronchus	*broncolito*
-bundo	condition or situation	*meditabundo,* *moribundo*
calco-	copper or bronze	*calcografía*
cali-, calo-	rightness, beauty	*caligrafía*
carcino-	cancer	*carcinoma*
-cardia, -cardio	heart	*taquicardia,* *pericardio*
-carpio, carpo-, *-carpo*	fruit	*endocarpio,* *carpófago,* *macrocarpo*
carni-, carn-	relative to meat or flesh	*carnívoro, carnaval*
cata-	downward	*cataclismo,* *catacumba*
caum-, caus-, *-causto,* *cauter-*	relative to burns	*caumestesia,* *causalgia,* *holocausto,* *cauterizante*
cefal-, -cefalia, *cefalo-,* *-céfalo*	head	*cefalalgia,* *hidrocefalia,* *cefalópodo,* *dolicocéfalo*
-cele	tumor	*hidrocele*
cel-, celo-	empty	*celentéreo, celoma*
centi-	hundredth part	*centímetro*
-ceo, -cea	similarity	*rosáceo*
cera-, cerato-, *-cero*	with horn or horn-shaped	*cerastes, ceratoi-* *deo, ropalocero*
ciclo-, -ciclo	circle	*ciclómetro, triciclo*
-cida, -cidio	action and effect of killing	*homicida, suicidio*
cimo-	relative to the fermentation process	*cimógeno*

PREFIX OR SUFFIX	MEANING OR USE	EXAMPLES
cin-, cino-	dog	cinegético, cinocéfalo
cinema-, cinesi-, -cinesis, cineto-	movement	cinematógrafo, cinesiterapia, cariocinesis, cinetogénesis
-ción, -ación, -ición	action	acción, aclamación, cocción, prohibición
cir-, quir-, quiro-	hands, handicraft	cirugía, quiralgia, quiromancia
circum-, circun-	around	circumpolar, circunvolar
cirro-	yellowish	cirronosis
cis-	on this side	cisalpino
cisti-, cisto-, -cisto	bladder	cistitis, cistoespasmo, microcisto
cito-, -cito	relative to the organic cells	citoplasma, fagocito
citra-	on this side	citramontano
-clasta, -clástico	action and effect of break	iconoclasta
clepto-	theft	cleptomanía
co-	jointly	codirector, comando
-cola	to live on	terrícola
cole-	bile	colesterina
com-, con-	jointly	compadre, condiscípulo
condro-, -condrio	cartilage	condrología, hipocondrio
coni-	cone	conífera
contra-	against or contrary	contracultura, contraventana
copr-, copri-, copro-	excrement	coprémesis, coprívoro, coprolito
-cordio	cord	clavicordio
cosmo-, -cosmo	universe	cosmografía, macrocosmo
cox-, coxi-	hip	coxidinia
-cracia, -crata	power, authority	democracia, demócrata

PREFIX OR SUFFIX	MEANING OR USE	EXAMPLES
-crasia, crasio-	group	idiosincrasia, crasiología
crimo-, crio-	in relation to cold	crimoterapia, criómetro
cripto-, -crifo	hidden, covered	criptografía, apócrifo
cris-, criso-	gold	crisantemo
cromato-, -cromía, -cromático, cromo-	color	cromatología, policromía, fotocromático, cromolitografía
crono-, -cronía	relative to time	cronómetro, isocronía
cruci-	cross	crucifixión
cuadri-, cuadru-	four	cuadrivio, cuadrúpedo
cuasi-	similarity	cuasicontrato
-culo	diminutive	tubérculo
-cultor, -cultura	cultivator, cultivate	apicultura
cupro-	copper	cuprotipia
dacrio-	relative to tears	dacriocistitis
dactili-, -dactilia, dactilo-	finger	dactiliforme, microdáctila, dactilografía
-dad	quality	levedad, generosidad
	-ble + -dad = -bilidad	debilidad
de-, des-	separation	desaparecer
	reduction	devaluar
deca-	ten	decasílabo
deci-	tenth part	decilitro
dema-, -demia, -démico, demo-	people	demagogo, epidemia, endémico, democracia
dendro-, -dendro	tree	dendómetro, cinamodendro
derm-, derma-, dermato-, -dermia, -dermis	skin	dermitis, dermatología, dermatólogo, epidermis

PREFIX OR SUFFIX	MEANING OR USE	EXAMPLES
-dero, -dera	instrument	regadera
	place	matadero
	capacity (feminine and plural)	entendederas
	possibility	hacedero
des-	with the absence	descamisado
	do the opposite of	desactivar
	insistence	desgañitarse
	excess	deslenguado
	error	descaminado
	derived from	descompuesto
deutero-, deuto-	secondary	Deuteronomio, deutóxido
dexio-	right	dexiocardia
dextro-, -dextro	right	dextrogiro, ambidextro
di-	twice, twofold, double	dítono
di-, dia-	(from Greek) dispersion	diáspora
	through	diapositiva
di-, dis-	(from Latin) do the opposite of	disentir
	separation	dislocar
	origin	dimanar
	intensity	dilapidar
dico-	in two parts	dicotomía
-díctico, -digma	example	apodíctico, paradigma
dino-	terrifying, frightful	dinosaurio
diplo-, -diplosis	double	diplonomo, epanadiplosis
dipso-	thirsty	dipsomanía
dis-	difficulty	disnea
	alteration	discromía
dodeca-	twelve	dodecasílabo
dolico-	long	dolicocéfalo
-dor, -dora	action agent	trabajador
	instrument	batidora
	location	comedor
	profession	aguador
-doxia, doxo-, -doxo	belief	ortodoxia, heterodoxo
dromo-, -dromo	course, racecourse	dromómetro, hipódromo

PREFIX OR SUFFIX	MEANING OR USE	EXAMPLES
-dura	action or effect	*dictadura, mordedura*
	instrument	*cerradura*
-e	action or effect	*aguante, goce*
-ear	inchoative	*alborear*
	frequentative	*martillear*
	property	*agujerear, pasear*
-ececito, -ececillo, -ececico, -ececuelo	diminutive for monosyllabic word	*piececito*
-ecer	inchoative	*atardecer*
ecto-	extreme	*ectoplasma*
-edo, -eda	group, place	*robledo, arboleda*
-edal	*-edo + -al:* abundance, place	*robledal*
ego-	self	*egocentrismo, egoísmo*
-ego, -ega	one that is of or belonging to	*gallego*
-ejo	pejorative diminutive	*animalejo*
-el	noun derivative	*cordel*
electro-	electric	*electromotriz*
eleo-	oil	*eleófago*
-elo, -ela	diminutive	*libelo, cuidadela*
embrio-	embryo	*embriogenia*
-emesia, -emesis, emet-	vomit	*copremesia, hematemesis, emético*
-emia	blood	*leucemia*
en-	within, over	*encubrir, ensangrentar*
	negation	*enemigo*
-encia	result of an action	*permanencia, querencia*
-enco, -enca	belonging to	*ibicenco*
	quality	*azulenco*
endo-	within	*endoplasma*
-endo	necessity	*estupendo*
enea-	nine	*eneágono*
eno-	wine	*enólogo*

PREFIX OR SUFFIX	MEANING OR USE	EXAMPLES
-eno, -ena	group	quincena
	order	onceno, docena
	-en- + -ar	centenar
-ense	one that is of or belonging to	hispalense, circense
-ente, -iente	quality, person or thing that performs	durmiente, sirviente
entero-	intestine	enterotomía
ento-	within	entocito
-ento, -enta, -iento	condition	amarillento
	result of an action	calenturiento
entomo-	insect	entomología
entre-	between	entrecano
	relation	entrelazar
-eño, -eña	quality	almizcleño
	one that is of or belonging to	puertorriqueño
	similarity	marfileño
eo-	earliest	eolito
-eo, -ea	result of an action	paseo
	quality	marmóreo
epi-	upon, besides	epidermis
	after	epígono
	repetition	epifora
equi-	equally	equidistante
-erio	result of an action	vituperio
erit-, eritro-	red	eritremia
-ero, -era	profession	aduanero
	tree	melocotonero
	location	leonera
	belonging or relating to	dominguero
	quality	flojera
eroto-	love	erotógeno
-érrimo, -érrima	superlative	misérrimo
es-, ex-	out of, outside	escoger, expresidente
-és, -esa	one that is of or belonging to	aragonés, montañés
	quality	cortés

PREFIX OR SUFFIX	MEANING OR USE	EXAMPLES
-esa	feminine noun	alcaldesa, abadesa
-escato-	excrement or the latest	escatología
-esco, -esca	in the manner or style of, but with a pejorative meaning	oficinesco, soldadesca
eso-	inside	esotérico
esperma-, -spermo	seed	espermatorrea, estatospermo
esplacno-	viscera	esplacnomancia
esplen-	arm	esplenalgia
espor-, -spora, -sporangio	seed	esporangio, diáspora, zoosporangio
esquizo-	split	esquizofrenia
estafil-	cluster	estafilococo
estear-, estearo-, esteato-	grease	estearina
esten-, esteno-	narrow	estenocardia
estereo-	solid	estereómetro
-estesia, estesio-	sensation	anestesia
esteto-	thorax	estetoscopio
estomat-, estomato-	mouth	estomatitis, estomatología
-estre	belonging or relating to	terrestre, rupestre
-ete, -eta	pejorative diminutive	mozalbete, mujereta
	one that is of or belonging to	lisboeta
etno-	race or ethnicity	etnografía
-eto, -eta	diminutive	folleto, paleto
eu-	good, well, easily	eutanasia, eugenesia
extra-	outside, beyond	extraterrestre
-evo, -eva	long duration	longevo
-ez	patronymic	López
	quality	honradez
-eza	quality	delicadeza
-ezno, -ezna	diminutive	osezno, torrezno
-fagia, -fago, -faga	eat	antropofagia
fanero-	manifest	fanerógamo
-fano	manifest	quirófano

PREFIX OR SUFFIX	MEANING OR USE	EXAMPLES
feo-	dark	*feofíceo*
-fero, -fera	reason	*salutífero*
	participant	*aurífero*
-fíceo, fico-	algae	*feofíceo, ficología*
-fico, -fica	reason	*maléfico*
	quality	*clarífico*
	similarity	*deífico*
fil-, fili-, filo-, fila-	leaf	*filanteo, filito, filófago*
fil-, -filia, filo-, -filo, -fila	love	*filantropía, bibliófilo*
fil-, filo-	race	*filarca, filogenia*
-física, fisio-	nature	*astrofísica, fisiología*
fito-, -fito	plant	*fitogenesia, fitomorfismo*
fleb-, flebo-	vein	*flebitis*
flori-, -floro	flower	*floricultura, trifloro*
-fobia, -fobo	dread of, phobic aversion toward	*hidrofobia, anglófobo*
foli-, -folio	leaf	*foliforme, caducifolio*
fono-, -fono	sound	*fonógrafo, teléfono*
-foro	bearer of	*cromóforo, semáforo*
fos-, foto-, -foto	light	*fósforo, fotocopia, telefoto*
-frenia, freno-	intelligence	*esquizofrenia, frenopatia*
-fugo, -fuga	to drive away	*centrífugo*
fungi-	fungus	*fungívoro*
galact-, galacto-	milk	*galactemia*
gameto-, -gamia, gamo-, -gamo	union	*gametocito, poligamia, gamopétala, gamogénesis*
gastero-, gastr-, -gastrio, gastro-	stomach	*gasterópodo, gastronomía, gastroenteritis*

PREFIX OR SUFFIX	MEANING OR USE	EXAMPLES
gen-, genea-, -génesis, -genia, geno-, -geno	birth, origin	génesis, genealogía, biogénesis, genocidio, hidrógeno
geo-, -geo	earth, ground	geografía, apogeo
geri-, gero-, -geronto	old age	geriatría, gerontología
gimn-, gimnas-, gimno-	naked	gimnasia, gimnosperma
gin-, gine-, gineco-, -ginia, gino-, -gino	feminine genre	ginántropo, ginecólogo, misoginia, ginostemo
glicer-, glici-, glico-, gluco-	sweet	glicerina, glicicarpo, glucometría
glifo-, glipto-, -glifo, -glífico	carving	glifografía, gliptografía, anáglifo
gloso-, -glota, -glotis	language	glosomanía, políglota, epiglotis
gnoseo-, -gnosis, gnost-	knowledge	gnoseología, diagnosis, gnosticismo
gona-, gonado-, gono-, -gono	generation	gonaducto, gonococo, epígono
-gonal, gonio-, -gono	angle	diagonal, polígono
-grafe, grafo-, -grafo, grama-, -grama, gramo-	letter, writing	epígrafe, grafología, bolígrafo, gramática, telegrama
hagio-, -agio	saint	hagiografía, trisagio
haplo-	simple	haplopétalo
hecto-	hundred	hectómetro
helio-, heli-, -elio	sun	heliógrafo
hema-, hemato-, hemo-, -emia	blood	hemafobia, hemorragia, leucemia

PREFIX OR SUFFIX	MEANING OR USE	EXAMPLES
hemero-, -emérides, -ímero	short duration event	hemeroteca, efemérides, efímero
hemi-	half	hemiplejia
hepta-	seven	heptasílabo
hetero-	the other of two, other, diversity	heterosexual
hex-, hexa-	six	hexámetro
hial-, hialo-	glass	hialografía
hidato-, hidra-, -hidrato, hidro-	water	hidrógeno, hidráulico
hilo-	material	hilomorfismo
hiper-	excessive, unusual	hipertrofia
hipno-, -ipnosis	sleep	hipnosis, hipnotizar
hipo-	under, below	hipodermis
hipo-	horse	hipódromo
histo-	tissue	histología
holo-	whole, entire	holocausto
homeo-	similar	homeopatía
homo-	same, identical	homosexual, homoerótico
-í	one that is of or belonging to	ceutí
-ia, -ía	employment or dignity, and territory	alcaldía, abadía
	group	judería
	country	Alemania
	quality	alevosía
	ero + -ía > ería	bellaquería
	nouns ending in -dor: o > u	habladuría
-iatra, -iatría	healing, medical practice	siquiatría
-icia	abstract quality	avaricia
-icie	quality	calvicie
-icio, -icia	action and effect	ejercicio
	belonging	alimenticio
-ico, -ica	diminutive	garbancico
icono-	image, likeness	iconografía
ictio-	fish	ictiófago

PREFIX OR SUFFIX	MEANING OR USE	EXAMPLES
-idad	quality	divinidad
	state	virginidad
ideo-	idea	ideograma
-ido, -ida	result of an action	ronquido, aullido
ido-, ídolo-	image	idolatría
-iego, -iega	one that is of or belonging to	mujeriego, pasiego
-iento, -ienta	quality or similarity	polvoriento
-ificar	to form causative verbs	deificar, mortificar
igni-	fire	ignífugo
-ijo, -ija	diminutive	lagartijo
	result of an action	amasijo
	location	escondrijo
-il	one that is of or belonging to	mujeril, dócil
	diminutive	tamboril, ministril
-illo, -illa	diminutive	canastillo
-imbre	result of an action	urdimbre
-imo	ordinals	séptimo
	superlatives	óptimo, pésimo
in-, im-, ir-, i-	negation or privation	incoloro, impermeable
	location where	implantar
	im- before p or b	imposible
	ir- before l or r	irresoluto
	i- before l	ilegal
-ín, -ina	diminutive	botiquín
	one that is of or belonging to	mallorquín
	person that performs	bailarín
-íneo, -ínea	similarity	jazmíneo
	belonging to	sanguíneo
infra-	below	infradesarrollado
-ino, -ina	diminutive	cebollino
	one that is of or belonging to	bilbaíno
	state	mortecino
inter-	between, among	intercambio
intra-	within	intravenoso
intro-	inside, within	introversión
-iño, -iña	diminutive	corpiño, lampiño
-ío, -ía	belonging to	bravío
	group	mujerío
	ero + ío (group)	vocerío

PREFIX OR SUFFIX	MEANING OR USE	EXAMPLES
-is	popular humoristic suffix	*mieditis, locatis*
-isa	feminine employment or dignity	*papisa, profetisa*
-isco, -isca	similarity or belonging to	*morisco, arenisca*
-ísimo, -ísima	superlative	*altísimo*
	n or *r* + *-ísimo* = *-císimo*	*jovencísimo*
-ismo	suffix of nouns denoting action or practice, state or condition, principles, doctrines, devotion or adherence	*ateísmo, platonismo, individualismo, analfabetismo, kantismo*
iso-	equal	*isómero*
-ista	employment, profession, person who holds certain principles, doctrines	*marmolista, organista, activista, comunista*
-ita	one that is of or belonging to	*moscovita*
-itis	inflammation or disease in a given part of the body	*bronquitis*
-ito, -ita	affective diminutive	*librito*
-itud	abstract names	*esclavitud*
-ivo, -iva	quality, similarity, tendency disposition	*expresivo, abortivo deportivo*
-izo, -iza	quality, similarity	*enfermizo*
	state	*fronterizo*
	tendency	*antojadizo*
	location (feminine)	*porqueriza*
-izar	action	*islamizar*
kilo-	thousand	*kilogramo*
lacti-, lacto-	milk	*lactífero*
laring-, laringo-	larynx	*laringitis*
latero-, -látero	side	*equilátero*
lati-	large extension or duration	*latifundio*
-latra, -latría	religious veneration	*egolatría*
lepido-	scale	*lepidóptero*
lepro-	leprosy	*leprofobia*
lepto-	thin, fine, slight	*leptofonía*
leuc-, leuco-	white	*leucocito*
levo-	left	*levógiro*
linf-, linfo-	water	*linfotomía*

PREFIX OR SUFFIX	MEANING OR USE	EXAMPLES
lip-, liparo-, lipo-	fat	*liposoluble, lipoblasto*
lis-, -lisia, -lisis	breakdown, decomposition	*lisemia, análisis, electrólisis*
lit-, lito-, -lito, -lítico	stone, calculus	*litografía, mono-lito, neolítico*
log-, logo-, -logo, -logismo	word, speech	*logomaquia, filólogo, neologismo*
-logía	field of scientific study, discipline	*teología*
longi-	long	*longímano*
macro-	large, abnormally large significant extended over a broad area	*macrocosmo macroevolución macroclima*
mal-	bad, wrongful, ill	*maldecir, malherido*
malaco-	softness	*malacodermo*
-mancia	divination	*necromancia*
mani-, -mano, -mania	craze	*manicomio*
	enthusiasm, often of an extreme nature	*bibliomanía*
mani-, manu-	hand	*manuscrito*
mast-, masto-	breast	*mastitis*
matri-	mother	*matriarcado*
mecano-	mechanical	*mecanografía*
mega-, megalo-	extremely large, huge equal to one million	*megalomanía megatón*
mela-, melan-, melano-	black	*melanoma, melancolía*
meli-	honey	*melifluo*
melo-	music	*melomanía*
meno-	month	*menopausia*
-menta, -mienta	collection	*vestimenta, herramienta*
-mente	mode of action	*fácilmente*
-mento	action or effect	*salvamento*
meri-, mero-, -mero	part, partial	*meristemo, polímero*

PREFIX OR SUFFIX	MEANING OR USE	EXAMPLES
mes-, meso-	middle	*mesocracia*
-mestral,	month	*trimestral*
-mestre		
met-, meta-	after, beyond	*metafísica*
metr-, metro-	uterus	*metropatía*
-metría, metro-,	measure	*simetría,*
-metro		*termómetro*
metro-	center	*metrópoli*
mi-, mio-	muscle	*miocardio*
miceto-,	fungus	*micetografía,*
-miceto,		*micófago*
mico-		
micro-	small	*microbio*
-miento	action or resulting state	*hundimiento*
mili-	a thousandth part	*milímetro*
mim-, -mima,	imitate, copy	*pantomima,*
mimo-		*mimógrafo*
mini-	small or reduced size in comparison with others	*minifalda,* *minifundio*
mio-	less	*Mioceno*
miria-	ten thousand	*miriámetro*
mis-, miso-	hate	*misógino*
mixa-, mixe-,	mucous	*mixodermia*
mixo-		
mnemo-,	memory	*mnemotecnia,*
-mnesia		*amnesia*
mon-, mono-	one, single, alone	*monoteísta*
morfo-, -morfo,	form, structure	*morfología,*
-morfismo,		*isomorfo*
-morfosis		
multi-	many, much, multiple, many times, more than one, more than two, composed of many like parts, in many respects	*multimillonario,* *multinacional,* *múltiplo*
naft-	petroleum	*naftalina*
nano-	very small, minute, one billionth (10^{-9})	*nanosegundo*

PREFIX OR SUFFIX	MEANING OR USE	EXAMPLES
naso-	nose	*nasofaríngeo*
nau-, naut-, -nauta	navigate	*naufragio, astronauta*
ne-, neo-	new, recent	*neologismo, neófito*
neci-, necro-, nigro-	dead, corpse	*necrópolis, nigromancia*
nefelo-, nefo-	cloud	*nefelómetro*
nefr-, nefro-	kidney	*nefrología*
nema-, nemat-, nemato-	thread, threadlike organism	*nematócero*
neuma-, neumato-, neumo-	lung	*neumograma*
neur-, neuro-, -neurosis	nerve, nervous system	*neurología, neuralgia*
neutro-	neutral	*neutrófilo*
nict-, nicti-, nicto-	night	*nictitropismo, nictofobia*
nitro-	presence of nitrogen	*nitroglicerina*
noct-, nocti-	night	*noctámbulo*
nom-, -nomia, nomo-	custom, law	*autonomía, nomografía*
nomen-, nomin-	name	*nomenclator, nominativo*
nos-, noso-	disease	*nosocomio*
nudi-, nudo-	nude	*nudícolo*
nuli-	null, nothingness	*nulípara*
numi-	coins or paper money	*numismática*
ob-	because of	*obstáculo, obturar*
octa-, octi-, octo-	eight	*octacordio, octifolio, octosílabo*
odo-	way	*odómetro*
odont-, -odonte, odonto-, -odontosia	teeth	*odontología, mastodonte*
odor-, odoro-	smell	*odorífero, odorografía*
ofido-, ofi-, ofio-	reptile	*ofidosaurio*

PREFIX OR SUFFIX	MEANING OR USE	EXAMPLES
oftalm-, -oftalmia, oftalmo-	eye	*oftalmología*
-oide, -oideo, -oides, -oidal	resembling, like	*humanoide, comunistoide, coloidal*
-ojo, -oja	pejorative	*pintojo*
olei-, oleo-	oil	*oleicultura, oleómetro*
olig-, oligo-	few, little, scant	*oligarca, oligocarpo*
-oma	tumor	*fibroma*
omni-	all	*omnipresencia*
-ón, -ona	augmentative	*hombrón*
	abundance	*barrigón*
	ironically used, lack	*pelón, rabón*
	age	*cincuentón*
	habit	*mirón*
	violent action	*empujón*
onco-	tumor	*oncología*
-ongo/a	pejorative diminutive	*frailongo*
onic-, onico-	nail	*onicofagia*
onir-, oniro-	of or pertaining to dreams	*onirocrítica*
-onimia, -ónimo, onoma-, -onomasia, onomato-	word, name	*metonimia, topónimo, onomancia, antonomasia, onomatopeya*
onto-	being	*ontología*
oo-	egg	*oocito*
-ope, -opía	gaze	*miope, miopía*
opsi-, -opsia, -opsis, opto-, -optria, -orama	vision	*optometría, panorama, dioptría, autopsia, sinopsis*
-or, -ora	(added to nouns to form words designating) occupation	*escritor, actor*
	quality	*dulzor*
-orexia	appetite	*anorexia*
-orio, -oria	action or effect	*casorio*
ornit-, ornito-	bird	*ornitología*

PREFIX OR SUFFIX	MEANING OR USE	EXAMPLES
oro-	mountain	orografía
-orrio	pejorative	bodorrio
-orro	pejorative	tintorro
orto-	straight, correct	ortodoxia
-osis	disorders or abnormal states	tuberculosis
-oso, -osa	abundance	velloso
	quality	poderoso
	aptitude	habilidoso
ost-, osteo-, -osteon	bone	osteopatía, teleósteo
ot-, oto-	ear	otitis
-ote, -ota	pejorative augmentative or diminutive	islote, amigota
ovi-, ovo-, ovuli-	egg	ovíparo, ovulígero
paleo-	old, ancient	paleolítico
palin-	result of an action	palingenesia
palud-	swamp	paludismo
pan-, panto-	all	panorama, pantomima
par-, para-	at or one side of, side by side	parábola
	beyond, past	paradoja
	abnormal or defective	paranoia
pari-	equal	parisílabo
-paro, -para	bearing, producing	ovíparo
pato-, -pata, -patía	suffering, disease	patología, frenópata
patri-	father	patrimonio
ped-, peda-	child, boy	pedofilia, pedagogía
pedi-, -pedia	foot	pedicuro, ortopedia
-peda, -pedia	education	logopeda, enciclopedia
pen-, peni-	almost	península, penúltimo
penta-, pente-	five	pentagrama
pepsi-, pepto-, -pepsia	to digest	peptólisis, dispepsia
per-	intensity	pervivir
peri-	around	perímetro
	enclosing	pericardio

PREFIX OR SUFFIX	MEANING OR USE	EXAMPLES
petro-	rock, stone	petroglifo
-peya	to make	epopeya
pireto-, -pirético	fever	piretografía, antipirético
pir-, piri-, piro-	fire	pirita, pirotécnico
pisci-	fish	piscícola
pitec-, piteco-, -piteco	monkey	antropopiteco
plagio-	oblique	plagiocefalia
plasma-, -plasma, plasmo-	formation	protoplasma
-plastia, plasto-	to mold	rinoplastia
plat-, plati-, -plato	broad, wide	homóplato
pleo-, pletor-	complete	pleocromía
pleni-	complete	plenilunio
plio-	more	plioceno
pluri-	more than one	pluriempleo
pluto-	wealth	plutocracia
poli-	much, many	polígono
-poli, -polis, -polita	city	metrópoli, cosmopolita
pos-, post-	after, subsequent to, behind	posponer, postromántico
pre-	before, in front of, prior to, surpassing	predecir, prefacio, preconciliar
preter-	beyond, by, past	preternatural, preterición
pro-	in place of	pronombre, procónsul
	in front of	procesión
proto-	first, foremost, earliest form of	protomártir, protohistoria
psic-, psico-, -psicosis, psiqu-	soul	psicoanálisis, psiquiatría
ptero-, -ptero, tero-	wing	pterodáctilo
pueri-	boy	puericultura

PREFIX OR SUFFIX	MEANING OR USE	EXAMPLES
quili-, quilo-	numerous	quilópodo
quinque-	five	quinquefolio
quiro-	hand	quiromancia
radi-, radio-	radiant energy	radioactividad
radici-	root	radiciforme
re-	action in a backward direction	reacción
	action done again	reelaborar
	emphasize	rebonito
reo-, -rragia, -rrea	rupture, abnormal flow	hemorragia, menorrea
rete-	used to add emphasis in popular speech	retebueno
retro-	back, backward	retrógrado
rin-, rino-, -rrino	nose	rinoceronte
rizo-, -rrizo	root	polirrizo
sacar-, sacari-, sacaro-	sugar	sacarífero
sarco-, -sarco	flesh	sarcófago
-scopia, -scopio	examination, measurement	radioscopia
se-	apart	segregar
seleno-	moon	selenografía
sema-, semant-, semasio-, semio-	sign	semáforo, semántica
semi-	half, partially, somewhat	semicírculo, semihereje
-sepsia, septi-, -séptico	putrefaction, infection	aséptico, septicemia
sero-	serum	seroterapia
seud-, seudo-	false, pretended, unreal	seudónimo, seudointelectual
sex-	six	sexenio
sider-, sidero-	iron	siderurgia
silvi-	forest	silvicultura
simil-, simili-	similar	similar
sin-, sim-	with	sincronía
	sim- before b or p	simpatía
sin-	without	sinrazón

PREFIX OR SUFFIX	MEANING OR USE	EXAMPLES
so-, son-, sos-, su-, sub-, sus-	under, below	*soportar, sonreír, soslayar, suponer, submarino, suspender*
sobre-	beyond	*sobrealimentación*
-sofia, sofo-, -sofo	wisdom, knowledge	*filosofía, sofomanía*
-soma, somato-, somo-	body	*cromosoma, somatocroma*
somni-, somn-	sleep	*somnífero*
sota-, soto-	under	*sotoministro*
super-	above, beyond, to place or be placed above or over	*superestructura*
supra-	above, over, beyond the limits of	*supranatural*
-tanasia, tanato-	death	*eutanasia, tanatorio*
tauto-	same	*tautología*
taxi-, -taxia, -taxis, taxo-	order	*taxímetro, sintaxis, taxonomía*
tele-	reaching over a distance	*televisión*
teleo-, telo-	end, complete	*teleología*
teo-, -teo, -teón, -teosis	god	*teocracia, ateo, panteón*
-terapia	curative process	*radioterapia*
terato-	monster, malformation	*teratogenia*
-terio	place	*cementerio*
term-, termato-, termo-, -termo	heat, hot	*termoeléctrico, isotermo*
tetra-	four	*tetraedro*
-timia	soul	*lipotimia*
tipo-	image	*tipología*
-tomia, tomo-, -tomo	cutting, dissection, division	*anatomía, átomo*
top-, topo-, -topo	place	*toponimia, isótopo*
-torio	place or object appropriate for an activity	*dormitorio*

PREFIX OR SUFFIX	MEANING OR USE	EXAMPLES
	aptitude	*laudatorio*
tox-, toxi-, toxico-, toxo-	toxin, poison	*toxicología, toxicómano*
trans-, tras-	across, through	*transgresión, trasponer, transbordo*
tri-	three	*tridimensional*
-triz	feminine agent	*emperatriz*
trofo-, -trofia	nutrition, development	*hipertrofia*
tropo-, -tropismo, -tropo	turn, reaction	*tropología, geotropismo*
-ucar	pejorative	*besucar*
-ucho, -ucha	pejorative	*medicucho*
-uco, -uca	pejorative	*casuca*
-ud	quality	*juventud*
-udo, -uda	abundance	*cornudo*
-uelo, -uela, -zuelo, -ezuelo, -ecezuelo, -achuelo, -ichuelo	diminutive	*aldehuela, copichuela, jovenzuelo, piecezuelo, patizuelo*
-ueño, -ueña	agent	*pedigüeño, risueño*
-ujar	pejorative	*apretujar*
-ujo, -uja	pejorative diminutive	*pequeñujo*
-ulento, -ulenta	abundance	*flatulento*
-ullar	diminutive	*mascullar*
ultra-	on the far side, beyond	*ultramar*
	carrying to the furthest degree possible	*ultraderecha*
	extremely	*ultraligero*
-umbre	group	*muchedumbre*
	quality	*pesadumbre*
uni-	one	*unicelular*
-uno, -una	belonging to	*perruno*
-ura	result of an action	*quemadura*

PREFIX OR SUFFIX	MEANING OR USE	EXAMPLES
ura-, ureo-, *-urético,* *-uria,* *urino-, uro-*	urine	*diurético,* *urinógeno*
urano-	sky	*uranolito*
uro-, -uro	tail	*anuro*
-urrio	pejorative	*blandurrio*
-urro, -urra	pejorative	*beaturro*
-usco, -usca	similarity	*pardusco*
-uza	pejorative	*gentuza*
-uzco, -uzca	similarity	*negruzco*
-uzno	result of an action	*rebuzno*
vermi-	worm	*vermífugo*
vi-, vice-, viz-	in place of	*virrey, vicerrector,* *vizconde*
vini-	wine	*vinícola*
-voro, -vora	one that eats	*carnívoro*
xant-, xante-	yellow	*xantina*
xeno-	foreign, strange	*xenofobia*
-xera, xero-	dry	*filoxera*
xilo-	wood	*xilografía*
-zoario, -zoico, *zoo-, -zoo*	animal	*protozoario,* *zoología*
-zón	action or effect augmentative	*comezón* *cabezón*

CHAPTER 5

CAPITALIZATION

GENERAL RULES

The following must be written in Spanish with the initial letter capitalized:

Names of people: *Carmen, Ernesto*
Surnames or last names: *Martínez, García Lorca*
Place-names: *Asunción, Perú*
Nicknames: *Azorín, Clarín*
Institutions and organizations: *Ministerio de Cultura, Real Academia Española*
Qualifying adjectives of proper names: *Castilla la Vieja, el Gran Buenos Aires, Alfonso X el Sabio*
God's appellatives: *el Redentor, el Cordero de Dios* (see under Religious Names, below)
Titles of rank:[1] *el Rey, el Papa*
Abbreviations of titles of address: *Sra.* (*señora*), *S.A.R.* (*su alteza real*)

The following have capital initial letters (*letras mayúsculas*) in English but lowercase (*letras minúsculas*) in Spanish:

Gentilicios (nouns or adjectives denoting inhabitants of continents, countries, regions, towns, etc.) and their derivatives:
  los mexicanos: Mexicans
  la industria argentina: Argentine industry
  una peruana: a Peruvian woman
Nouns or adjectives denoting members of political parties or religious groups:
  los demócratas: the Democrats

---

[1] Such titles are written with lowercase initial letters when followed by the name of the person, as in *el papa Juan Pablo I;* or when used in an unspecified sense, as in *los reyes españoles.*

los judíos: the Jews
Points of the compass, unless abbreviated (*N, S, E, O*) or part of a place-name: *America del Sur* (South America), *el Polo Norte* (the North Pole).

CALENDAR AND TIME DESIGNATIONS

Month, season, and day of the week designations are written in lowercase letters: *el cuatro de julio es el día de la Independencia norteamericana; se encontraron el dos de octubre; los meses de verano son lluviosos; se reúnen sábados y domingos.* The same principle applies to non-Gregorian designations: *en el mes de ramadán.*

Dates are given in the following order: day/month/year. Examples: *el 25 de mayo de 1973* or *25-5-73.* Sometimes Roman numerals are used for months: *25-V-73.*

Words denoting units of time are spelled out in the text: *segundo, minuto, semana, mes, año, lustro, década, siglo.*

Some time designations are used only in abbreviated form: *a.m., p.m., a.C.* (antes de Cristo), and *d.C.* (después de Cristo). Note the capitalization in the latter two.

RELIGIOUS NAMES

God's designations are written with the initial letters capitalized: *el Señor, el Salvador.* The word *virgen* should also be written with capitalized initial letters when referring to the Mother of God: *la Virgen* and *la Virgen María.*

San and *santo* are written with capital initial letters when referring to individuals: *San José, Santa Bárbara, Santo Tomás.* In other cases, they must be written in all lowercase letters: *santo Dios, santo cielo.*

Expressions such as *año santo, año jubilar,* and *año de jubileo* are written in all lowercase letters.

An ecclesiastical hierarch's designations are usually written in all lowercase letters: *el papa reinante, el arzobispo de Buenos Aires, el patriarca de Alejandría.* Capital initial letters are to be used when referring to a historical figure without indicating the proper name: *el Papa* or *el Santo Padre.*

The words *evangelios* and *escrituras* are written with initial capital letters when referring to specific sacred books: *predicar el Evangelio, el Evangelio según San Mateo, las Sagradas Escrituras.*

Other religion-related designations are mostly written in lowercase letters: *la basílica de Luján, el monasterio de El Escorial, los apóstoles de Cristo, la iglesia de San Patricio.* One exception is the word *apóstol* when used as a nickname for *San Pablo: el Apóstol de los Gentiles.*

TITLES OF PUBLICATIONS

In titles of books and other works, current practice in Spanish differs from that in English. Whereas English normally capitalizes the first letter of all first and last words and all nouns, pronouns, adjectives, verbs, adverbs, and subordinating conjunctions, Spanish does not use capitals after the first word (except for those proper nouns listed above that are always capitalized):

> *Cien años de soledad: One Hundred Years of Solitude*
> *La muerte de Artemio Cruz: The Death of Artemio Cruz*

CHAPTER 6

TITLES OF PERSONS

TITLES OF NOBILITY

archiduque, archiduquesa: archduke, archduchess
barón, baronesa: baron, baroness
baronet: baronet
conde, condesa: count, countess
delfín: dauphin
duque, duquesa: duke, duchess
emperador, emperatriz: emperor, empress
hidalgo: hidalgo, noble
infante, infanta: prince, princess
marqués, marquesa: marquess, marchioness
menina: maid of honor
príncipe, princesa: prince, princess
rey, reina: king, queen
señor, señora: sir, lady
virrey, virreina: viceroy, vicereine
vizconde, vizcondesa: viscount, viscountess

RELIGIOUS TITLES

abad, abadesa: abbot, abbess
acólito: acolyte
archidiácono: archdeacon
arzobispo: archbishop
cardenal: cardinal
coadjutor: coadjutor
cura: priest
diácono, diaconisa: deacon, deaconess
fraile: friar

hermano, hermana: brother, sister
lego, lega: lay brother, lay sister
madre: mother
madre superiora: mother superior
ministro: minister
misionero, misionera: missionary
monaguillo: altar boy
monje: monk
monja: nun
monseñor: monsignor
obispo: bishop
padre: father
Papa, Sumo Pontífice: pope
pastor: pastor, clergyman
patriarca: patriarch
presbítero: presbyter, priest
rabino: rabbi
sacerdote, sacerdotisa: priest, priestess
sacristán, sacristana: sacristan, vestry nun
sochantre: succentor
vicario: vicar

ACADEMIC, DIPLOMATIC, AND POLITICAL TITLES

alcalde/alcaldesa: mayor
canciller: chancellor
cónsul: consul
decano/a: dean
diputado/a: congressman, congresswoman
diputado provincial: county councillor
doctor/a: doctor
embajador/a: ambassador
gobernador/a: governor
ministro/a: minister
ministro/a de Asuntos Exteriores: minister of foreign affairs, secretary
    of state
ministro/a de Comunicaciones: postmaster general
ministro/a de Educación: secretary of education
ministro/a de Hacienda: secretary of the treasury
ministro/a de Interior: secretary of the interior
ministro/a de Justicia: attorney general
ministro/a de Trabajo: secretary of labor

presidente/a: president
primer/a ministro/a: prime minister
profesor/a: professor
rector/a: rector
secretario/a municipal: town clerk
senador/a: senator
teniente de alcalde: deputy mayor
vicepresidente/a: vice president

MILITARY TITLES

abanderado: standard-bearer
alférez: second lieutenant
alférez de fragata: ensign
alférez de navío: lieutenant junior grade
almirante: admiral
cabo de escuadra: corporal
cabo de marina: leading seaman
cabo de policía: sergeant
cabo de vara: prison guard
capitán: captain
capitán de corbeta: lieutenant commander
capitán de fragata: commander
capitán general: field marshal
comandante: major
coronel: colonel
general: general
general de brigada: brigadier general
sargento: sergeant
sargento mayor: sergeant major
soldado: soldier
soldado de artillería: artilleryman
soldado de caballería: cavalryman
soldado de infantería: infantryman
soldado de infantería de marina: marine
soldado voluntario: volunteer
teniente: lieutenant
teniente coronel: lieutenant colonel
teniente general: lieutenant general

CHAPTER 7

PROFESSIONS AND OCCUPATIONS

abaniquero: fan manufacturer, fan dealer
abarrotero: storekeeper
abastecedor: supplier
abogado: lawyer
abogado acusador: prosecuting attorney
abogado de oficio: public defender
abogado penalista: criminal lawyer
acabador: finisher
acarreador: transporter
aceitero: oil seller
aceitunero: olive seller, olive harvester
acólito: altar boy
acomodador: usher
acordeonero: accordion manufacturer
acordeonista: accordionist
acróbata: acrobat
actor: actor
actriz: actress
actuario de seguros: actuary
actuario de tribunal: clerk of the court
acuafortista: etcher
acuanauta: aquanaut
acuarelista: watercolorist
acupuntor: acupuncturist
administrador: manager
administrador judicial: administrator
aduanero: customs officer
aeromozo: flight attendant
afilador: knife grinder
afinador: tuner
aforador: estimator, assessor

agente artístico: artistic agent
agente comercial: sales representative
agente de bolsa: stockbroker
agente de la propiedad inmobiliaria: real estate agent, realtor
agente del orden: police officer
agente de patentes: patent agent
agente de policía: police officer
agente de publicidad: advertising agent
agente de seguros: insurance broker
agente de tráfico: traffic policeman
agente de viajes: travel agent
agente literario: literary agent
agente secreto: secret agent
agiotista: money changer
agricultor: farmer
agrimensor: surveyor
agrobiólogo: agrobiologist
agrónomo: agronomist
aguador: water carrier
ajedrecista: chess player
alambrista: tightrope walker
albañil: bricklayer
albañil constructor: builder
alcaide: jailer
alcalde: mayor
alfarero: potter
algodonero: cotton planter, cotton farmer, cotton dealer
alguacil: bailiff
almacenero: grocer
almacenista: wholesaler
almuecín or *almuédano:* muezzin
alpinista: mountain climber
alquimista: alchemist
ama de llaves: housekeeper
amaestrador: animal trainer
ambulanciero: ambulance driver
analista: analyst
analista de inversiones: investment analyst
analista de presupuestos: budget analyst
analista de sistemas: systems analyst
anatomista: anatomist
anestesiólogo: anesthesiologist
anestesista: anesthetist

animadora: cheerleader
animador cultural: events organizer
animador de un hotel: social director
animador de un programa: host
antropólogo: anthropologist
anunciador: advertiser
aparejador: quantity surveyor
apicultor: beekeeper, apiarist
aprendiz: trainee
árbitro (en fútbol, boxeo): referee
árbitro (en tenis, béisbol): umpire
archivero or *archivista:* archivist
armador: shipowner
armero: gunsmith, armorer
arpista: harpist
arponero: harpooner
arqueólogo: archaeologist
arquero (fútbol): goalkeeper
arquitecto: architect
arreglista: arranger
arrendatario: tenant, lessee
arriero: mule driver, mule skinner, muleteer
arrocero: rice grower
artesano: craftsperson, artisan
artillero: artilleryman, gunner
artista (pintor, escultor): artist
ascensorista: elevator operator
aserrador: sawyer
asesor de imagen: public relations consultant
asesor fiscal: tax consultant
asesor militar: military consultant
asesor técnico: technical consultant
asistente: assistant
asistente social: social worker
astrólogo: astrologist
astronauta: astronaut
astrónomo: astronomer
auditor: auditor
autor: author, writer
auxiliar: assistant
auxiliar administrativo: administrative assistant
auxiliar de laboratorio: laboratory assistant
auxiliar de vuelo: flight attendant

avicultor: poultry farmer
ayudante: assistant
ayudante de campo: aide-de-camp
ayudante de cátedra: assistant professor
ayudante de cocina: kitchen porter
ayudante de dirección: assistant to the director
ayudante de producción: production assistant
ayudante técnico sanitario (ATS): registered nurse
azafata: flight attendant
azafata de congresos: conference hostess
azafata de tierra: ground stewardess, airline employee

bacaladero: cod fisherman
bacteriólogo: bacteriologist
bailaor: flamenco dancer
bailarín: dancer
bajista: bass player, bassist
balandrista: yachtsman
baloncestista: basketball player
ballenero: whaler
balsero: ferryman
bancario: bank employee
banderillero: banderillero
banquero: banker
bañista: bather
barítono: baritone
barman: bartender, barman
barquero: boatman
barrendero: road sweeper, street cleaner
basquetbolista: basketball player
bastonero: cane maker or seller
basusero: garbage collector
batelero: boatman
baterista: drummer
batidor de caza: beater in a hunt
bedel: porter
beisbolista: baseball player
bencinero: service station attendant
bibliotecario: librarian
biógrafo: biographer
biólogo: biologist
bioquímico: biochemist
bodeguero: wine producer, shopkeeper, warehouseman

boleador: bootblack
bolero: bootblack
boletero: ticket seller
bolichero: small store keeper
bolsista: stockbroker
bombero: firefighter, fireman
bordador: embroiderer
botánico or *botanista:* botanist
botellero: ragman
boticario: pharmacist, druggist
botones: bellboy
boxeador: boxer
boyero: drover, oxherd
bracero: temporary farmworker
bufón: jester
burgomaestre: burgomaster
buscador de oro: gold prospector
buscador de tesoros: treasure hunter
buzo: diver

caballerizo: groom
caballista: horseman
cabañero: herdsman, drover
cabaretera: cabaret dancer, showgirl, nightclub hostess
cabinista: projectionist
cabrerizo: goatherd
cafetalero or *cafetista:* coffee grower
cafetero: coffee grower or planter
caficultor: coffee grower
cajero: cashier
cajista: typesetter, compositor
calderero: tinker, boilermaker
caletero: longshoreman
callista: chiropodist
camarero: waiter, barman
camarógrafo: cameraman
camaronero: shrimper
cambista: money changer
camellero: camel driver
camillero: stretcher bearer, orderly, porter
camionero: truck driver, bus driver
camisero: shirt maker
campanero: bell ringer, campanologist

campero: farmworker
canastero: basket maker, basket weaver, basket seller
cancerbero: goalkeeper, keeper
cancerólogo: cancer specialist, oncologist
cantante or *cantor:* singer
cantaor: flamenco singer
cantautor: singer-songwriter
cantinero: barman
cañero: sugar plantation owner, sugar plantation worker, cane cutter
capataz: foreman
carabinero: police officer, policeman, border guard, mounted policeman
carbonero: coal merchant, coalman
carcelero: jailer
cardiocirujano: heart surgeon
cardiólogo: cardiologist
cargador de aviones: baggage handler
cargador de barcos: longshoreman
cargador de camiones: loader
caricaturista: caricaturist
carnicero: butcher
carpintero: carpenter
carretero: cart driver
carrocero: coach builder
cartelero: bill poster, bill sticker
cartero: mail carrier
cartógrafo: cartographer
cartomante: fortune-teller
casero: landlord, caretaker
castañero: chestnut seller
catador: tester
catavinos: wine taster
catedrático: professor
catequista: catechist
cazacriminales: bounty hunter
cazador: hunter
cazador de cabezas: headhunter
cazador de fortunas: fortune hunter
cazador de pieles: trapper
cazador furtivo: poacher
cazarecompensas: bounty hunter
cazatalentos: talent scout
celador de un museo: security guard

celador de una cárcel: prison guard
censista: census enumerator
censor: censor, critic, enumerator
censor de cuentas: auditor
censor jurado de cuentas: certified public accountant
centinela: guard
ceramista: ceramicist, ceramist
cerealista: grain farmer
cerillero: match seller
cerrajero: locksmith
cervantista: Cervantes scholar
cestero: basket maker, basket weaver, basket seller
chacarero: farmer
chacinero: person who makes/sells salami or sausages
chanchero: pig farmer, pork butcher
changador: porter
chef: chef
chelista: cellist
chichero: chicha seller
chiclero: street vendor (selling chewing gum)
chinchinero: street performer
chistulari: Basque flute player
chofer de autobús: bus driver
chofer de taxi: taxi driver
chofer particular: chauffeur
chumero: apprentice
churrero: person who makes/sells *churros*
ciclista: cyclist
científico: scientist
cineasta: filmmaker, moviemaker
cirquero: circus performer
cirujano: surgeon
cobrador a domicilio: collector, debt collector
cobrador de autobús: bus conductor
cochero: coach driver
cocinero: cook
codificador: encoder
colaborador: contributor
colectivero: bus driver
colmenero: beekeeper
colonialista: colonialist
columnista: columnist
comadrona: midwife

comediante: actor
comediógrafo: playwright, dramatist
comendador: commander
comentador or *comentarista:* commentator
comerciante: storekeeper, dealer, trader
cómico: comedy actor, comic actor, comedian, comic
comisario: captain
comisario (delegado): commissioner
comisario de carreras: steward
comisario de la quiebra: official receiver
comisario de una exposición: organizer
comisionista: commission agent
comparsa: extra
compilador: compiler
compositor: composer
comprador: buyer, purchaser
computista: computer programmer
concejal: town/city councilor, councilman
concertista: soloist
concertista de piano: concert pianist
conductor: driver
conductor de un programa: host, presenter
confeccionista: clothes manufacturer, clothes retailer
confitero: confectioner
congresista: congressperson
consejero: adviser
consejero delegado: chief executive
consejero de una embajada: counsel
conserje de un colegio: custodian, janitor
conserje de un edificio de apartamentos: superintendent
conserje de un hotel: receptionist
conservador de un museo: curator
consignatario de buques: shipping agent
constructor: builder, building contractor
constructor de coches: car manufacturer
contable or *contador:* accountant
contador público: certified public accountant
contorsionista: contortionist
contrabajista or *contrabajo:* double-bass player, double bassist
contrabandista: smuggler
contralor: comptroller
contratista: contractor
contramaestre: boatswain

controlador: controller
controlador de tráfico aéreo: air traffic controller
cónsul: consul
consultor: consultant
consultor jurídico: legal consultant
coordinador: coordinator, controller
copera: hostess
copiloto de avión: copilot
copista: copyist
coquero: person involved in the cocaine trade
cordelero: rope maker
coreógrafo: choreographer
corista: chorus girl
cornetista: bugler, cornet player
corrector de estilo: copy editor
corrector de pruebas de imprenta: proofreader
corredor: runner
corredor de bola: halfback, ball carrier
corredor de bolsa: stockbroker
corredor de carros: racing driver
corredor de fincas: real estate broker
corredor de fondo: long-distance runner
corredor de poder: fullback
corredor de seguros: insurance broker
corredor de vallas: hurdler
corregidor: judge, mayor
corresponsal: correspondent
cortador: cutter
cortijero: overseer
cosechador: harvester
cosmetólogo: beautician, cosmetologist
costurera: seamstress
coyote: person who helps illegal immigrants enter the United States
criada: servant, maid
criado: servant
criminalista: criminal lawyer
criminologista: criminologist
criptógrafo: cryptographer
cristalero: glazier, window cleaner
crítico: critic
cronista: journalist, reporter
cronista de radio: radio broadcaster
cronometrador: timekeeper

cuchillero: cutter, knife maker, knife seller
cuentista: short-story writer
cuidador de coches: attendant
cuidador de niños: childcare worker, childminder
cultivador: grower
culturista: bodybuilder
cupletista: singer or composer of *cuplés*
curandero: folk healer, witch doctor
currito: worker
curtidor: fanner
custodio: guardian

dactilógrafo: typist
dama de una reina: lady-in-waiting
decano: dean
decorador de interiores: interior decorator
defensor: defender, defense lawyer
defensor del pueblo: ombudsman
delantero centro: central forward
delegado apostólico: papal envoy
delegado de curso: student representative
delegado de Sanidad: director of regional health department
delineante: draftsman
demógrafo: demographer
dentista: dentist
dependiente: salesperson, salesclerk
deportista: sportsman
dermatólogo: dermatologist
deshollinador: chimney sweep
destilador: distiller
detective: detective
detective privado: private detective
diácono: deacon
diariero: newspaper vendor, newspaper delivery man or boy
dibujante: draftsman
dibujante de comics: comic book artist, strip cartoonist
dibujante publicitario: commercial artist
diestro: matador, bullfighter
dietista: dietitian
dinamitero: dynamite or explosives expert
director adjunto: deputy director
director de división: divisional director
director de escena: stage manager

director de escuela: principal
director de orquesta: conductor
director de periódico: editor, editor in chief
director de ventas: sales manager
director ejecutivo: executive director
director espiritual: father confessor
director general: general manager
director gerente: managing director
director técnico: head coach
disecador: taxidermist
diseñador de modas: fashion designer
diseñador de productos industriales: industrial or technical designer
distribuidor: distributor
doctor: doctor
documentalista: documentary maker
domador: tamer
domador de caballos: horse breaker
doméstico: servant
dramaturgo: dramatist, playwright

ebanista: cabinetmaker
echador de cartas: fortune-teller
ecólogo: ecologist
economista: economist
edecán: aide-de-camp, escort
editor: publisher, editor
editorialista: editorialist
educador: teacher, educator
ejecutante: performer
ejecutivo: executive
ejecutivo de ventas: sales executive
electricista: electrician
embajador: ambassador
embalador: packer
embalsamador: embalmer
embolador: bootblack
empacador: packer
empastador: bookbinder
emperador: emperor
empleada de hogar: maid, domestic servant
empleado: employee
empleado de banco: bank clerk, teller
empleado de oficina: office or clerical worker

empleado de tienda: clerk
empleado del Estado: civil servant
empleado público: civil servant
empleador: employer
empresario: businessman
empresario de boxeo: promoter
encargado de un negocio: manager
encuadernador: bookbinder
encuestador: pollster, survey taker
endocrinólogo: endocrinologist
enfermero: nurse
enfermero jefe: senior nurse
ensamblador: assembler, assembly worker
ensayista: essayist
enterrador: gravedigger
entomólogo: entomologist
entrenador: coach, trainer
entrevistador: interviewer
envasador: packer
ergoterapeuta: occupational therapist
ertzaina: Basque police officer
escalador (ciclista): mountain biker
escalador de montañas: mountaineer, climber
escalador de rocas: rock climber
escaparatista: window dresser
escenógrafo: scenographer
escolta: escort
escribano: scribe
escribano (notario): notary, notary public
escribano (secretario judicial): scrivener
escribiente: clerk
escritor: writer, author
escrutador: scrutineer, inspector
escultor: sculptor
esgrimista: fencer
especialista: specialist, expert
especialista en explosivos: bomb disposal expert
espeleólogo: spelunker, speleologist
espía: spy
espiritista: spiritualist
esquiador: skier
esquilador: sheep shearer, clipper
estadista: statesman

estadístico: statistician
estanquero: tobacconist
estenógrafo: stenographer
estenotipista: shorthand typist
esteticien: aesthetician, beautician
estibador: stevedore, longshoreman
estilista: stylist
estilista (peluquero): hairstylist
estilista de modas (diseñador): designer
estomatólogo: stomatologist
estraperlista: black marketeer
estudiante: student
etimólogo: etymologist
etiquetador: labeler
etnólogo: ethnologist
eurodiputado: member of the European Parliament
evangelizador: evangelist, missionary
examinador: examiner
excursionista: hiker
expedicionario: member of an expedition
expendedor de lotería: lottery ticket seller
expendedor de tabaco: tobacconist
explorador: explorer
explotador de un negocio: operator
exportador: exporter
expositor: exhibitor

fabricante: manufacturer
fabulista: fabulist, writer of fables
falsificador: forger
farmacéutico: pharmacist
farmacólogo: pharmacologist
feriante: exhibitor, stall holder, trader
ferretero: hardware dealer
ferroviario: railroad worker
filatelista: stamp collector, philatelist
figurinista: costume designer
filólogo: philologist
filósofo: philosopher
fiscal: district attorney
Fiscal General del Estado: Attorney General
físico: physicist
fisiculturista: bodybuilder

fisiólogo: physiologist
fisioterapeuta: physical therapist
flautista: flute player
floricultor: flower grower
florista: florist
fogonero: stoker, fireman
folklorista: folklorist
fondista: long-distance runner; innkeeper
foniatra or *fonoaudiólogo:* speech therapist
fontanero: plumber
forense: forensic scientist
fotógrafo: photographer
fresador: milling machine operator
frigorista: refrigeration engineer
frutero: fruit seller, greengrocer
fruticultor: fruit grower, fruit farmer
funcionario de correos: mail service employee
funcionario público or *funcionario del Estado:* government employee
fundidor: foundry worker
futbolista: soccer or football player
futurólogo: futurologist

gacetillero: reporter, article writer, gossip columnist
gaitero: bagpiper, piper, flautist
galeno: physician
galerista: gallery owner
ganadero: rancher
gandolero: truck driver
gasfitero: plumber
gaucho: gaucho (South American cowboy)
geneticista or *genetista:* geneticist
geógrafo: geographer
geólogo: geologist
gerente comercial: business manager
gerente de banco: bank manager
gerente general: general manager
geriatra: geriatrician, geriatrist
germanista: Germanist
gestor: agent
gimnasta: gymnast
ginecólogo: gynecologist
gladiador: gladiator
gobernador: governor

gobernanta (institutriz): governess
gobernanta en un hotel: staff manager
golfista: golfer
gomero: tire merchant
gondolero: gondolier
grabador: engraver
grafista: graphic artist, graphic designer
grafólogo: graphologist
gramático: grammarian
granjero: farmer
guachimán: watchman
guarda: guard
guarda de edificio público: security guard
guarda de un museo: museum keeper
guarda forestal: forest ranger
guarda jurado: security guard
guardabarrera: grade-crossing keeper
guardabosque (parque nacional): warden, forest ranger
guardabosque (particular): gamekeeper
guardacoches: parking lot attendant
guardacostas: coast guard
guardaespaldas: bodyguard
guardafaro: lighthouse keeper
guardagujas: switchman
guardalíneas: line judge
guardameta: goalkeeper
guardaparque: national park ranger
guardia: police officer
guardia civil: civil guard
guardia de tráfico: traffic policeman
guardia jurado: security guard
guardia marina: midshipman
guardia municipal/urbano: police officer
guardián: security guard
guerrero: warrior
guerrillero: guerrilla
guía: guide
guía de turismo: tourist guide
guionista: scriptwriter
guitarrista: guitarist

hacendista: expert in public finance
hagiógrafo: hagiographer

halconero: falconer
halterófilo: weightlifter
hechicero: sorcerer, wizard, witch doctor
heladero: ice-cream vendor, ice-cream seller
hematólogo: hematologist
herrador: blacksmith
herrero: blacksmith
higienista: hygienist
higienista dental: dental hygienist
hilandero: spinner
hipnotizador: hypnotist
hispanista: Hispanist, Hispanicist
historiador: historian
historiógrafo: historiographer
hojalatero: tinsmith
homeópata: homeopath
hortelano: truck farmer
horticultor: horticulturalist, gardener
hostelero: landlord
hotelero: hotel manager
humorista: humorist, comic writer, cartoonist

ilusionista: illusionist
imitador: imitator
impresor: printer
impulsador de ventas: sales promoter
industrial: industrialist
ingeniero: engineer
ingeniero agrícola: agricultural engineer
ingeniero eléctrico: electrical engineer
ingeniero industrial: industrial engineer
ingeniero mecánico: mechanical engineer
ingeniero químico: chemical engineer
inmunólogo: immunologist
inspector: inspector
instructor de vuelo: flight instructor
instrumentista: instrumentalist
intendente: manager
intérprete: interpreter
inventor: inventor
investigador privado: private investigator

jardinero: gardener
jefe: manager

jefe de crédito: credit manager
jefe de cuentas corrientes: checking account manager
jefe de publicidad: advertisement manager
jinete: jockey
jornalero: day laborer
joyero: jeweler
juez: judge
jurista: jurist

karateka: karate expert
kinesiterapeuta: masseur, masseuse

laboratorista: laboratory technician
labrador: farmer
ladrillador: bricklayer
ladrillero: brick maker
lancero: lancer
lanchero: boatman
laringólogo: laryngologist
latero: tinsmith
lavandera: laundress, washerwoman
lavandero: launderer, laundryman
lavaplatos: dishwasher
lector: reader
lechero: milkman
legislador: legislator
legista: jurist
lencero: draper
leñador: woodcutter
leñero: dealer in wood
letrado: lawyer
letrista: songwriter
lavantador de pesos: weightlifter
lexicógrafo: lexicographer
librero: bookseller
licenciado: graduate
licitador: bidder
lidiador: fighter
limpiabotas: bootblack
limpiachimeneas: chimney sweep
limpiacristales: window cleaner
lingüista: linguist
linotipista: linotypist

litigante: litigant
litógrafo: lithographer
locutor: announcer
loquero: psychiatric nurse
lotero: seller of lottery tickets
luchador: fighter
lugarteniente: deputy
luminotécnico: light technician
lustrabotas: bootblack
lustrador: polisher

machetero: cane cutter
maestro: teacher
magistrado: magistrate
mago: magician
maître: head waiter
malabarista: juggler
maletero: porter
mandadero: office boy
manisero: peanut seller
manicurista or *manicuro:* manicurist
maquillador: makeup artist
maquinista: engine driver
mariachi: mariachi
marinero: sailor
maromero: acrobat
masajista: masseur, masseuse
matarife: slaughterer
matemático: mathematician
mayoral: foreman
mayordomo: butler
mayorista: wholesaler
mecánico: mechanic
mecanógrafo: typist
mecanotaquígrafa: stenographer
médico: doctor
mensajero: messenger
mercader: merchant
mesera: waitress
mesero: waiter
metalúrgico: metallurgist
meteorólogo: meteorologist
microbiólogo: microbiologist

militar: military man
mimo: mime
mineralogista: mineralogist
minero: miner
ministro: minister, secretary
modelador: modeler
modelo: model
modisto: fashion designer
molinero: miller
monitor: monitor
motociclista: motorcyclist
motorista: motorist
mucama: maid
mucamo: servant
muralista: muralist
músico: musician

nadador: swimmer
naturista: naturalist
navegante: navigator
naviero: shipowner
negociador: negotiator
neurocirujano: neurosurgeon
neurólogo: neurologist
niñera: nanny
nodriza: wet nurse
notario: notary
novelista: novelist
numismático: numismatist
nutricionista: nutrition specialist

obrero: worker
oceanógrafo: oceanographer
oculista: oculist
odontólogo: dentist
oficinista: clerk
oftalmólogo: ophthalmologist
operador: operator
operario de máquina: machinist
orador: speaker
orfebre: goldsmith or silversmith
organista: organist
organizador: organizer

ornitólogo: ornithologist
ortopedista: orthopedist
osteópata: osteopath
ostrero: oyster catcher

paisajista: landscape painter
pajarero: bird catcher
paje: page, cabin boy
palafrenero: groom
paleógrafo: paleographer
panadero: baker
papelero: paper manufacturer
paracaidista: parachutist
parlamentario: parliamentarian
partera: midwife
párroco: parish priest
pastelero: baker, pastry cook
pastor: shepherd, minister
patinador: skater
patólogo: pathologist
patrocinador: sponsor
payador: gaucho minstrel
payaso: clown
peajero: toll collector
pedagogo: teacher/pedagogue
pediatra: pediatrician
pedicuro: chiropodist
peinador: hairdresser
peletero: furrier
peluquero: barber
penalista: expert in criminal law
pensionado: pensioner
peón: unskilled worker
periodista: journalist
perito: expert
perito agrónomo: agronomist
perito forense: legal expert
pescador: fisherman
pesquisidor: investigator
pianista: pianist
picador: horse trainer, picador
picapedrero: stonecutter

piloto: pilot
pinchadiscos: disc jockey
pintor: painter
pirófago: fire-eater
pistolero: gunman
pitonisa: fortune-teller
planificador: planner
platanero: dealer in bananas
platero: silversmith
plomero: plumber
poeta: poet
policía: police officer
político: politician
pollero: chicken farmer
portavoz: spokesperson
portero: porter; goalkeeper
preceptor: teacher, tutor
predicador: preacher
prefecto: prefect
prendero: pawnbroker
presentador: compère, master of ceremonies
presidente: president
prestamista: moneylender
probador: taster
proctólogo: proctologist
procurador: attorney
productor: producer
profesor: professor
programador: programmer
promotor: promoter
propagandista: propagandist
prostituta: prostitute
proveedor: supplier
proxeneta: go-between
psicoanalista: psychoanalyst
psicólogo: psychologist
psicoterapeuta: psychotherapist
psiquiatra: psychiatrist
publicista: publicist
puestero: market vendor
púgil: boxer

pulidor: polisher
pulpero: storekeeper

quesero: cheese maker, cheese seller
químico: chemist
quiromántico: palmist
quiropráctico: chiropractor

rabino: rabbi
radiólogo: radiologist
radioperador: radio operator
ranchero: rancher
rastreador: tracker
realizador: producer
recadero: messenger
recepcionista: receptionist
recluta: recruit
rector: head, chief
redactor: writer, editor
refinador: refiner
regente: regent, manager
registrador: registrar
relator: teller, narrator
religiosa: nun
religioso: monk
relojero: watch or clock maker
rematista: auctioneer
remolcador: tugboat operator
rentista: bondholder
reparador: repairer
repartidor: distributor
repartidor de periódicos: paperboy
reportero de prensa: news reporter
reportero gráfico: photojournalist
repostero: pastry cook
representante: representative
representante artístico: artist manager
reservista: reservist
restaurador: restorer
revelador de fotografía: film developer

sacerdote: priest
sacristán: verger

salvaguarda: guard
sargento: sergeant
sastre: tailor
saxofonista: saxophonist
secretario: secretary
segador: harvester
sembrador: sower
seminarista: seminarian
senador: senator
sepulturero: gravedigger
sereno: night watchman
sirvienta: maid
sirviente: servant
sismólogo: seismologist
sobrecargo: purser
sociólogo: sociologist
socorrista: first-aid worker, lifesaver
soldado: soldier
soldador: welder
solista: soloist
sombrerero: hat maker
soprano: soprano
subastador: auctioneer
subsecretario: assistant secretary
suministrador: supplier
superintendente: supervisor
supervisor: supervisor
suplente: deputy

tabacalero: tobacconist, tobacco grower
tabernera: barmaid
tabernero: barman
tallador: carver
tamalero: tamale maker
tamborilero: drummer
tanteador: scorer
tapicero: upholsterer
taquígrafo: stenographer
taquillero: clerk
taurómaco: bullfighting expert
taxidermista: taxidermist
taxista: taxi driver

taxonomista: taxonomist
técnico: technician
tecnólogo: technologist
tejedor: weaver
telecomunicador: telecommunicator
telefonista: operator
telegrafista: telegraphist
teleimpresor: teleprinter
teletipista: teletypist
tendero: shopkeeper
tenedor de libros: bookkeeper
tenor: tenor
tenista: tennis player
teñidor: dyer
teólogo: theologian
terapeuta: therapist
tesorero: treasurer
testaferro: front man
timonel: steersman
tintorero: dry cleaner
tinturador: dyer
tipógrafo: typographer
titiritero: puppeteer
tomatero: tomato grower or dealer
tonelero: cooper
topógrafo: topographer
torero: bullfighter
tornero: machinist, turner
toxicólogo: toxicologist
trabajador social: social worker
traductor: translator
tramoyista: stagehand
transportador: transporter
trapecista: trapeze artist
trapichero: sugar mill worker
tratadista: writer, essayist
traumatólogo: traumatologist
trazador: planner, designer
trillador: thresher
tripulante: crew member

trompetista: trumpet player
tutor: tutor

urbanista: town planner
urólogo: urologist

vaquero: cowboy
velador: watchman
vendedor: seller
ventero: innkeeper
ventrílocuo: ventriloquist
verdugo: executioner
verdulero: greengrocer
verificador: inspector
veterinario: veterinarian
vicepresidente: vice-president
vidriero: glazier
vigilante: watchman
vinatero: wine merchant
vinicultor: wine grower
violinista: violinist
violoncelista: cellist
vocalista: vocalist, singer
voceador: news vendor
volatinero: acrobat
voluntario: volunteer

xilografista: xylographer

yesero: plasterer
yuguero or *yuntero:* plowman

zapatero: shoemaker
zoólogo: zoologist
zurrador: tanner

CHAPTER 8

TERMINOLOGY

GEOGRAPHICAL TERMS

In general, Spanish writing convention accepts the original spelling of geographical denominations: "Mississippi" is better than "Misisipi," "México" is better than "Méjico." However, when the expression is already incorporated into the Spanish language, the use of the foreign form may sound unnatural: "Londres" and not "London," "Nueva Delhi" and not "New Delhi," "Nueva York" and not "New York," "San Pablo" and not "São Paulo," and so on.

COUNTRIES OF THE WORLD

Abjasia: Abkhaz Republic
Afganistán: Afghanistan
Alemania: Germany
Arabia Saudí: Saudi Arabia
Argelia: Algeria
Azerbaiyán: Azerbaijan or Azerbaidzhan or Azerbaijan Republic
Bahrein: Bahrain or Bahrein
Bélgica: Belgium
Bielorrusia: Belorussia
Belice: Belize
Bofutatsuana: Bophuthatswana
Botsuana: Botswana
Brasil: Brazil
Cabo Verde: Cape Verde
Camboya: Cambodia
Camerún: Cameroon
Canadá: Canada
Chipre: Cyprus

Comoras (Islas): Comoro Islands
Corea del Norte: North Korea
Corea del Sur: South Korea
Costa de Marfil: Ivory Coast
Croacia: Croatia
Dinamarca: Denmark
Egipto: Egypt
Emiratos Árabes Unidos: United Arab Emirates
Eslovaquia: Slovakia
Eslovenia: Slovenia
España: Spain
Estados Unidos: United States [1]
Etiopía: Ethiopia
Filipinas: Philippines
Finlandia: Finland
Fiyi (Islas): Fiji
Francia: France
Gabón: Gabon
Gambia: The Gambia
Georgia: Georgian Republic
Gran Bretaña (Reino Unido): Great Britain (United Kingdom)
Grecia: Greece
Guinea: Conakry
Guinea Ecuatorial: Equatorial Guinea
Haití: Haiti
Hungría: Hungary
Irak/Iraq: Iraq
Irán: Iran
Irlanda: Ireland
Islandia: Iceland
Italia: Italy
Japón: Japan
Jordania: Jordan
Kazajistán: Kazakhstan
Kenia: Kenya

---

[1] The use of the article is optional with *Estados Unidos:* "Proviene de Estados Unidos" or "Proviene de los Estados Unidos." When the article is omitted, the word is considered as singular: "Proviene de Estados Unidos que es el principal exportador."

Kirguizistán: Kirghiz Republic
Lesoto: Lesotho
Líbano: Lebanon
Libia: Libya
Luxemburgo: Luxembourg
Malasia: Malaysia
Malaui: Malawi
Maldivas: Republic of Maldives
Mauricio: Mauritius
Marruecos: Morocco
Níger: Niger
Noruega: Norway
Nueva Zelanda: New Zealand
Omán: Oman
Osetia del Norte: North Ossetian Republic
Países Bajos, Reino de los: Netherlands
Pakistán: Pakistan
Panamá: Panama
Papúa Nueva Guinea: Papua New Guinea
Perú: Peru
Polonia: Poland
República Centroafricana: Central African Republic
República Checa: Czech Republic
República Dominicana: Dominican Republic
República Popular China: People's Republic of China
Ruanda: Rwanda
Rusia: Russia
Sierra Leona: Sierra Leone
Singapur: Singapore
Siria: Syria
Suazilandia: Swaziland
Sudáfrica: South Africa
Sudán: Sudan
Suecia: Sweden
Suiza: Switzerland
Surinam: Suriname
Tailandia: Thailand
Taiwán: Taiwan
Tayikistán: Tadzhik Republic or Tadzhikistan
Túnez: Tunisia
Turkmenistán: Turkmen Republic
Turquía: Turkey
Tuvalú: Tuvalu

Ucrania: Ukrainian Republic or Ukraine
Uzbekistán: Uzbek Republic
Yibuti: Djibouti
Zimbabue: Zimbabwe

NATIONALITIES AND OTHER PLACE IDENTIFIERS

Abisinia o Etiopía: *abisinio, etíope*
Afganistán (Asia): *afgano, paropamisio*
Alaska (Estados Unidos): *alasqueño, alasquiano, alasquense,
    alascense*
Albania: *albanés, albano*
Albi (Francia): *albigense*
Alcalá de Henares (España): *alcalaíno, alcalaeño, complutense*
Alcántara (cualquier ciudad): *alcantarino*
Alejandría (Egipto): *alejandrino*
Algarve (Portugal): *algarveño, algarvio*
Alto Volta (Burkina Faso, Africa): *voltense*
Amberes (Bélgica): *amberino, amberiense, antuerpiense*
Ammán (Jordania): *ammonita, ammami, rabbatita*
Amsterdam (Holanda): *amsterdamés, amstelodamense,
    amstelodamés*
Ángeles, Los (Estados Unidos): *angeleno, angelopolitano, angelino*
Angola: *angoleño*
Angora o Ankara (Turquía): *angorino, angorense, ancirense*
Antigua, isla (Antillas): *antiguano*
Antigua (Guatemala): *antigüeño*
Antioquia (Colombia): *antioqueño*
Antioquía (Siria): *antioqueno, antioquense, antioqueño*
Arabia Saudí: *saudí, saudita*
Aranjuez (España): *ribereño*
Argelia: *argelino*
Asunción (Paraguay): *asunceño*
Australia: *australiano*
Australia (población indígena): *australiense*
Ávila: *avilés, abulense*

Babilonia: *babilonicense, babilonio*
Badajoz: *pacense*
Bagdad (Irak): *bagdadí*
Bahamas o Lucayas, islas: *bahamense, lucayo, bahameño*
Basilea (Suiza): *basilés, basilense, basileense*
Belén (Israel): *betlemita*
Belgrado (Yugoslavia): *belogradense, belgradense, singidunense*

Belice: *beliceño*
Berbería (Africa): *bereber, berebere*
Bermudas: *de Bermudas*
Berna (Suiza): *bernés*
Betania (Palestina): *betanita*
Bielorrusia: *bielorruso*
Bogotá (Colombia): *bogotano*
Bolivia: *boliviano*
Bolonia (Italia): *boloñés*
Bosnia-Herzegovina: *bosnio*
Braga (Portugal): *bracarense*
Brasil: *brasileño*
Brasília (Brasil): *brasiliense*
Bretaña (Francia): *bretón*
Bruselas (Bélgica): *bruselense*
Buenos Aires (capital de Argentina): *porteño*
Buenos Aires (provincia de Argentina): *bonaerense*
Bulgaria: *búlgaro*
Burdeos (Francia): *bordelés*
Burundi: *burundiano, burundés*

Cabo de Hornos (Chile): *caphornicense*
Cabo Verde: *caboverdiano*
Cali (Colombia): *caleño, calima, caliqueño, caliense*
Callao, El (Perú): *chalaco*
Camboya: *camboyano*
Cambridge (Estados Unidos/Gran Bretaña): *cantabrigense*
Camerún: *camerunés*
Canadá: *canadiense*
Carolina (Colombia): *carolineño, carolinita, carolinense*
Casablanca (Colombia): *casablanqués, casablancuno*
Ceilán: *cingalés*
Cerdeña (Italia): *sardo*
Ceuta: *ceutí, septense*
Chachapoyas (Perú): *chachapoyense, chachapoyuno*
Chaco (provincia de Argentina): *chaqueño*
Chaco (región de América del Sur): *chaquense, chaqueño*
Chaco de Bolivia: *calchaquí*
Chad: *chadiano, chadí*
Checa, República: *checo*
República Chechén: *checheno*
Chichicastenago (Guatemala): *maxeno*

Chile: *chileno*
China: *chino*
Chipre: *chipriota*
Ciudad Real: *ciudadrealeño, cluniense*
Coimbra (Portugal): *conimbricense*
Colombia: *colombiano*
Comoras: *comorano*
Concepción (Chile): *penquisto*
Concepción (Colombia, Cuba y Paraguay): *concepcionero*
Concepción (Honduras): *concepcioneño*
Congo: *congoleño*
Constantinopla (Turquía): *constantinopolitano*
Córdoba (Argentina): *cordobés*
Córdoba (Bolívar, Colombia): *cordobense*
Córdoba (España): *cordobés, cordubense, patriciense*
Córdoba (Nariño, Colombia): *cordobeño*
Corea del Norte: *norcoreano*
Corea del Sur: *surcoreano*
Corrientes (Argentina): *correntino*
Costa de Marfil: *marfilense, marfileño*
Costa Rica: *costarricense*
Croacia: *croata*
Cuba: *cubano*
Cuenca (Ecuador): *cuencano*
Cuenca (España): *cuencano, conquense*
Curazao o Curaçao (islas, Antillas Holandesas): *curazoleño, curaso-*
   leño, curassaviense, curazaense
Cuzco (Perú): *cuzqueño, cuzcoense*

Dinamarca: *danés*
Dominica: *de Dominica*
Durango (España): *durangués*
Durango (estado de México): *duranguense*
Durango (México): *durangueño*

Ecuador: *ecuatoriano*
Egipto: *egipcio*
El Salvador: *salvadoreño*
Emiratos Arabes Unidos: *de los Emiratos Arabes Unidos*
Eslovaquia: *eslovaco*
Eslovenia: *esloveno*
España: *español*
Estados Unidos: *estadounidense*

Estonia: *estoniano*
Etiopía: *etíope*

Fernando Poo (isla, Guinea): *fernandino, fernandense*
Filadelfia (Colombia): *filadelfano*
Filadelfia (cualquier ciudad): *filadelfino*
Filadelfia (Estados Unidos): *filadelfiense, filadelfiano*
Filipinas: *filipino*
Finlandia: *finés, finlandés*
Fiyi: *fiyiano*
Florencia (Italia): *florentino*
Florida, La (Colombia): *florideño, floridano*
Florida (Estados Unidos): *floridiano, floridense, floridiano*
Florida (Honduras): *florideno*
Formosa (Argentina): *formoseño*
Francia: *francés*

Gabón: *gabonés*
Gambia: *gambiano*
Georgia: *georgiano*
Ghana: *ghanés*
Ginebra (Suiza): *ginebrino*
Granada (Antillas): *granadense*
Granada (Colombia): *granadino*
Granada (España): *granadino, iliberitano*
Granada (Nicaragua): *granatense*
Grecia: *griego*
Groenlandia: *groenlandés*
Guadalajara (España): *caracense, carriacense, arriacense, guadalaja-
reño, alcarreño*
Guadalajara (México): *guadalajarense, tapatío*
Guadalupe (Colombia): *guadalupeño*
Guadalupe (España): *guadalupense, guadalupeño*
Guadalupe (isla, Antillas): *guadalupeño, guadalupiense*
Guadalupe (México): *guadalupano*
Guatemala: *guatemalteco*
Guayana Francesa: *de la Guayana Francesa*
Guinea: *guineo*
Guinea Ecuatorial: *guineano, ecuatoguineano*
Guyana: *guyanés*

Haití: *haitiano*
Holanda: *holandés* (Países Bajos, *neerlandés*)
Honduras: *hondureño*

Huelva: *olvisino, onubense, huelveño*
Huesca: *oscense*
Hungría: *húngaro*

India: *indio (no hindú)*
Indonesia: *indonesio*
Irak: *iraquí*
Irán: *iraní*
Irlanda: *irlandés*
Islandia: *islandés*
Islas Caimán: *de las islas Caimán (no caimanes)*
Islas Malvinas: *malvinense*
Islas Vírgenes: *de las Islas Vírgenes*
Israel: *israelí (no israelita)*
Italia: *italiano*

Jamaica: *jamaiquino, jamaicano*
Japón: *japonés, nipón*
Jericó (Colombia, Antioquia): *jericoano*
Jericó (Colombia, Boyacá): *jericó, jericoense*
Jerusalén (Colombia): *jelusaleño, salemita*
Jerusalén (Israel): *jerosolimitano*
Jordania: *jordano*

Kenia: *keniano*

La Habana (Cuba): *habanero*
La Paz (Bolivia): *paceño*
León: *leonés*
Lérida: *ileriense, leridano, leridense*
Letonia: *letón*
Líbano: *libanés*
Liberia: *liberiano*
Libia: *libio*
Lisboa (Portugal): *lisboeta*
Lituania: *lituano*
Logroño: *logroñés, lucroniense*
Londres (Gran Bretaña): *londinense*
Lugo: *lucense, luqués*

Madagascar: *malgache*
Madrid: *madrideño, madrileño, matritense*
Málaga: *malagueño, malagués*
Maldivas: *maldivo*
Malta: *maltés, maltense*

Managua (Nicaragua): *manguero, manguense*
Manizales (Colombia): *caldense, manizaleño, manizalita*
Maracaibo (Venezuela): *maracucho, maraibero, marabino*
Marruecos: *marroquí*
Martinica: *de Martinica o martiniqueño*
Mauricio: *mauriciano*
Mauritania: *mauritano*
Medellín (Colombia): *medellinense, medellense*
Medellín (España): *metelinense, metilinense*
Mérida (España): *emelitense, merideño*
México: *mexicano*
México, D.F.: *defeño*
Moldavia: *moldavo*
Mónaco: *monegasco*
Mongolia: *mongol*
Montevideo (Uruguay): *montevideano*
Montserrat, islas (Antillas): *montserratiano*
Mozambique: *mozambiqueño*

Nautla (México): *nauteco*
Nepal: *nepalés*
Nicaragua: *nicaragüense*
Níger: *nigerino*
Nigeria: *nigeriano*
Noruega: *noruego*
Nueva York (Estados Unidos): *neoyorquino*
Nueva Zelanda: *neozelandés*
Numancia (antigua Soria, España): *numantino*

Oaxaca (estado de México): *oaxaqueño, zapoteca, oaxacano*
Orense: *orensano, auriense*
Oviedo (España): *ovetense*
Oxford (Gran Bretaña): *oxoniano, oxoniense, oxfordiense, oxfordiano, oxfordense, oxenfordense*

Pakistán: *paquistaní*
Palma, La, isla (España): *palmero*
Palma de Mallorca (España): *palmesano, palmense*
Palmas, Las (España): *palmense*
Pamplona (España): *pamplonense, pamplonica, pamplonés*
Panamá: *panameño*
Papúa (Nueva Guinea): *papuano, papú*
Paraguay: *paraguayo*
París (Francia): *parisiense, parisino*

Perú: *peruano*
Polonia: *polaco*
Portugal: *portugués*
Posadas (Argentina): *posadense, posadeño*
Posadas (España): *maleño*
Puerto Rico: *borinqueño, puertorriqueño*
Puerto Rico (Bolivia): *puertorriquense*

Quezaltenango (Guatemala, departamento): *quezalteco*
Quimbaya (Colombia): *quimbaya, quimbayuno*
Quintana Roo (territorio federal de México): *quintanarroense*
Quito (Ecuador): *quiteño*

Reino Unido de Gran Bretaña e Irlanda del Norte: *británico*
República Centroafricana: *centroafricano*
República Dominicana: *dominicano*
Río de Janeiro (Brasil): *fluminense, carioca*
Rosario, El (España): *rosariero*
Rosario (Argentina): *rosarino*
Rosario (Colombia): *rosario*
Rosario (Uruguay): *rosarino*
Rumania: *rumano*
Rusia: *ruso*

Salamanca: *charro, salmantino, salmanticense, helmántico, sala-
    manquino, salamanqués, helmanticense*
Samoa: *samoano*
San Antonio (Estados Unidos): *sanantoniano*
San Antonio de las Vegas (Cuba): *veguero*
San Antonio de los Baños (Cuba): *ariguanense*
San Carlos (Chile): *sancarlino*
San Carlos (Nicaragua): *carleño*
San Carlos (Uruguay): *carolino*
San Carlos (Venezuela): *carlense*
San Felipe (Chile): *sanfilipeño*
San Felipe (Cuba): *filipeño*
San Felipe (Venezuela): *filipense*
San Marino: *sanmarinense*
Sancti-Spíritus (Cuba): *guayabero, espirituano*
Santa Cruz (Bolivia): *cruceño*
Santa Cruz de la Palma (España): *palmero*
Santa Cruz de Tenerife (España): *candelariero, tinerfeño*
Santa Sede: *de la Santa Sede, vaticano*
Santiago de Chile (Chile): *santiaguino*

Santiago de Compostela (España): *compostelano, santiagués*
Santiago de Cuba (Cuba): *santiaguero*
Santiago del Estero (Argentina): *santiagueño*
Santo Domingo (República Dominicana): *dominicano*
Santo Tomé y Príncipe: *santomense*
São Paulo (Brasil, ciudad): *paulistano (city), paulista (province),*
  sampaulero
Senegal: *senegalés*
Serbia: *serbio*
Sevilla: *hispalense, hispaleto, hispaliense, sevillano*
Sierra Leona: *sierraleonés*
Singapur: *singapurense*
Siria: *sirio*
Somalia: *somalí*
Sri Lanka: *srilanqués, cingalés*
Suazilandia: *suazi*
Sudáfrica: *sudafricano*
Sudán: *sudanés*
Suecia: *sueco*
Suiza: *suizo*
Surinam: *surinamés*

Tailandia: *tailandés*
Tanzania: *tanzano*
Tarragona: *tarraconense, tarraconita, cesetano, cosetano*
Teruel: *turolense, turboleta*
Texas: *texano*
Togo: *togolés*
Trento (Italia): *tridentino*
Trinidad (Bolivia): *trinitario*
Trinidad (Colombia): *trinitense*
Trinidad (Cuba): *trinitario*
Trinidad (Honduras): *triniteco*
Trinidad (Uruguay): *trinitario*
Trinidad y Tobago: *de Trinidad y Tobago, trinitario, trinitense*
Túnez: *tunecino*
Turquía: *turco*

Ucrania: *ucranio, ucraniano*
Uganda: *ugandés*
Uruguay: *uruguayo, oriental*

Venezuela: *venezolano*
Vietnam: *vietnamita*

Washington, D.C. (Estados Unidos): *washingtoniano*

Yemen: *yemení*
Yucatán (México): *yucateco*
Yugoslavia: *yugoslavo*

Zambia: *zambiano*
Zimbabue: *zimbabuense, zimbabuano*

Designations of oceans, seas, lakes, and rivers are masculine:

el Océano Ártico
el Océano Atlántico/el Atlántico
el Océano Índico
el Océano Pacífico/el Pacífico

el (mar) Caribe
el Mar Caspio
el Mar de Bering
el Mar del Norte
el (mar) Mediterráneo
el Mar Muerto

el Great Salt Lake (el lago Great Salt)
el (lago) Maracaibo
el (lago) Titicaca

el Amazonas
el Danubio
el Éufrates
el Nilo
el Yenisei

Referring to waterfalls, the expression *cataratas de* is used in all cases:

las cataratas del Ángel
las cataratas del Iguazú
las cataratas del Niágara

Mountains, volcanoes, and desert designations are masculine:

el Aconcagua
el Chimborazo
el Monte Blanco
el (monte) Everest
el Orizaba

el Cotopaxi
el Etna
el Mauna Loa
el Tupungatito
el Vesubio

el desierto de Atacama[2]
el desierto de Gobi
el Sahara

Many geographical names have a traditional Spanish form:

Amberes: Antwerp
Antioquía: Antakya
Aquisgrán: Aachen
Basilea: Basel
Birmania: Burma (Myanmar)
Burdeos: Bordeaux
Carolina del Norte: North Carolina
Carolina del Sur: South Carolina
Cayo Hueso: Key West
Colonia: Cologne
Dresde: Dresden
Fráncfort: Frankfurt
Friburgo: Freiburg
Ginebra: Geneva
Gotinga: Göttingen
Granada (*isla*): Grenada
La Haya: The Hague
Maguncia: Mainz
Malasia: Malaysia
Meca, La: Mecca
Milán: Milan
Moscú: Moscow
Munich: Munich
Pekín: Beijing
Ruán: Rouen
Salónica: Thessaloníki
Turín: Turin

---

[2] However, the expression *la puna de Atacama* is used frequently.

PLANETS OF THE SOLAR SYSTEM

Mercurio
Venus
Tierra (la Tierra/el planeta Tierra)
Marte
Júpiter
Saturno
Urano
Neptuno
Plutón

NAMES OF ORGANIZATIONS

SPANISH CULTURAL INSTITUTIONS

Acadèmia de Ciències (Academia de Ciencias de Cataluña; founded 1770)
Academia de Nobles Artes (1744–1873), later known as Real Academia de Bellas Artes de San Fernando
Real Academia de la Historia (founded 1738)
Real Academia de las Buenas Letras de Barcelona (founded 1759)
Real Academia de las Buenas Letras de Sevilla (founded 1751)
Real Academia Española or Academia Española (founded 1714). It is recommended to avoid the expression "Academia de la Lengua."

HISPANIC CULTURAL INSTITUTIONS

Academias correspondientes

Academia Boliviana (La Paz, 1927)
Academia Chilena (Santiago, 1885)
Academia Colombiana (Bogotá, 1871)
Academia Costarricense (San José, 1923)
Academia Cubana (La Habana, 1926)
Academia Dominicana (Santo Domingo, 1927)
Academia Ecuatoriana (Quito, 1874)
Academia Filipina (Manila, 1924)
Academia Guatemalteca (Guatemala, 1887)
Academia Hondureña (Tegucigalpa, 1949)
Academia Mexicana (México, 1875)
Academia Nicaragüense (Managua, 1928)
Academia Norteamericana (Nueva York, 1973)

Academia Panameña (Panamá, 1926)
Academia Paraguaya (Asunción, 1927)
Academia Peruana (Lima, 1887)
Academia Puertorriqueña (San Juan, 1955)
Academia Salvadoreña (San Salvador, 1876)
Academia Venezolana (Caracas, 1883)

Academias asociadas

Academia Argentina de Letras (Buenos Aires, 1931)
Academia Nacional de Letras de Uruguay (Montevideo, 1943)

FREQUENTLY MENTIONED INTERNATIONAL INSTITUTIONS AND ORGANIZATIONS

Agencia Central de Información[3] (Central Intelligence Agency)
Amnistía Internacional (Amnesty International)
Asociación Latinoamericana de Libre Comercio (ALALC)
Comisión Económica para la América Latina (CEPAL)
Comunidad Económica Europea (CEE), also known as Mercado Común
Fondo Monetario Internacional (FMI)
Organización de Estados Americanos (OEA)
Organización de las Naciones Unidas (ONU)
Organización de las Naciones Unidas para la Educación, la Ciencia y la Cultura (UNESCO)
Organización del Atlántico Norte (OTAN)[4]

HISTORICAL TERMS

PERIODS

Traditional Designations

Edad de Oro: Golden Age
Edad de Piedra: Stone Age
Edad de Bronce: Bronze Age
Edad de Hierro: Iron Age
Edad Antigua: Antiquity
Edad Media: Middle Ages

---

[3] In Spanish, it is generally referred to with the English acronym, "CIA."
[4] The English acronym "NATO" is also frequent.

Edad Moderna: Modern Age
Edad Contemporánea: Contemporary Age

Geologic Time Divisions

Cenozoico
    Cuaternario (Reciente, Pleistoceno)
    Terciario (Plioceno, Mioceno, Oligoceno, Eoceno y Paleoceno)
Mesozoico
    Cretáceo
    Jurásico
    Triásico
Paleozoico
    Pérmico
    Carbonífero
    Devoniano
    Siluriano
    Ordoviciano
    Cámbrico
Precámbrico
    Proterozoico
    Arqueozoico

RELIGIONS AND RELIGIOUS MOVEMENTS

el Budismo
el Cristianismo
el Hinduismo
el Islam

CULTURAL MOVEMENTS AND STYLE DESIGNATIONS

These may be written in capital letters or not: *el barroco/el Barroco, el romanticismo/el Romanticismo, la vanguardia/la vanguardia.*[5] In general, when referring to a movement as a precise historical period, it should be written with an initial capital letter: *el Renacimiento* versus *el renacimiento de una nación.*

anarquismo: anarchism
art nouveau: art nouveau

---

[5] Even though *avant-garde* is used, the word *vanguardia* is more common.

arte conceptual: conceptual art
barroco: baroque
budismo: Buddhism
catolicismo: Catholicism
churrigueresco: churrigueresque
clasicismo: classicism
comunismo: communism
confucionismo: Confucianism
cubismo: cubism
deísmo: deism
determinismo: determinism
edad isabelina: Elizabethan Age
era augusta: Augustan Age
escepticismo: skepticism
esteticismo: aestheticism
etapa jacobina: Jacobean Age
existencialismo: existentialism
expresionismo: expressionism
fatalismo: fatalism
feudalismo: feudalism
futurismo: futurism
gótico: Gothic
gótico flamígero: flamboyant Gothic
gótico tardío: late Gothic
hinduismo: Hinduism
humanismo: humanism
Ilustración, la: the Enlightenment
impresionismo: impressionism
islamismo: Islam
judaísmo: Judaism
manierismo: mannerism
marxismo: Marxism
monarquía: monarchy
monarquía absoluta: absolute monarchy
monarquía constitucional: constitutional monarchy
nacionalismo: nationalism
naturalismo: naturalism
nazismo: Nazism
neoclasicismo: neoclassicism
neoliberalismo: neoliberalism
neorrealismo: neorealism
nihilismo: nihilism
nuevo humanismo: new humanism

objetivismo: objectivism
ocultismo: occultism
oligarquía: oligarchy
panteísmo: pantheism
platonismo: Platonism
protestantismo: Protestantism
puntillismo: pointillism
puritanismo: puritanism
realismo: realism
Restauración, la: the Restoration
románico: romanesque
socialismo: socialism
surrealismo: surrealism
vanguardia: avant-garde
vanguardismo: avant-gardism

WARS

Guerra de los Cien Años (1337–1453)
Guerra de las Comunidades (1520–1521)
Guerras de las Germanías (1521–1523)
Guerra de los Treinta Años (1618–1648)
Guerra de la Independencia Española (1808–1814)
Guerras de Independencia (1811–1829)
Guerras Carlistas (1833–1876)
Guerra Austro-prusiana (1866)
Guerra Franco-prusiana (1870–1871)
Guerras Balcánicas (1912–1913)
Primera Guerra Mundial (1914–1918)
Guerra Civil Española (1936–1939)
Segunda Guerra Mundial (1939–1945)
Guerra Fría (ca. 1945–1992)
Guerra de Corea (1950–1953)
Guerra de Vietnam (ca. 1960–1975)
Guerra de Oriente Medio (1980–1988)
Guerra de Malvinas/Guerra del Atlántico Sur (1982)
Guerra del Golfo (1991)

HISPANIC NATIONAL HOLIDAYS

Argentina: July 9, Día de la Independencia (Independence Day)
Bolivia: August 6, Día de la Independencia
Chile: September 18, Día de la Independencia

Colombia: July 20, Día de la Independencia
Costa Rica: September 15, Día de la Independencia
Cuba: January 1, Aniversario de la Revolucíon (Revolution
   Anniversary)
Ecuador: August 10, Día de la Independencia
El Salvador: September 15, Día de la Independencia
España: July 25, Día de Santiago, patrón de España (Saint James the
   Greater Day); December 6, Día de la Constitución
Guatemala: September 15, Día de la Independencia
Honduras: September 15, Día de la Independencia
México: September 16, Día de la Independencia
Nicaragua: September 15, Día de la Independencia
Panamá: November 3, Día de la Independencia
Paraguay: May 15, Día de la Independencia
Perú: July 28 and 29, Día de la Independencia
Puerto Rico: July 25, Día de la Constitución
República Dominicana: February 27, Día de la Independencia
Uruguay: August 25, Día de la Independencia; July 18, Día de la
   Constitución
Venezuela: September 18, Día de la Independencia

RELIGIOUS CONGREGATIONS

Adoratrices Esclavas del Santísimo Sacramento; *Adoratrices*[6]
Agustinianos de la Asunción; *Asuncionistas*
Agustinos
Agustinos Recoletos

Benedictinos

Canónigos Regulares de la Inmaculada Concepción
Canónigos Regulares Lateranenses
Capuchinos
Carmelitas
Carmelitas de la Caridad
Carmelitas de María Inmaculada
Carmelitas Descalzos
Cartujos
Cistercienses
Cistercienses Reformados; *Trapenses*
Clarisas

---

[6] Italic type indicates the common name of the congregation.

Clérigos de San Víctor

Clérigos Descalzos de la Santísima Cruz y Pasión de Nuestro Señor
Jesucristo; *Pasionistas*

Clérigos Regulares de la Madre de Dios y de las Escuelas Pías;
Escolapios

Clérigos Regulares de San Pablo; *Barnabitas*

Clérigos Regulares Menores

Clérigos Regulares Ministros de los Enfermos; *Camilos*

Compañía de Jesús; *Jesuitas*

Compañía de María; *Marianistas*

Compañía de María Nuestra Señora; *Religiosas de la Enseñanza*

Compañía de Santa Teresa de Jesús

Concepcionistas Misioneras de la Enseñanza; *Concepcionistas de la
Enseñanza*

Congregación de Jesús y María; *Eudistas*

Congregación de la Fraternidad Sacerdotal

Congregación de la Misión; Paúles; *Lazaristas*

Congregación de los Sagrados Corazones

Congregación de la Santa Cruz

Congregación del Corazón Inmaculado de María

Congregación del Espíritu Santo

Congregación del Oratorio de San Felipe Neri; *Oratorianos*

Dominicas de la Anunciata

Ermitaños de San Agustín

Esclavas del Sagrado Corazón de Jesús

Estigmatizados

Franciscanas Misioneras de María

Franciscanos

Franciscanos Conventuales

Hermanas de la Caridad de Santa Ana

Hermanitos de Jesús

Hermanos de la Sagrada Familia

Hermanos de las Escuelas Cristianas

Hermanos de Nuestra Señora de la Misericordia

Hermanos de San Francisco Javier

Hermanos de San Juan de Dios; *Hospitalarios de San Juan de Dios;
Hospitalarios*

Hermanos del Sagrado Corazón

Hermanos Maristas de las Escuelas; *Maristas*

Hermanos Misioneros de San Francisco de Asís

Hijas de Cristo Rey

Hijas de Jesús
Hijas de la Caridad
Hijos de la Sagrada Familia
Hijos del Sagrado Corazón de Jesús; *Misioneros Combonianos*;
  Combonianos

Institución Teresiana

Jerónimos

Mercedarias Misioneras de Berriz
Mercedarios
Misioneros de Africa; *Padres Blancos*
Misioneros de la Preciosísima Sangre
Misioneros de la Sagrada Familia
Misioneros de los Sagrados Corazones de Jesús y María
Misioneros del Espíritu Santo
Misioneros del Sagrado Corazón de Jesús
Misioneros Hijos del Inmaculado Corazón de María; *Hijos del Cora-
  zón de María; Claretianos*

Oblatos de María Inmaculada
Operarios Diocesanos
Oratorianos
Orden de los Mínimos
Orden de Predicadores; *Dominicos*
Orden Tercera Regular de San Francisco

Premostratenses

Redentoristas
Religiosas de Jesús y María
Reparadoras
Resurreccionistas

Sacerdotes de San Basilio
Sacerdotes del Sagrado Corazón de Jesús; *Reparadores*
Sacramentinos
Sagrados Corazones
Siervos de María; *Servitas*
Sociedad de la Santa Cruz; *Opus Dei*
Sociedad de María; *Marianistas*
Sociedad de San Francisco de Sales; *Salesianos*
Sociedad de San Pablo; *Paulinos*
Sociedad del Sagrado Corazón de Jesús; *Religiosas del Sagrado
  Corazón*

Sociedad Salesiana de San Juan Bosco; *Salesianos*

Teatinos
Trinitarios

Ursulinas
Ursulinas de Jesús

ACRONYMS OF RELIGIOUS CONGREGATIONS

A.A.: Asuncionistas
A.C.I.: Esclavas del Sagrado Corazón de Jesús
CC.RR.MM.: Clérigos Regulares Menores
C.F.S.: Congregación de la Fraternidad Sacerdotal
C.F.X.: Hermanos de San Francisco Javier
C.I.C.M.: Congregación del Inmaculado Corazón de María
C.I.M.: Congregación de Jesús y María
C.M.: Congregación de Misioneros Paúles
C.M.F.: Hijos del Corazón de María
C.M.I.: Carmelitas de María Inmaculada
C.M.S.F.: Hermanos Misioneros de San Francisco de Asís
C.O.: Oratorianos
C.P.: Pasionistas
C.P.P.S.: Misioneros de la Preciosísima Sangre
C.P.S.: Estigmatizados
C.R.: Clérigos Regulares Teatinos
C.R.: Resurreccionistas
C.R.I.C.: Canónigos Regulares de la Inmaculada Concepción
C.R.L.: Canónigos Regulares Lateranenses
C.S.B.: Sacerdotes de San Basilio
C.S.C.: Congregación de la Santa Cruz
C.S.Sp.: Congregación del Espíritu Santo
C.SS.R.: Redentoristas
C.S.V.: Clérigos de San Viator
F.D.M.: Hermanos de Nuestra Señora de la Misericordia
F.M.M.: Franciscanas Misioneras de María
F.S.C.: Hermanos de las Escuelas Cristianas
F.S.C.J.: Combonianos
F.S.F.: Hermanos de la Sagrada Familia
HH.MM.: Maristas
H.J.: Hermanitos de Jesús
Jer.: Jerónimos
M.C.S.: Misioneros del Sagrado Corazón de Jesús

M.I.: Camilos
M.M.B.: Mercedarias Misioneras de Berriz
M.S.F.: Misioneros de la Sagrada Familia
M.Sp.S.: Misioneros del Espíritu Santo
M.SS.CC.: Misioneros de los Sagrados Corazones de Jesús y María
O.C.: Carmelitas
O.Cart.: Cartujos
O.C.D.: Carmelitas Descalzos
O. Cist.: Cistercienses
O.C.S.O.: Trapenses
O. de M.: Mercedarios
O.E.S.A.: Ermitanos de San Agustín
O.F.M.: Franciscanos
O.F.M.Cap.: Capuchinos
O.F.M.Conv.: Franciscanos Conventuales
O.H.: Hermanos de San Juan de Dios
O. Minim.: Orden de los Mínimos
O.M.I.: Oblatos de María Inmaculada
O.P.: Dominicos
O. Prem.: Premostratenses
O.R.S.A.: Agustinos Recoletos
O.S.A.: Agustinos
O.S.B.: Benedictinos
O.S.M.: Servitas
O.SS.T.: Trinitarios
P.B.: Padres Blancos
R.C.: Concepcionistas de la Enseñanza
R.S.C.J.: Religiosas del Sagrado Corazón
S.C.: Hermanos del Sagrado Corazón
Sch.P.: Escolapios
S.C.J.: Reparadores
S.D.B.: Salesianos
S.I.: Jesuitas
S.M.: Marianistas
SS.CC.: Congregación de los Sagrados Corazones
S.S.P.: Sociedad de San Pablo
S.S.S.: Sacramentinos
S.T.J.: Compañía de Santa Teresa de Jesús
T.O.R.: Orden Tercera Regular de San Francisco

CHAPTER 9

CITATION OF BOOKS, PERIODICALS, AND OTHER WORKS

In a text in English, the titles of works written in Spanish should be cited in conformance with the practices of that language. Thus, no words will be capitalized except for proper names and the absolutely first word of the title; note that adjectives of national origin and languages are not capitalized in Spanish: *Un tratado sobre el español mexicano según su uso en Guadalajara.* Periodical titles are customarily cited in the same fashion: *Revista interamericana de bibliografía,* although some sources will capitalize all words in the title: *Revista Iberoamericana de Bibliografía.* This usage is not recommended.

Newspaper and magazine titles present a somewhat different circumstance. Since so many titles of such publications consist of a single-word title preceded by an article, that single word seems to get "lost" on the page. Thus, it is far more common to see *La Nación, La Prensa, La Gazeta* than *La nación, La prensa, La gazeta.* However, consistency of usage would argue for the latter practice, especially since there are also many book titles that consist of identical single-word titles preceded by an article: *El aleph, El matadero, Los de abajo.* Capitalization of anything other than the absolute first word would be inconsistent.

When Spanish-language titles are incorporated into texts in English, it is important that word division for them follow the rules of Spanish and not those of English. See the section on rules of word division in Spanish in chapter 2 of this manual.

The alternation between norms that have evolved in Spain and the various Latin American countries, the influence of the norms used for other languages, and the lack of rigorous academic style manuals have resulted in not only extremely different structures for the statement of bibliographic information but also the tendency either to undercite information or to overcite it. Along with the need to adhere to a principle of consistency is the advisability of presenting only that information necessary for the verification and location of a bibliographic item. In addition to variation related to capitalization, other typical problem areas have been criteria for alphabetization of entries, the citation of volume references for periodicals, and the distinguishing use of italicized titles versus those enclosed in comillas.

The purpose here is to cover material that is problematical with reference to Spanish-language citations. For details not covered here, consult the most recent edition of the *MLA Style Manual* or the *University of Chicago Manual of Style*.

A distinction is customarily made between freestanding titles, such as books and other monographs, pamphlets, plays, films, and videos; and items that appear as part of a larger whole, such as poems, short stories, essays, and chapters. Of course, a poem may be freestanding, especially a long poem, such as José Hernández's gaucho epic *Martín Fierro* or José de Espronceda's Romantic lyrical narrative, *El estudiante de Salamanca*. Conversely, normally freestanding units may be incorporated within larger works, such as anthologies. Texts that normally are part of larger collections but that may be published separately are treated as though they were freestanding. Texts usually published as freestanding continue to be treated as such (i.e., the title is italicized) when they are published as part of larger units, and the publication data of the larger unit are also given.

MONOGRAPHS

Albuquerque, M. A. *Antología de tangos.* 8ª ed. aum. México, D.F.: Medina, 1970.[1]

Avellaneda, Andrés. *Censura, autoritarismo y cultura: Argentina 1960–1983.* Buenos Aires: Centro Editor de América Latina, 1986.[2]

Baker, Edward. *Materiales para escribir Madrid: literatura y espacio urbano de Moratín a Galdós.* Madrid: Siglo Veintiuno de España, 1991.

Borges, Jorge Luis y Silvina Bullrich. *El compadrito: su destino, sus barrios, su música.* Buenos Aires: Compañía General Fabril Editora, 1963.

Feierstein, Ricardo. *Historia de los judíos argentinos.* Buenos Aires: Editorial Planeta Argentina, 1993.

---

[1] If supported by the software being used, *8a* and similar ordinals should be written as 8ª.

[2] The Centro Editor de América Latina is one of a number of publishers that are frequently cited via an acronym (CEDAL). It is preferable to avoid this practice, as it assumes knowledge that all may not possess. Another frequent example is the Modern Language Association, cited as MLA. Of course, should the actual imprint use an acronym, that is what should be cited; clarification may be added in brackets. Such an example is EUDEBA (also cited as Eudeba), which is the Editorial de la Universidad de Buenos Aires.

The general practice in Spanish has been to adhere to the same capitalization format adopted by the U.S. Library of Congress: only the absolute first letter of a title is capitalized, along with the first letter of proper names. It is not necessary to capitalize the first letter of a subtitle given after a colon, semicolon, dash, or within parentheses, although, should the main title end in a period, the subtitle would consequently constitute a new unit opened with a capital. Some users will, however, prefer to capitalize the first word in a subtitle always, and this use should be respected.

Julián Pérez, Alberto. *Modernidad, vanguardias, posmodernidad. Ensayos de literatura hispanoamericana.* Buenos Aires: Corregidor, 1995.
Méndez, Priscilla. *La dramaturgia hispanoamericana: teatralidad y autoconciencia.* Madrid: Pliegos, 1990.
Verani, Hugo J. *Las vanguardias literarias en Hispanoamérica. (Manifiestos, proclamas y otros escritos).* 3ª ed. México, D.F.: Fondo de Cultura Económica, 1995.

The names of authors other than the primary author are cited in normal word order (i.e., first name[s] first). The *y* used to introduce the last author in a series should not be preceded by a comma. (Note that this differs from *Chicago Manual* style.)

Borges, Jorge Luis y Adolfo Bioy Casares. *Cuentos breves y extraordinarios.* Buenos Aires: Losada, 1957.
Kohut, Karl y Andrea Pagni, eds. *Literatura argentina hoy. De la dictadura a la democracia.* Frankfurt: Vervuert, 1993.

If an author's name varies from one publication to another, that variation should be captured in the bibliographic citation, which may mean that an author may be listed in more than one fashion; consistency may be achieved via the use of bracketed information.

Martini, Juan Carlos. *Composición de lugar.* Buenos Aires: Bruguera, 1984.
Martini, Juan [Carlos]. *La máquina de escribir.* Buenos Aires: Perfil, 1997.

Even though it may be customary to refer to an author in the main body of the text in conformance with usual critical usage—Lorca, rather than García Lorca—the listing in the bibliography should conform to normal name patterns, since such patterns will determine the entry in an index or database listing. In the case of pseudonyms, if the listing is by the preferred pseudonym, but databases in fact use the author's original given name, a note to this effect should be included: Quino (pseud. of Joaquín Salvador Lavado). Even when an author is referred to with a title in the main body of a text, listing should be in terms of database conventions: Sor Juana, Sor Juana Inés de la Cruz, Juana de Asbaje are all reference forms, but the only citational form should be Juana Inés de la Cruz, Sister (not, Cruz, Juana Inés de la).

It should be born in mind that many individuals of Hispanic descent have two family names, a patronymic followed by a matronymic, with or without intervening connectors. In the case of women's names, information may include her patronymic followed (with or without a connective, typically *de*) by her husband's patronymic. Listing should be by the patronymic, or, in the case of women, by the patronymic she chooses to use (customarily, the one other than her husband's—i.e., her father's):

> Bioy Casares, Adolfo
> Ortega y Gasset, José
> Zayas de Lima, Perla
> Fernández Latour de Botas, Olga
> Kaiser-Lenoir, Claudia

The particle *de,* when uncapitalized, is understood to be a genealogical connector; when capitalized, it is considered to be part of the name and is therefore counted in alphabetization.

> De Garayalde, Giovanna
> *but* Onís, Federico de

This is also true of names based on other languages.

> Di Giorgio, Marosa

The same is true of the variants *de la/De la* and *del/Del*

> Río, Ana María del
> Parra, Marco Antonio de la
> Del Río, Fernando

In cases of doubt, a database should be consulted, preferably that of the U.S. Library of Congress. Note that in the case of Luso-Brazilian culture, the order of names is reversed, with the first being the matronymic and the second the patronymic. Even though João Guimarães Rosa is frequently referred to as Guimarães Rosa, he should be listed as Rosa, João Guimarães.

Publishers' notes should be recorded accurately from the title page. If they do not appear on the title page, they may usually be found on the verso of the title page. Colophons may be the only place where a publication date is given. Colophons tend to cite the printing plant used, however, rather than a publisher. If no publisher is given, the name of the printing plant should not be substituted for it. In this case, only place and date, the second separated from the latter by a comma, are given.

"Editorial" and similar designations are usually included as part of the name of the publisher, although they may be consistently omitted for reasons of brevity and the fact that they may be so referred to customarily: "Sudamericana" rather than "Editorial Sudamericana." Information appended to the name of the publisher may be routinely omitted: "e hijos," "Cía." However, when such notes precede the main name of the publisher, they should be included: "Viuda de Suárez," "Hijos de Pérez."

Cities of publication should be followed by the name of the country only if there is the possibility of confusion between two or more locales with the same name: Córdoba, España, versus Córdoba, Argentina (see Chapter 10 for proper abbreviations for countries). However, it is customarily assumed that when more than one city exists with the same name, the one cited without a country designation is to be considered the most important one historically: Córdoba, understood as referring to the Spanish city, versus Córdoba, Arg. City names should be cited as they appear in the publication—that is, not translated into Spanish: London, not Londres. Usage varies regarding citing the capital city of Mexico, but México, D.F., is the preferable form to ensure that the city rather than the country is understood. Unfortunately, there is no convenient way of citing Guatemala as city rather than as country. Country names are always cited in their standard abbreviated form, as are states and provinces. U.S. states are preferably cited in their traditional abbreviated form rather than with their post office code: Wash. versus WA, Ariz. versus AZ.

Spanish has not traditionally distinguished between "printing" (a new press run, with or without discreet corrections of minor typos) and "edition" (understood as incorporating significant textual modifications). The term *edición* has historically been used in both senses, although some publishers are now beginning to distinguish between *impresión* and *edición*. In general, it is not necessary to incorporate a printing note, but it is important in the case of different editions. The date given should be the date of the actual edition being cited. If necessary, the original date of publication may be cited in one of two ways: "1980, 1974" or "1980. Orig. 1974." Since, however, it is often the case that, when a title is referred to in the main body of text, the original date of publication is given, this may not need to be repeated in the bibliographic note. Notes like "rev." for revised, "aum." for augmented, and "ampl." for amplified are usually included.

Names should be alphabetized in the manner of databases and not telephone books, in such a way that commas and spaces are counted, in that order, as first letters before *a*. Hyphens matter only in the case of items that are identical except for the hyphen; in such cases, the item without a hyphen precedes the item with a hyphen. Thus:

González, José Luis
González Álvarez, Juan
González-Álvarez, Juan
González Álvarez, Julio

If an item contains a double imprint, a semicolon is used to separate the two publishers' notes:

Ficción y política. La narrativa argentina durante el proceso militar. Buenos Aires: Alianza; Minneapolis: Institute for the Study of Ideologies and Literature, 1987.

Series notes are usually only included if titles in the series are numbered:

Martínez, Elena M. *Lesbian Voices from Latin America: Breaking Ground.* Garland Reference Library of Social Sciences. Latin American Studies 7. New York: Garland, 1996.
Blecua, Alberto. *Manual de crítica textual.* Literatura y sociedad 33. Madrid: Castalia, 1983.

Scholarly publishing may cite various editions of a creative work: the first edition, a definitive edition, an edition with an important critical introduction, or a translation. Note that in the latter three cases, the citation may or may not include information about the first edition. The example given here includes full information, although it may often suffice simply to provide the date of the first edition. The second example provides an alternative citation format:

Borges, Jorge Luis. *Historia universal de la infamia.* Buenos Aires: Tor, 1935. Buenos Aires: Emecé Editores, 1954.
Borges, Jorge Luis. *Historia universal de la infamia.* Buenos Aires: Emecé Editores, 1954. Orig. Buenos Aires: Tor, 1935.
Cortázar, Julio. *Rayuela.* 1963. 12ª ed. Buenos Aires: Sudamericana, 1970.

Since no information is provided as to the publisher of the first 1963 edition, one could reasonably assume that it was Editorial Sudamericana (it was).

Cortázar, Julio. *Rayuela.* Buenos Aires: Sudamericana, 1963. 3ª ed. Madrid: Alfaguara Literaturas, 1993.

This noncritical edition is by a publisher different from that of the first edition; hence the two separate full publishers' citations. Moreover, the Alfaguara Literaturas edition is the third under their imprint. While it would not normally be necessary to cite the first Alfaguara Literaturas edition, should it be necessary (if, for example, editions were being compared), then the citation might be as follows:

Cortázar, Julio. *Rayuela.* Buenos Aires: Sudamericana, 1963. Madrid: Alfaguara Literaturas, 1984. 3ª ed. Madrid: Alfaguara Literaturas, 1993.

Or, simply: 3ª ed., 1993.

Cortázar, Julio. *Rayuela.* Buenos Aires: Sudamericana, 1963. Prólogo y cronología de Jaime Alazraki. Caracas: Biblioteca Ayacucho, 1988.

In this case, the critical edition being cited (Biblioteca Ayacucho, 1988) belongs to a different publisher than the first edition, as this case is duly noted, and the author of the critical apparatus is credited.

The following provides a format for the first edition of the English translation and its subsequent paperback reissue:

Cortázar, Julio. *Hopscotch.* Trad. del español por Gregory Rabassa. New York: Pantheon Books, 1966.
Cortázar, Julio. *Hopscotch.* Trad. del español por Gregory Rabassa. New York: New American Library, 1967. Orig., New York: Pantheon Books, 1966.

In either case, note may be made of the original-language edition, either the first edition or the specific edition on which the translation is based; full publication citation or only the year may be given:

Cortázar, Julio. *Hopscotch.* Trad. del español por Gregory Rabassa. New York: Pantheon Books, 1966. Trad. de *Rayuela.* Buenos Aires: Sudamericana, 1963.

Title variations may be handled in the same way:

Neruda, Pablo. *El hondero entusiasta.* Santiago de Chile: Empresa Letras, 1933. *El hondero entusiasta y otras obras.* Buenos Aires: Torres Agüero, 1974.
Neruda, Pablo. *El hondero entusiasta y otras obras.* Buenos Aires: Torres Agüero, 1974. Orig. como *El hondero entusiasta.* Santiago de Chile: Empresa Letras, 1933.

If necessary, the scope of "otras obras" can be added:

Neruda, Pablo. *El hondero entusiasta y otras obras [Anillos. Tentativa del hombre infinito. El habitante y su esperanza].* Buenos Aires: Torres Agüero Editor, 1974. Orig. como *El hondero entusiasta.* Santiago de Chile: Empresa Letras, 1933.

If standard information is unavailable from the item itself, but is obtainable from other sources, it may be provided in brackets. If the information cannot be obtained, an indication of the omission may be provided (see abbreviations below). Finally, if the information is questionable, it may be followed by an interrogative sign:

Martínez, Emir. *Cantos errantes.* s.l.: Ediciones Signos, s.f. s.p.
Martínez, Emir. *Cantos errantes.* [Guatemala?]: Ediciones Signos, [1889]. [132 págs.]
Martínez, Emir. *Otros cantos errantes.* Guatemala: s.e., 1892. 98 págs.

    s.l.: sin lugar
    s.e.: sin editorial
    s.f.: sin fecha
    s.p.: sin paginación

PERIODICALS

The greatest problems arise in the adequate listing of information for periodicals, especially with reference to titles and volume and issue numbers.

Carreira, André. "Teatro callejero en la ciudad de Buenos Aires después de la dictadura militar."[3] *Latin American Theatre Review* 27.2 (1944): 103–14.
Foster, David William y Naomi Lindstrom. "Jewish Argentine Authors: A Registry." *Revista interamericana de bibliografía* 41.3 (1991): 478–503; 41.4 (1991): 655–82.
Roy-Cabrerizo, Joaquín. "Claves de Cortázar en un libro olvidado: *Buenos Aires. Buenos Aires.*" *Revista iberoamericana* 84–85 (1973): 471–82.

---

[3] A particular problem is created with the order of periods/commas and quote marks between Spanish and English. American English places the period and comma inside the closing quote mark, while Spanish (and British English) place the period and comma outside. However, when citing references written in Spanish in a text written in English, the English-language norm should be observed.

If a journal repaginates with every issue, the issue number needs to be provided along with the volume number (first example). If a journal numbers continuously throughout an entire volume, providing the issue number is optional; in the second example it is given only to underscore the fact that there are two parts to the entry distributed between two issues of a journal that, however, paginates continuously throughout the entire volume. If a journal numbers each issue separately, providing the volume number is not necessary (third item).

Note that, in the pagination note, following the dash, only the last two digits of the second number are given, unless the first would be a zero, in which case the hundred's place is repeated. If the journal does not paginate, either the indication "no p." may be given or the pages may be numbered and provided in brackets.

In the case of titles that may belong to more than one journal, the city or institutional affiliation may be provided in either parentheses or brackets following the title to assist in the location of the specific title.

Because of the similarity of so many newspaper titles, it is advisable to specify the city: *La Nación* (Buenos Aires).

BOOK CHAPTERS

Bartís, Ricardo. *Postales argentinas*. En *Otro teatro después de Teatro Abierto*. Recopilación y banda: Jorge A. Dubatti. Buenos Aires: Libros del Quirquincho, 1990. 5–23.

Borges, Jorge Luis. "Las inscripciones de los carros." Jorge Luis Borges y José E. Clemente, *El lenguaje de Buenos Aires*. Buenos Aires: Emecé, 1968. 49–59.

Brant, Herbert J. "Marco Denevi." *Latin American Writers on Gay and Lesbian Themes: A Bio-Critical Sourcebook*. Ed. David William Foster. Westport, Conn.: Greenwood Press, 1994. 34–37.

Walter, Richard J. "Buenos Aires." *Encyclopedia of Latin American History and Culture*. Ed. Barbara A. Tenenbaum et al. New York: Charles Scribner's, 1996. 1.480–83.

There are various formats for indicating the pagination of book chapters. The model chosen here follows the example of the Modern Language Association. The University of Chicago *Manual of Style* would, for example, place the pagination following the editor's name, separated by a comma: Recopilación y banda: Jorge A. Dubatti, 5–23.

In the first example, the text included within a collection is a primary unit, a full-length play that could be published as a freestanding volume.

The second example records a separately named chapter in a book by the author of that book (or, in this case, the coauthor). The third example records an essay in an edited volume. Note the different position of authors in the first case and editor in the second case. In both of these cases, the chapter and essay are considered secondary units.

In the case of multivolume titles, the volume and pagination are given, separated by a period (fourth example).

BIBLIOGRAPHY PREPARATION

Information that is added (for example, elements of an author's name) that does not appear complete in the item being cited is usually enclosed in square brackets: García-Lorca, F[ederico].

The items attributed to an author should be arranged alphabetically (not chronologically) by title, discounting articles (note that so-called neuter *lo*, as in "lo importante," does not count as an article and is, therefore, counted in alphabetization). Should a publisher so demand, items may be arranged chronologically, following a social sciences format:

Sosnowski, Saul. 1975. "El verbo cabalístico en la obra de Borges." *Hispamérica* 9: 33–54.
———. 1987. *La orilla inminente; escritores judíos argentinos.* Buenos Aires: Legasa, 1987.

If more than one item by an author is listed, items subsequent to the first are introduced by six hyphens or a three-em dash in place of the author name. When a repeated author is also the first of a series of coauthors, the dash is followed by the names of the coauthors:

Jodorowsky, Alejandro. *Las ansias carnívoras de la nada.* Santiago: Hachette, 1991.
———y Juan Giménez. *La Caste des Méta-Barons: Othon le Trisaïeul.* Paris: Les Humanoïdes Associés, 1992.

Anonymous books and articles are listed by title and alphabetized accordingly. "Anonymous" or "Anónimo" are not used.

Corporate authors are treated as any author. If the name is made up of multiple units, each unit is separated by a period. The listing of the units follows organizational hierarchy, beginning with the highest unit:

Argentina. Comisión Nacional sobre la Desaparición de Personas. *Nunca más; informe de la Comisión Nacional sobre la Desaparición de Personas.* Buenos Aires: EUDEBA, 1984.

If an item has been reprinted, the reprint note follows the original reference, preceded by the phrase "Reproducido en," unless the title has been modified, in which case the phrase "Reproducido como" is used, followed by the revised title:

Bruce-Novoa, Juan. "Homosexuality and the Chicano Novel." *Confluencia; revista hispánica de cultura y literatura* 2.1 (1986): 69–77. Reproducido en *European Perspectives on Hispanic Literature of the United States.* Ed. Genvieve Fabre. Houston: Arte Público Press, 1988. 98–106.

Foster, David William. "Algunos espejismos eróticos [*De Ausencia* de María Luisa Mendoza]." *Revista de la Universidad de México* 37 (1984): 36–38. Reproducido como "Espejismos eróticos: 'De Ausencia,' de María Luisa Mendoza." *Revista iberoamericana* 132–133 (1985): 657–63.

Material, typically prefatory, containing generic titles such as "Introducción," "Prefacio," "Prólogo," or "Palabras preliminares" need not be cited with quotation marks (first example). If, however, it is a distinctive title, preceded or not by a generic designation, it is quoted as any other fragment of a larger whole (second example):

Borges, Jorge Luis. Foreword. *Selected Poems, 1923–1967.* Ed. Norman Thomas Di Giovanni. New York: Delta-Dell, 1973. xv–xvi.

Borré, Omar. "Prólogo: las colaboraciones de Arlt en Don Goyo." *Aguafuertes uruguayas y otras páginas.* Por Roberto Arlt. Montevideo: Ediciones de la Banda Oriental, 1996. 5–14.[4]

An alternative casting of this citation might be:

Borré, Omar. "Prólogo: las colaboraciones de Arlt en Don Goyo." Roberto Arlt, *Aguafuertes uruguayas y otras páginas.* Montevideo: Ediciones de la Banda Oriental, 1996. 5–14.

In the first example, it is understood that Borges has prefaced a collection of his own poetry. When this is not the case, an indication is made that the work being prefaced is by a different author than the preface.

When several sections of a single work are listed separately, it is appropriate to provide a simple key to the main comprehensive reference:

---

[4] A preface or prologue may be numbered consecutively in arabic numerals with the main body of text, or it may be numbered separately, typically in roman numerals. The citation should reflect the actual usage in the item being cited.

DuPouy, Steven M. "Fernando Vallejo." Foster, 439–42.

Foster, David William, ed. *Latin American Writers on Gay and Lesbian Themes: A Bio-critical Sourcebook.* Westport, Conn.: Greenwood Press, 1994.

Muñoz, Elías Miguel. "Manuel Puig." Foster, 339–45.

Should there be several entries by Foster, it would be necessary to provide a short title:

Muñoz, Elías Miguel. "Manuel Puig." Foster, *Latin American Writers,* 339–45.

CHAPTER 10

ABBREVIATIONS

*: (This sign is used to mark a hypothetical form in etymologies; in linguistics, it is used to mark an ungrammatical form.)

a: área

a.: antes

a), (a): alias

A., AA.: autor, autores; alteza, altezas

a. al.: alto alemán

AA.VV.: autores varios

A.B.: *Artium Baccalaureus* (Bachiller en Artes)

abg.: abogado

abl.: ablativo

abr.: abril

abrev.: abreviación

abs.: absoluto

a/c.: a cuenta de; a cargo de

a.C.: antes de Cristo

A.C.: año de Cristo

acad.: academia

acep., aceps.: acepción, acepciones

acept.: aceptación

act.: actualmente, actualizado

Act.: Hechos de los Apóstoles

acus.: acusativo

adapt.: adaptador

a. de J.C., a.J.C.: antes de Jesucristo

a D.g.: a Dios gracias

adj.: adjetivo

adm., admón.: administración

adm. púb.: administración pública

adv.: adverbio o adverbial

adv. afirm.: adverbio de afirmación

adv. c.: adverbio de cantidad
adv. correlat. cant.: adverbio correlativo de cantidad
advers.: adversativo
advert.: advertencia
adv. interrog. l.: adverbio interrogativo de lugar
adv. m.: adverbio de modo
adv. neg.: adverbio negativo
adv. ord.: adverbio de orden
adv. prnl. excl.: adverbio pronominal exclamativo
adv. relat. cant.: adverbio relativo de cantidad
adv. relat. l.: adverbio relativo de lugar
adv. t.: adverbio de tiempo
aer.: aeronáutica
ag., agost.: agosto
agric.: agricultura
agrim.: agrimensura
al., alem.: alemán
álg.: álgebra
al. mod.: alemán moderno
alt.: alto, altura, altitud
Am.: Amós
a.m.: antes del mediodía (del latín *ante meridiem*)
A.M.: *Artium Magister* (Maestro en Artes)
amb.: ambiguo
amer.: americanismo
Amér.: América
Amér. Central: América Central
Amér. Lat.: América Latina
Amér. Mer.: América Meridional
amp.: ampliada
anagr.: anagrama
anat.: anatomía
anón.: anónimo
anot.: anotador
ant.: anticuado, antiguo, antología
Ant.: Antillas
ant. al.: antiguo alemán
antep.: anteportada
ant. fr.: antiguo francés
antífr.: antífrasis
Antrop.: antropología
ap.: apéndice
apais.: apaisado

apl.: aplicado
apl. a pers., ú.t.c.s.: aplicado a persona, úsase también como
   sustantivo
apóc.: apócope
Apoc., Ap.: Apocalipsis
apócr.: apócrifo
aprox.: aproximadamente
ár.: árabe
arag.: aragonés
arauc.: araucano
arc.: arcaico
arch.: archivo
Arg., Argent.: Argentina
arit.: aritmética
arq.: arquitectura
arqueol.: arqueología
arr.: arreglador
art.: artículo
ast.: asturiano
astrol.: astrología
astron.: astronomía
A.T.: Antiguo Testamento
atm.: atmósfera
atte.: atentamente
aum.: aumentativo, aumentada
Aust.: Austria
autobiog.: autobiografía
autógr.: autógrafo
aut.: autor
av., Avda.: avenida, Avenida
aviac.: aviación
azt.: azteca

b.: bajo, barrio
B.A.: Bachiller en Artes
B.A., B. Art.: Bellas Artes
bact., bacteriol.: Bacteriología
B. Aires, Bs.As.: Buenos Aires
Bar.: Baruc
Barc.: Barcelona
bbl., bib., bibl.: biblioteca
b. bret.: bajo bretón
bco.: banco

Bélg.: Bélgica
b. gr.: bajo griego
Bibl.: Biblia
bibliogr.: bibliografía
biol.: biología
bioquím.: bioquímica
b.l., b. lat.: bajo latín
B.Lit.: Bachiller en Literatura
b.l.m.: besa la mano
Bln.: Berlín
B.Mús.: Bachiller en Música
Bol.: Bolivia
bot.: botánica
br., Br.: bachiller
Bras.: Brasil
Bret.: Bretaña
B.S.: Bachiller en Ciencias
Bulg.: Bulgaria
burg.: burgalés

c.: como, ciudad
C.: Celsius (grados centígrados)
c/: cargo, cuenta, calle
c: copyright
c., ca.: *circa* (hacia)
caligr.: caligrafía
Can.: Canadá, Canarias
Cap.: Capital
cap., c.: capítulo
Cap. Fed.: Capital Federal
carp.: carpintería
cast.: castellano
cat.: catalán, catálogo
c.c.: centímetros cúbicos
c/c., cta., cte.: cuenta corriente
célt.: céltico
celtolat.: celtolatino
cf., cfr.: *confer* (compárese)
Chil.: Chile
Cía, cía., C.ª: compañía
ciber.: cibernética
cinem., cinemat.: cinematografía
cir.: cirugía

cit.: citado
cm: centímetros
co., comp.: compañía
coaut.: coautor
col.: columna, colaborador, colección, color
Col.: Epístola de San Pablo a los Colosenses
Col., Colomb.: Colombia
colect.: colectivo
coloq.: coloquial
com.: sustantivo común de dos, comentarista, comercio
comp.: comparativo, compilador
compl.: complementario
comunic.: comunicación
conc.: concesivo
cond.: condicional
conj.: conjunción
constr.: construcción
contracc.: contracción
coord.: coordinador
copul.: copulativo
Cor.: Epístola de San Pablo a los Corintios
Córd.: Córdoba
corrup.: corrupción
C.P.: código postal
C.R., C. Rica: Costa Rica
C. Real: Ciudad Real
cronol.: cronológico, cronología
c.s.p.: cantidad suficiente para
cta.: cuenta
cte.: corriente
c/u.: cada uno
cub.: cubierta
Cub.: Cuba

d.: diminutivo
D., dn.: don
D.ª: doña
Dan.: Daniel
dat.: dativo
d.C., d. de J.C: después de Cristo
dcha.: derecha
ded.: dedicado, dedicatoria
defect.: (verbo) defectivo

del m.or.: del mismo origen
dep.: deporte
dep., depto.: departamento
d.e.p.: descanse en paz
der.: derivado, derecho
despect.: despectivo
desus.: desusado
deter.: determinado
Deut., Dt.: Deuteronomio
D.F.: Distrito Federal
dial.: dialéctica
dialect.: dialectal
dic.: diciembre
diplom.: diplomático
dir.: director, dirección
distrib.: distributivo
disyunt.: disyuntivo
dm, dms : decímetro(s)
doc.: documento, docena
dom.: domingo
D.P.: distrito postal
Dr.: doctor
Dra.: doctora
dram.: dramaturgo, dramático
dupdo., dupl.: duplicado

E: este (punto cardinal)
Ecl.: Eclesiastés
ecolog.: ecología
econ.: economía
Ecuad.: Ecuador
ed.: edición, editor
ed.: editorial
ed. lit.: editor literario
e.g.: *exempli gratia* (por ejemplo)
ej., ejs.: ejemplo, ejemplos
ejempl.: ejemplar
electr.: electricidad
electrón.: electrónica
El Salv.: El Salvador
en.: enero
ep.: epílogo
e.p.d.: en paz descanse

Eph., Ef.: Epístola de San Pablo a los Efesios
esc.: escultura
escand.: escandinavo
escr.: escritor
Esdr.: Esdras
esp.: español, especialmente
Esp.: España
estad.: estadísticas
Esth.: Ester
et al.: *et alii* (y otros)
etc.: etcétera
etim.: etimología
E.U., EEUU, EE.UU., E.U.A.: Estados Unidos
Eur.: Europa
Evang.: Evangelio
Ex.: Éxodo
excl.: exclamativo
exclam.: exclamación
explet.: expletivo
expr.: expresión
expr. elípt.: expresión elíptica
Ez.: Ezequiel

f., fem.: femenino
f., fol.: folio
F: Fahrenheit (grados)
f.ª, fra.: factura
Fac.: facultad
fac., facs.: facsímil
fam.: familiar
Farm.: farmacia
fasc.: fascículo
feb.: febrero
Ferr.: ferrocarriles
fest.: festivo
fha.: fecha
fig.: figurado, figura
fil., filos.: filosofía
Fil., Flp.: Epístola de San Pablo a los Filipenses
File., Flm.: Epístola de San Pablo a Filemón
Filip.: Filipinas
filol.: filología
filós.: filósofo

fís.: física
fisiol.: fisiología
flam.: flamenco
fon.: fonética, fonología
for.: forense
fotogr., fot.: fotografía, fotógrafo
fr.: francés
Fr.: fray
fr., frs.: frase, frases
fr. proverb.: frase proverbial
frec., frecuent.: frecuencia; (verbo) frecuentativo
fut.: futuro

g, gr.: gramo
g/: giro
gaél.: gaélico
Gál., Gal.: Epístola de San Pablo a los Gálatas
gall.: gallego
gal. port.: galaico portugués
gén.: género
Gén., Gen.: Génesis
genit.: genitivo
geogr.: geografía
geol.: geología
geom.: geometría
ger., Ger.: gerundio
ger. comp.: gerundio compuesto
germ.: germánico
gob.: gobierno, gobernación, gobernador
gót.: gótico
g.p., g/p.: giro postal
gr.: griego
gral.: general
gram.: gramática
grecolat.: grecolatino
gr. mod.: griego moderno
guar.: guaraní
Guat.: Guatemala

h.: hora, habitante, hoja
H.: hermano (de una orden religiosa)
Ha: hectárea(s)
Hab.: Habacuc
hebr.: hebreo

Hebr.: Epístola de San Pablo a los Hebreos
hig.: higiene
hist.: historiador, histórico, Historia
hm.: hectómetro
hnos.: hermanos
hol.: holandés
Hond.: Honduras
hros.: herederos

Iac.: Iacobi (Epístola de Santiago)
ib., ibíd.: *ibídem* (en el mismo lugar)
ibér.: ibérico
íd.: *ídem* (lo mismo)
i.e.: *id est* (lo mismo)
il.: ilustración, ilustrador
ilat.: ilativo, ilativa
imp.: imprenta
imp., impr.: imprenta, impresor
imper., imperat.: imperativo
impers.: (verbo) impersonal
incl.: incluido
incoat.: (verbo) incoativo
incomp.: incompleto
ind.: industria
indef.: indefinido
indet.: indeterminado
indic.: indicativo
infinit.: infinitivo
inform.: informática
ingen.: ingeniería
ingl.: inglés
inic.: iniciales
intens.: intensivo
interj.: interjección
interrog.: interrogativo
intr.: (verbo) intransitivo
invar.: invariable
irl.: irlandés
Io.: Ioannes (Evangelio de San Juan)
irón.: irónico
irreg.: irregular
Is.: Isaías
ít.: *ítem* (también)

ital.: italiano, italianismo
iterat.: (verbo) iterativo
izq., izqda.: izquierda

jap.: japonés
Jap.: Japón
J.C.: Jesucristo
Jds.: Judas
Jdt.: Judit
Jer.: Jeremías
jerig.: jerigonza
Jl.: Joel
Jn.: Evangelio de San Juan
Jon.: Jonás
Jos.: Josué
Jud., Jue.: Iudicum (Libro de los Jueces)
juev.: jueves
jul.: julio
jun.: junio
jurisp.: jurisprudencia

kg, Kg., kgs: kilogramo(s)
km, kms: kilómetro(s)
kv., kw.: kilovatio

l: litro(s)
l., lib.: libro
L/: letra de cambio
lám.: lámina
Lam.: Lamentaciones
lat.: latino
lat., l.: latín
Lc.: Evangelio de San Lucas
Ldo., Lda.: licenciado, licenciada
legisla.: legislación
leng.: lenguaje, lengua
leon.: leonés
Lev.: Levítico
l. gót.: letra gótica
Lic.: licenciado
ling.: lingüística
lit.: literalmente
lit.: literatura
litogr.: litografía, litografiado

loc.: locución
loc. adj.: locución adjetiva
loc. adv.: locución adverbial
loc. adv. interrog.: locución adverbial interrogativa
loc. cit., l.c.: *loco citato* (en el lugar citado)
loc. conjunt.: locución conjuntiva
loc. conjunt. advers.: locución conjuntiva adversativa
loc. conjunt. condic.: locución conjuntiva condicional
loc. interj.: locución interjectiva
loc. prepos.: locución preposicional
lóg.: lógica
l. rom.: letra romana
ltda.: limitada
lun.: lunes

m: metro(s)
m., mañ.: mañana
m.: moderno (siglos XVIII y XIX)
M.: medieval (siglos V al XV), madre (de una orden religiosa)
m., mas.: masculino
M.ª: María
M.A.: *Magister Artium* (Maestro en Artes)
Mac.: Macabeos
Magn.: magnetismo
Mal.: Malaquías
map.: mapa
mar.: marzo
Mar.: marina
mart.: martes
mat.: matemáticas
Mat., Mt.: Evangelio de San Mateo
may.: mayo
Mc.: Evangelio de San Marcos
M.D.: *Medicinae Doctor* (Doctor en Medicina)
mec.: mecánica
mecanogr.: mecanografía
med.: medicina
metal.: metalurgia
metát.: metátesis
meteor.: meteorología
métr.: métrica
mex.: mexicanismo

Méx., Méj.: México
miérc.: miércoles
min.: minuto
mineral.: mineralogía
Miq.: Miqueas
míst.: mística
mit.: mitología
mm: milímetro(s)
mod.: moderno
m.or.: mismo origen
mozár.: mozárabe
ms., mss.: manuscrito(s)
m. tipogr.: marca tipográfica
Mtro.: maestro
mús.: música
m. y f.: masculino y femenino

N: norte (punto cardinal)
n.: nació, nacido, neutro, noche, nota
NA: Norte América
n.a., n. del a.: nota del autor
N.ª S.ª: Nuestra Señora
Nah.: Nahum
náut.: náutica
N.B.: *nota bene* (nótese bien), obsérvese
ne: noreste
n.e., n. del e.: nota del editor
neerl.: neerlandés
neg., negat.: negación, negativo
Neh.: Nehemías
neol.: neologismo
Nicar.: Nicaragua
no: noroeste
nominat.: nominativo
nov.: noviembre
n.p., n.pr.: nombre propio
n.s.: nueva serie
N.T.: Nuevo Testamento
n.t., n. del t.: nota del traductor
ntro.: nuestro
NU: Naciones Unidas
num.: numerado

Núm.: Libro de los Números
núm., núms., n., N.º: número, números

O: oeste (punto cardinal)
o/: orden
ob. cit.: obra citada
obst.: obstetricia
oct.: octubre
odont.: odontología
oftalm.: oftalmología
onomat.: onomatopeya
op. cit.: *opere citato* (en la obra citada)
opt.: óptica
opúsc.: opúsculo
orig.: original
ortogr.: ortografía
ortop.: ortopedia
Os.: Oseas

p.: página
P.: padre (en una orden religiosa), papa
p., ps., Part.: participio, participios
p.a.: participio activo
pag. dupl.: paginación duplicada
pag. var.: paginación variada
pág., págs.: página (s)
paleog.: paleografía
paleont.: paleontología
Pan.: Panamá
Par.: Paralipómenos
Par., Parag.: Paraguay
párr.: párrafo
part. comp.: partícula comparativa
part. conj.: partícula conjuntiva
part. insep.: partícula inseparable
Pat.: Patología
Pcia.: provincia
P.D.: posdata
ped.: pediatría
pedag.: pedagogía
p.ej., por ej.: por ejemplo
Per.: Perú
perg.: pergamino

pers.: persona
persp.: perspectiva
Pet.: Epístola de San Pedro
p.f.: participio de futuro
p.f.p.: participio de futuro pasivo
Ph.D.: *Philosophiae Doctor* (Doctor en Filosofía)
pint.: pintura
pl.: plural
Pl.: plaza
p.m.: después del mediodía (del latín *post meridiem*)
P.º: paseo
P.O., p.o., p/o.: por orden
poét.: poético
polít.: política
pop.: popular
por anal.: por analogía
por antonom.: por antonomasia
por excel.: por excelencia
por ext.: por extensión
port.: portugués, portada
Port.: Portugal
post.: postgraduado
pp.: páginas
p.p.: participio pasivo
ppal., pral.: principal
pr.: prologista
precede al tít.: precede al título
pref.: prefijo, prefacio
prehist.: prehistoria
prelat.: prelatino
prelim.: preliminares
prep.: preposición
prep. insep.: preposición inseparable
pres.: presente
pret.: pretérito
P. Rico, Puerto R., P.R.: Puerto Rico
priv., privat.: privativo
prnl.: pronominal
prof.: profesor
prof.ª: profesora
pról.: prólogo
pron.: pronombre

pron. correlat. cant.: pronombre correlativo de cantidad
pron. dem.: pronombre demostrativo
pron. excl.: pronombre exclamativo
pron. interrog.: pronombre interrogativo
pron. pers.: pronombre personal
pron. poses.: pronombre posesivo
pron. relat.: pronombre relativo
pron. relat. cant.: pronombre relativo de cantidad
pronun.: pronunciación
pronun. and.: pronunciación andaluza
pronun. esp.: pronunciación española
pros.: prosodia
prov.: provenzal
Prov.: Libro de los Proverbios
ps.: personas
P.S.: *post scriptum* (posdata)
psicoanál.: psicoanálisis
psicol.: psicología
psiquiat.: psiquiatría
pta., ptas.: peseta(s)
publ.: publicado
p.us.: poco usado

q.b.s.m.: que besa su mano
q.b.s.p.: que besa sus pies
quech.: quechua
quím.: química

R.: renacimiento, renacentista (siglos XVI y XVII)
R., Rda., Revda.: reverendo, reverenda
R.A., Rep. Arg.: República Argentina
Radio.: radiodifusión
R.ᵇⁱ: recibí
Rda. M., R. M.: reverenda madre
R. de la Plata: Río de la Plata
rec.: (verbo) recíproco, recopilador
red.: redactor
Rdo., Revdo.: reverendo
Rdo. P., R. P.: reverendo padre
ref., refs.: refrán, refranes, refundidor
reform.: reformada
reg.: regular
Reg.: Regum (Libro de los Reyes), registro

regres.: regresivo
reimp.: reimpresión
rel.: religión
Rep. Domin.: República Dominicana
reprod.: reproducción
ret.: retórica
retr.: retrato
R.I.P.: *requiescat in pace* (en paz descanse)
Rmo., Rma. reverendísimo, reverendísima
Rom.: Epístola de San Pablo a los Romanos
Rp.: *recipe* (tómese)
rpm., r.p.m.: revoluciones por minuto
Rte.: remitente
rúst.: rústico

S: sur (punto cardinal)
s.: segundo, sustantivo
s.a.: sin año
S.ª: señora
S.A.: Sociedad Anónima; Su Alteza
Sab.: Libro de la Sabiduría
sáb.: sábado
Sal.: Salmos
Salv.: San Salvador
Sam.: Samuel
sánsc., sánscr.: sánscrito
Sant.: Epístola de Santiago
s/c.: su cuenta
sdad.: sociedad
s.e.: sin editor
sel.: selección, seleccionador
sent.: sentido
sep.: separata
separat.: separativo
sept., septbre.: septiembre
ser.: serie
seud.: seudónimo
seud. colect.: seudónimo colectivo
s.e.u o.: salvo error u omisión
s.f.: sin fecha
sig., sigs., s. ss.: siguiente(s)
sign.: signatura

símb.: símbolo
sing.: singular
s.l.: sin lugar, sus labores
s/L.: su letra (de cambio)
s.l.n.a.: sin lugar ni año
s.n., s/n.: sin número
s/o.: su orden
sociol.: sociología
Sof., Soph.: Sofonías
S.O.S.: socorro
S.P.: servicio público
Sr., Sres., Srs.: señor, señores
Sra., Sras.: señora, señoras
s.r.c.: se ruega contestación
Srta., Srtas.: señorita, señoritas
S., s., ss.: siglo, siglos
S., Sta., Sto.: san, santa, santo
s.s.: seguro servidor
ss.: siguientes
SS.$^{\underline{mo}}$ P.: Santísimo Padre
s.s.s.: su seguro servidor
Sto. Dom.: Santo Domingo
subj.: subjuntivo
subtít.: subtítulo
suf.: sufijo
sup.: superlativo
supl.: suplemento
s.v.: *sub voce* (bajo la voz, en el artículo)

t: tonelada(s)
t.: temporal, tiempo, tarde
t., to., tom.: tomo
tall. gráf.: talleres gráficos
taurom.: tauromaquia
tecn.: tecnicismo
tecnol.: tecnología
tel.: teléfono
telec.: telecomunicación
telev.: televisión
teol.: teología
terap.: terapéutica
term.: término, terminación
Tes., Thess.: Epístola de San Pablo a los Tesalonicences

test.: testamento
t.f.: terminación femenina
Tim.: Epístola de San Pablo a Timoteo
tít.: título
Tit.: Tito
tít. orig.: título original
t.m.: terminación masculina
Tob.: Tobías
topogr.: topografía, topográfico
trad.: traductor, traducción
transcrip.: transcriptor
tr.: (verbo) transitivo
TV: televisión

Ú., ú.: úsase
Ud., ud., Uds., uds.: usted, ustedes
unipers.: (verbo) unipersonal
univ.: universidad
urb.: urbanización
Urug.: Uruguay
usáb.: usábase

v.: verbo, verso, véase
v/: visto
v.a.: véase además
var.: variedad
vasc.: vascuence
vdo., vda.: viudo, viuda
Venez.: Venezuela
veter.: veterinaria
v.gr., v.g.: *verbi gratia* (verbigracia)
vid.: *vide* (véase)
vier.: viernes
V.º B.º, v.º b.º: visto bueno
vocat.: vocativo
vol., v.: volumen
vulg.: vulgar
vv.: versos

Xto.: Cristo

Zach.: Zacarías
zool.: zoología
zoot.: zootecnia

ANONYMOUS SPANISH CLASSICS

«A cazar va el caballero»
Abad don Juan de Montemayor
«Alora, la bien cercada»
Amadís de Gaula
Amadís de Grecia
«Andando por estos mares»
Auto de la destrucción de Jerusalén / ¡Ay Jherusalem!
Auto de la huida a Egipto
Auto de los Reyes Magos

Balandro del sabio Merlín
Berta

Caballería celestial de la rosa fragante
«Caballeros de Moclín»
Cancionero de Herberay des Essarts
Cancionero de Palacio
Cancionero de Stúñiga
Cantar de Roncesvalles
Cantar de los siete infantes de Lara
Chronica Adefonsi imperatoris
Clemades y Claramunda
Códice de autos viejos
«Conde Arnaldos»
«Conde Claros de Montalván»
Coplas de ¡Ay Panadera!
Coplas de Mingo Revulgo
Coplas del provincial
Crónica albeldense

Crónica de los reyes de Castilla
Crónica de veinte reyes
Crónica latina de los reyes de Castilla
Crónica najerense
Crónica particular del Cid
Crónica seudo-Isidoriana
Crónica silense
Crónica troyana
Cuestión de amor
Curial y Güelfa

Dança general de la muerte
Danse macabre
«De Francia partió una niña»
La degollación de san Juan Bautista
«Diálogo entre el amor, el viejo y la hermosa»
Diez mandamientos
Disputa del alma y del cuerpo
Disputa de Elena y María o Disputa del clérigo y del caballero
Don Fernando par del emperador
Don Rodrigo
Doncella Teodor
Doña Alda

Enrique Pi de Oliva

Farsa sacramental de las cortes de la Iglesia
Flores y Blancaflor

Gran conquista de ultramar

Historia del abencerraje y la hermosa Jarifa

Historia del caballero de Dios que había por nombre Zifar o Leyenda del caballero Cifar

Lazarillo de Tormes
Leyenda de Cerdeña
Leyenda de don Rodrigo
Leyenda de la condesa traidora
Libro de Alexandre
Libro de Apolonio
Libro de los engaños
Libro de los gatos o Libro de los cuentos
Libro de los tres reyes de Oriente (Libre dels tres reys d'Orient)
Libro de miseria del omne
Libro del caballero del Cisne o Leyenda del caballero del Cisne

Mainete y Galiana
El martirio de santa Bárbara
El martirio de santa Eulalia
Misteri de sant Esteve
Misterio de Elche
Mocedades del Cid
Mora Zaida

Oliveros de Castilla

Palmerín de Inglaterra
Palmerín de Oliva
Parsifal

Partinuplés

Peregrinación del rey Luis de Francia

La pícara Justina
Poema de Alfonso Onceno
Poema de Bernardo del Carpio
Poema de Fernán González
Poema de Mío Cid
Poema de Rodrigo y el Rey Don Fernando
Poema del Yuçuf
«Por los caños de Carmona»
Primaleón
«El prisionero»
Proverbios del rey Salomón

Razón de amor con los denuestos del agua y del vino
Reinaldos de Montalbán
Revelación de un ermitaño
Roberto el Diablo
Roman de la Rose
Romance del infante García

Sancho II y el Cerco de Zamora
Sansueña

Tablante de Ricamonte
Tirant lo blanc
Tristán de Leonís
Tristán e Iseo

Vida de Estebanillo González
Vida de san Ildefonso
Vida de santa María Egipciaca

LATIN AUTHORS

Accio, Lucio
Acron, Helenio
Afranio, Lucio
Albinovano, Peto
Antonio, Marco
Apuleyo, Celso
Apuleyo, Lucio
Aquilio Galo, Cayo
Asconio Pediano, Quinto
Asinio Polión, Cayo
Ateyo Capitón, Cayo
Aulo Ofilio, Cayo
Aurelio Víctor, Sexto
Ausonio, Décimo Magno
Aviano, Flavio
Avieno, Rufo Festo

Boecio, Anicio Manlio Torcuato
   Severiano
Bruto, Marco Junio

Calpurnio Sículo, Tito Julio
Capro, Flavio
Carisio, Aurelio Arcadio
Carisio, Flavio Sosípatro
Casio Hemina, Lucio
Casio Severo, Tito
Casio Severo de Parma, Cayo
Casiodoro, Magno Aurelio
Catón, Dionisio
Catón, Marco Porcio (Mayor)
Catón, Marco Porcio (Menor)

Catón, Valerio
Catón Liciniano, Marco Porcio
Catulo, Cayo Valerio
Celio Antípater, Lucio
Celio Rufo, Marco
Celso, Aulo Cornelio
Celso, Julio
César, Cayo Julio
Cicerón, Marco Tulio
Cicerón, Quinto Tulio
Cincio Alimento, Lucio
Claudiano, Claudio
Claudio, Apio (El Ciego)
Clodio, Servio
Columela, Lucio Junio Moderato
Cornelio Cetego, Marco
Cornelio Severo, Publio
Cornuto, Lucio Anneo
Coruncanio, Tiberio

Donato, Elio

Elio Tuberón, Lucio
Elio Tuberón, Quinto
Emilio Escauro, Marco (Mayor)
Emilio Escauro, Marco (Menor)
Ennio, Quinto
Escipión Nasica, Publio Cornelio
Estacio, Cecilio
Estacio, Publio Papinio
Estrabón, Cayo Julio César
Eutropio, Flavio

Fabio Píctor, Quinto
Fabio Píctor, Servio
Fedro
Fenestela, Lucio
Festo, Sexto Pompeyo
Fírmico Materno, Julio
Flavio, Cneo
Floro, Lucio Anneo
Frontino, Sexto Julio
Frontón, Marco Cornelio
Fulgencio, Fabio Furio Planciades
Furio Antiano

Galo, Cayo Cornelio
Gayo, Cayo
Gelio, Aulo
Gelio, Cneo
Graco, Cayo Sempronio
Graco, Tiberio Sempronio

Helvio, Cayo Cinna
Higinio, Cayo Julio
Horacio Flaco, Quinto
Hortensio Hortalo, Quinto

Juvenal, Decio Junio
Juvencio Celso, Publio (Mayor)
Juvencio Celso, Publio (Menor)
Juvenco, Cayo Aquilino Vecio

Laberio, Decio
Labieno, Tito
Lactancio, Lucio Celio Firmiano
Lampridio, Elio
Licinio Macer, Cayo
Livio Andrónico
Lucano, Marco Anneo
Lucilio, Cayo
Lucrecio Caro, Tito
Lutacio Catulo, Quinto (Mayor)
Lutacio Catulo, Quinto (Menor)

Macrobio, Ambrosio Aurelio
    Teodosio
Manilio, Lucio

Marcial, Gargilio
Marcial, Marco Valerio
Matio, Cneo
Mecenas, Cayo Cilnio
Mecenas, Cayo Meliso
Mela, Pomponio
Menandro, Arrio
Merobaudes, Flavio
Minucio Félix Capela, Marciano
Mucio Escévola, Publio
Mucio Escévola I, Quinto
Mucio Escévola II, Quinto
Mucio Escévola III, Quinto

Nemesiano, Marco Aurelio
    Olimpio
Nepote, Cornelio
Nevio, Cneo
Nevio, Quinto

Orosio, Paulo
Ovidio Nasón, Publio

Pacuvio, Marco
Paladio, Rutilio Tauro Emiliano
Papiniano, Emilio
Papirio, Cayo
Papirio Peto, Lucio
Paulo, Julio
Petronio Árbitro, Cayo
Pisón, Lucio Calpurnio
Pisón Calpurniano, Marco Pupio
Pisón Frugi, Lucio Calpurnio
Plauto, Tito Maccio
Plinio Cecilio Segundo, Cayo
Plinio Segundo, Cayo
Plinio Valeriano, Cayo
Plocio Galo, Lucio
Pomponio, Sexto
Porcio Latrón, Marco
Porfirio, Pomponio
Postumio Albino, Aulo
Próculo, Sempronio
Propercio, Sexto Aurelio

Prudencio Clemente, Aurelio
Publilio Siro

Quintiliano, Marco Fabio

Rabirio, Cayo
Remio Fanio Palemón, Quinto
Rutilio Namaciano, Claudio
Rutilio Rufo, Publio

Sabino, Aulo
Sabino, Celio
Sabino, Elio
Sabino, Masurio
Sabino, Paulo
Salustio Crispo, Cayo
Sempronio Aselión, Cayo
Sempronio Tuditano, Cayo
Séneca, Lucio Anneo
Séneca, Marco Anneo
Sereno Samónico, Quinto
Servio, Mauro Honorato
Silio Itálico, Cayo
Solino, Cayo Julio
Suetonio Paulino, Cayo
Suetonio Tranquilo, Cayo
Sulpicio Apolinario, Cayo
Sulpicio Rufo, Servio
Sulpicio Severo

Tácito, Cayo Cornelio
Terencio Africano, Publio

Terencio Escauro, Quinto
Tertuliano, Quinto Septimio
  Florente
Tibulo, Albio
Ticiano, Julio
Tito Livio
Trabeas, Quinto
Trebacio Testa, Cayo
Trebelio Polión

Ulpiano, Domicio

Valerio Antias, Quinto
Valerio Flaco, Cayo
Valerio Máximo, Publio
Valerio Severo
Valgio Rufo, Cayo
Vario Rufo, Lucio
Varrón, Marco Terencio
Varrón Atacino, Publio
Vegecio Renato, Flavio
Vegecio Renato, Publio
Veleyo Patérculo, Cayo
Veleyo Torcuato, Cayo
Verrio Flaco, Marco
Vibio Floro, Lucio
Vibio Pansa, Cayo
Virgilio Marón, Publio
Vitelio Eulogio, Quinto
Vitrubio Polión, Marco
Vulcacio Sedígito, Publio

GREEK AUTHORS

Agatón
Alcifrón
Alexis [de Turios]
Anacreonte
Anaxágoras
Anaximandro [de Mileto]
Anaxímenes
Andócides
Antífanes
Antifonte
Antímaco de Colofón
Antístenes [de Atenas]
Apolodoro de Atenas
Apolonio de Rodas
Aquiles Tacio
Arato de Soli
Arión
Aristarco de Samos
Arístides
Aristófanes
Aristóteles
Arquílogo [de Paros]
Arquímedes
Arriano, Flavio

Babrio
Baquílides

Calímaco
Calino
Caritón
Cecilio

Corina [de Tanagra]
Cratino
Crinágoras [de Mitilene]
Critias
Ctesias [de Cnido]

Demetrio Falereo
Demócrito
Demóstenes
Diodoro de Sicilia
Diógenes Laercio
Dionisio de Halicarnaso

Empédocles
Epicarmo
Epicteto
Epicuro
Eratóstenes
Esopo
Esquilo
Esquines
Estesícoro
Estesimbroto
Estrabón
Euclides
Euforión
Eupolis
Eurípides

Fedón
Ferécrates
Filemón

Filócoro
Focílides
Frínico

Gorgias

Hecateo [de Mileto]
Hegesias
Helánico
Heliodoro
Heráclides
Heráclito
Hermipo
Herodes Atico
Herodoto
Hesíodo
Hipérides
Hipócrates
Hipónax
Homero

Íbico
Ión
Iseo
Isócrates

Janto
Jenófanes
Jenofonte
Jenofonte de Efeso
Josefo, Flavio

Licofrón [de Calcis]
Licurgo
Lisias
Longo
Luciano de Samosata

Meleagro
Menandro
Mimnermo
Mosco de Siracusa

Nicandro
Nonnos

Paniasis
Parménides
Partenio de Nicea
Pausanias
Píndaro
Pisandro
Pitágoras
Platón
Plotino
Plutarco
Polibio
Porfirio
Pratinas de Fliunte
Praxífanes
Práxila
Pródico
Protágoras

Querilo de Samos
Quinto de Esmirna
Quiónides

Safo
Simónides
Simónides de Amorgos
Sófocles
Sofrón
Solón

Tales de Mileto
Telesila
Teócrito
Teodectes
Teofrasto
Teognis [de Mégara]
Teopompo
Terpandro
Timeo
Tirteo
Trasímaco
Tucídides

Zenódoto [de Éfeso]
Zenón

LATIN EXPRESSIONS

Latin expressions are considered foreign-language expressions, so there is a strong tendency in written Spanish to print them in italics, though often with Spanish accents. Both forms (the Latin form and Latin form with accents) are acceptable. (In this appendix, Latin terms are in boldface italics, Spanish in regular italics.)

a fortiori: con mayor razón (for a still stronger reason, all the more)

a posteriori: después de (based upon actual observation or upon experimental data)

a priori: antes de (not based on prior study or examination)

ab absurdo: por lo absurdo (in an absurd fashion)

ab aeterno: desde la eternidad (from the most remote antiquity)

ab initio: desde el comienzo (from the beginning)

ab origine / ab orígine: desde el origen (from the beginning, from the source or origin)

ad calendas graecas: lit. *calendas griegas, tiempo que no ha de llegar* (at no time, never)

ad hoc: para un fin determinado (for this purpose)

ad hominem / ad hóminem: argumento fundado en las opiniones o actos de la misma persona a quien se dirige (appealing to one's prejudices or special interests rather than to one's intellect or reason)

ad infinitum / ad infinítum: hasta el infinito (to infinity)

ad interim / ad ínterim: entretanto (in the time between)

ad libitum / ad líbitum: a voluntad (at one's pleasure)

ad litteram / ad lítteram: al pie de la letra (to the letter, exactly)

ad nauseam / ad náuseam: hasta la repugnancia (ad nauseam)

ad pedem litterae / ad pédem lítterae: al pie de la letra (strictly speaking)

alma mater: madre nutricia (para referirse a la patria o la universidad) (nourishing mother, a school, college, or university at which one has studied; in Spanish it is also used to refer to the homeland) *alter ego:* otro yo (a second self)

ante meridiem / ante merídiem: antes del mediodía (occurring before noon)

bona fide: de buena fe (in good faith)

casus belli: caso de guerra (an event that brings about a declaration of war)

cum laude: con opción a premio extraordinario (with honor)

de facto: de hecho (en oposición a *de jure*) (in fact)

de jure: de derecho (by right)

de visu: con la vista (visually evident)

desideratum / desiderátum (pl. *desiderata*): aspiración o deseo que aún no se ha cumplido (something wanted or needed)

deus ex machina / deus ex máchina: intervención de un ser sobrenatural; dios bajado por un mecanismo especial (any artificial or improbable device resolving the difficulties of a plot)

do ut des: doy para que des (I give so you give)

dura lex sed lex: la ley es dura pero es ley (the law is hard, but it is the law)

et alii (masc.) / *et alia* (neutr.): y otros (and others)

ex aequo: con igual mérito (with equal merit)

ex cathedra / ex cáthedra: con autoridad de maestro (with authority)

ex libris: perteneciente a la biblioteca de (from the library of)

ex profeso: a propósito (on purpose)

grosso modo: en líneas generales (generally speaking)

habeas corpus / hábeas corpus: auto de comparecencia (a writ requiring a person to be brought before a judge)

hic et nunc: aquí y ahora (here and now)

honoris causa: por razón de honor (honorary university degree)

ibidem / ibídem: en el mismo lugar (in the aforementioned place)

in absentia: en ausencia (in absence)

in aeternum / in aetérnum: para siempre (forever)

in extenso: por extenso (at full length)

in extremis: poco antes de morir (near death)

in fraganti (instead of *in flagranti*): en el momento de cometerse el delito (in the very act of committing the offense)

in illo tempore / in illo témpore: en aquella época (in past times)

in itinere / in itínere: en el camino (on the way)

in memoriam: en recuerdo de (in memory of)

in pectore / in péctore: en reserva (referido a las decisiones) (secretly)

in promptu: de repente (suddenly)
in situ: en el sitio (in the place or position)
inter nos / ínter nos: entre nosotros (between us)
inter vivos / ínter vivos: entre vivos (between living persons)
ipso facto: inmediatamente (immediately)
item / ítem: elemento (element)

lapsus calami / lapsus cálami: error de pluma (a slip of the pen)
lapsus linguae: equivocación al hablar (a slip of the tongue)

manu militari: por mano militar (by military authority)
mare magnum / mare mágnum: confusión de asuntos (a mess, a confusion)
mea culpa: por mi culpa (my fault, used as an acknowledgment of one's responsibility)
modus operandi: modo de obrar (mode of operating or working)
modus vivendi: modo de vivir (lifestyle)
motu proprio: voluntariamente (of one's own accord)
mutatis mutandis: cambiando lo que se deba cambiar (the necessary changes having been made)

nihil obstat / níhil óbstat: nada se opone (nothing stands in the way; permission to publish a piece of writing, granted by an official censor)
non plus ultra: no más allá (non plus ultra)

peccata minuta: error, falta o vicio leves (inconsequential error or fault)
per accidens / per áccidens: por accidente (accidentally)
per capita / per cápita: por individuo (by or for each individual person)
per fas et per nefas: por las buenas y por las malas (one way or another; this way or else)
per saecula saeculorum / per saécula saeculorum: por los siglos de los siglos (forever)
per se: por sí mismo, en sí (by, of, for, or in itself)
post meridiem / post merídiem: después del mediodía (of or pertaining to the afternoon)
post mortem: después de muerto (after death)
pro domo sua: en su propio beneficio (to one's own benefit)

quid pro quo: una cosa por la otra (anything in return for another)

sine die: sin fecha determinada (without fixing a day for future action or meeting)
sine qua non: condición sin la cual no (an indispensable condition)

statu quo: *en el estado actual* (the existing state or condition)

sub judice / sub júdice: *pendiente de resolución* (under consideration)

sui generis / sui géneris: *muy especial* (unique)

urbi et orbi: *a la ciudad y al orbe, universalmente* (to the city [Rome] and the world)

ut supra: *como arriba* (as above)

vade retro: *retrocede* (go back)

velis nolis: *quieras o no quieras* (whether you like it or not)

vox populi / vox pópuli: *de dominio público* (popular opinion)

LITERARY AND DRAMATURGICAL TERMINOLOGY

el/lo absurdo: absurd
la acción: action
la acción final (la catástrofe): falling action (catastrophe)
el acento: stress, emphasis
la acentuación: accentuation
la acepción: (lexical) meaning
el acontecimiento: event
la acotación: stage direction
la acronía: achrony
el acrónimo: acronym
el acróstico: acrostic
actancial (el modelo): actantial (model)
el actante: actant (acting force)
el acto: act
el acto de habla: speech act
el actor: actor
la actuación: performance
la actualización: actualization, concretization
el adagio: proverb, adage
la adaptación: adaptation
la adecuación: adequacy
el aforismo: aphorism
el agente: agent
el agon: agon
la alegoría: allegory
el alejandrino: alejandrino (a fourteen-syllable verse, divided into two hemistiches)

la aliteración: alliteration
la ambigüedad: ambiguity
el amor cortés: courtly love
la anábasis: anabasis
el anacoluto: anacoluthon
la anacronía: anachrony
la anáfora: anaphora
la anagnórisis (el reconocimiento): anagnorisis (recognition)
el anagrama: anagram
la analepsis: analepse
los anales: annals
el análisis del discurso: discourse analysis
el análisis del relato: narrative analysis
el anapesto: anapest
la anfibología: amphibology
la angustia de las influencias: anxiety of influence
el/la antagonista: antagonist
el antihéroe: antihero
la antinomia: antinomy
el antiteatro: antitheater
la antítesis: antithesis
la antología: anthology
el antónimo: antonym
el aparte: aside
la apelación al público: address to the audience
el apócope: apocopation, apocope

lo apolíneo / lo dionisíaco: Apollonian/Dionysiac

la apología: vindication, apology

el apólogo: apologue

la aporía: aporia

el/la apóstrofe: apostrophe

el apotegma: apothegm

la arbitrariedad del signo: arbitrariness of the sign

el área de actuación: play area

el argumento: argument

aristotélico (el teatro): Aristotelian theater

el arquetipo: archetype

el arte poética: poetics

el asíndeton: asyndeton

la asonancia: assonance

el aspecto: aspect

la astracanada: farce

el asunto (la fábula): subject (plot)

átono: atonic, unstressed

el auto sacramental: sacramental play

la autobiografía: autobiography

el autor dramático: dramatist, playwright

el autor implícito: implied author

la autoridad textual: textual authority

la balada: ballade, ballad

el bestiario: bestiary

el binarismo / la binariedad: binarism/binarity

la biografía: biography

bisílabo: two-syllable verse

el bordón: refrain

brechtiano: Brechtian

el breviario: breviary

el bricolage: bricolage

burlesco: burlesque

la cacofonía: cacophony

la cadencia: rhythm, cadence

el canal: channel

la canción: song

la canción de cuna: lullaby

el canon: canon

el cantar de gesta: chanson de geste, epic poem

el cante jondo: cante jondo, Andalusian folk music

la cantiga: song, poem, ballad

el canto: song, canto (of a poem)

la caricatura: caricature

carnavalesco: carnivalesque

la catálisis: catalysts/catalyses

la catarsis: catharsis

la catástrofe: catastrophe

el centón: cento

la cesura: caesura

el cielito: cielito, an Argentine folk song

la ciencia ficción: science fiction

la cinésica: kinesics

el circunloquio, la circunlocución: circumlocution

la cita: quotation, quote

el clímax: climax

los códigos teatrales: theatrical codes

la coherencia: coherence

el collage: collage

el colonialismo: colonialism

la comedia: comedia/comedy

la comedia antigua: old comedy

la comedia burguesa: bourgeois comedy

la comedia de capa y espada: cloak-and-dagger play

la comedia de carácter: character comedy, comedy of character

la comedia de costumbres: comedy of manners

la comedia de humores: comedy of humors

la comedia de intriga: comedy of intrigue

la comedia de salón: society play, play of drawing-room manners

la comedia de situaciones: situation comedy

la comedia ligera: light comedy

la comedia musical: musical

la comedia negra: black comedy

la comedia nueva: new comedy

la comedia pastoral: pastoral comedy

la comedia satírica: satirical comedy

la comedia sentimental: sentimental comedy

cómico: comic

la competencia (lingüística, comunicativa): competence (linguistic, communicative)

la comunicación teatral: theatrical communication

la comunidad interpretativa: interpretive community

el concepto: witticism, pun

la concordancia: concordance, agreement

la connotación: connotation

la consonancia: consonance

la constelación de personajes: grouping of characters

el contexto: context

el contrapunto: counterpoint

la convención: convention

la copla: verse, stanza, song, ballad

el corifeo: coryphaeus

el coro: chorus

el corpus: corpus

el correlato objetivo: objective correlative

la corriente de conciencia: stream of consciousness

la creación colectiva: collective creation

la criada: lady's maid

el criado: servant

la crónica: chronicle

la cuaderna vía: cuaderna vía, a composition formed with four Spanish *alejandrinos* (fourteen-syllable verses)

el cuadro: scene

el cuadro viviente: tableau vivant

la cuarta pared: fourth wall

la cuarteta: quatrain (short verses)

el cuarteto: quatrain (long verses)

el cuento de hadas: fairy tale

el dáctilo: dactyl

danza de la muerte, danza macabra: dance of death, *danse macabre*

el decasílabo: decasyllable

la décima: stanza of ten octosyllabic lines

los decires: short medieval poetry

la deconstrucción: deconstruction

el decorado: set

el decorado sonoro: sound scenery

el decorado verbal: word scenery

la deíxis: deixis

derecha e izquierda del escenario: stage right, stage left

el desenlace: conclusion

la desfamiliarización (ostrananie): defamiliarization

el destinatario: addressee

el/la deuteragonista: deuteragonist

el diacrítico: diacritic(al)

la diacronía: diachrony

diacrónico: diachronic

la dialéctica: dialectics

el dialogismo: dialogism

el diálogo: dialogue

el diario: diary

la diatriba: diatribe

el dicho de autor: out-of-character speech

lo dicho y lo no dicho: spoken and unspoken

didáctica (la obra): didactic play

las didascalias: didascalia, stage directions

la diégesis: diegesis

diegético: diégétique; diegetic

la diéresis: diaeresis

la digresión: digression

el dilema: dilemma

el díptico: diptych

la dirección (la puesta en escena): direction, production

el/la director/a: director, producer

el ditirambo: dithyramb

el discurso: discourse, speech

el disfraz: disguise

el dispositivo escénico: stage form

la distanciación: alienation

documental (el teatro): documentary play

el dodecasílabo: alexandrine, dodecasyllable

el drama: drama

el drama burgués: bourgeois drama

el drama histórico: historical drama

el drama litúrgico: liturgical drama

las dramatis personae: dramatis personae

la dramatización: dramatization

la dramaturgia: dramaturgy

dramatúrgico (el análisis): dramaturgical analysis

el/la dramaturgo/a: playwright

el efecto de actualización: concretization effect

el efecto de extrañamiento: alienation effect

el efecto de realidad: reality effect

los efectos de sonido: sound effects

la égloga: eclogue, short pastoral poem

la elegía: elegy

la elipsis: ellipse

la empatía (la identificación): empathy

el encabalgamiento: enjambment

el encadenamiento: connection, order of scenes

el endecasílabo: hendecasyllable

la endecha: quatrain with lines of six or seven syllables, usually assonant

el enredo: imbroglio

el ensayo (dramático): repetition, rehearsal

el ensayo: essay

el entreacto: interval

el entremés: interlude, short comedy

la enunciación: enunciation

el enunciado: énoncé; utterance; that which is enunciated

épico: epic

el epigrama: epigram

el epílogo: epilogue

el episodio: episode

la episteme: episteme

la epístola: epistle, letter

el epitafio: epitaph

el epitalamio: epithalamium, epithalamion

el epíteto: epithet

el epítome: epitome

el epónimo: eponymous, eponymic

la epopeya: epic poem, epopee

el equívoco (el quidproquo): mistaken identity

la escena: stage, scene

el escenario: stage

la escenificación: staging

el espacio dramático: dramatic space
el espacio escénico: stage room
el espacio textual: textual space
la especificidad teatral: theatrical specificity
el espectáculo: performance show
el espondeo: spondee
la estancia: stanza
el estereotipo: stereotype
la estética teatral: aesthetics of drama
el estilo (directo, indirecto): style (direct, indirect)
el estrambote: extra verses added to a poem
el estreno: opening performance
el estribillo: refrain
la estrofa: verse, stance, strophe
la estructura dramática: dramatic structure
la estructura profunda: deep structure
la estructura superficial: surface structure
el estructuralismo (post-): structuralism (post-)
el eufemismo: euphemism
la eufonía: euphony
el exordio: exordium, preamble
la expectativa: expectation
la experiencia estética: aesthetic experience
experimental (el teatro): experimental theater
la expresión corporal: body language
el expresionismo: expressionism
el extrañamiento (ostrananie): defamiliarization, estrangement

la fábula: plot, fable
la farsa: farce

la ficción: fiction
la figura: figure, character
el fluir de conciencia: stream of consciousness
la focalización: focalization
la folía: folia, a dance of Portuguese origin
el folletín: newspaper serial, melodrama
la forma abierta: open form
la forma cerrada: closed form
el formalismo: formalism
las fuentes: sources
la función: function

el género: genre
el genotexto / el fenotexto: genotext/phenotext
el gesto: gesture
el gestus: gestus
la ginecrítica: gynocriticism
la glosa: gloss
el glosario: glossary
el goliardo: goliard
el gracioso: gracioso, a comic character, buffoon in Spanish comedy
la gramática generativa: generative grammar
la gramatología: grammatology
la greguería: greguería, a type of aphorism created by the Spanish writer Ramón Gómez de la Serna
grotesco: grotesque
el guión: script

el habla: parole; speech act
la hagiografía: hagiography
el hecho teatral: theatrical event
el hemistiquio: hemistich
el heptasílabo: heptasyllable
el hermetismo: hermetism
el héroe: hero

la heteroglosia: heteroglossia
el heterónimo: heteronym
el hexasílabo: hexasyllable
el hiato: hiatus
el himno: hymn
el hipérbaton (pl. hiperbatones, hipérbatos): hyperbaton
la hipérbole: hyperbole
el hipograma: hypogram
la historia: history, story
el homónimo: homonym
el horizonte de expectativas: horizon of expectations

el ícono/icono: icon
la iconología: iconology
el ideologema: ideologeme
la iluminación: lighting
el iluminismo: Enlightenment
la imagen: image
el imaginario: imaginary
la imaginería: imagery
la imitación: imitation
el inconsciente colectivo: collective unconscious
el inconsciente político: political unconscious
la indeterminación: indeterminacy
el incidente: incident
el indicio (el índice): index
la intención(alidad): intention(ality)
el intermedio: interval
el interpretante: interpretant
el intérprete: performer
la intersubjetividad: intersubjectivity
la intertextualidad: intertextuality
la intriga: story
la intriga secundaria: subplot
la ironía: irony
la isotopía: isotopy

la jácara: jácara, a picaresque ballad
el juego de lenguaje, de palabras: language play, pun
el juego dramático: dramatic play
el juego escénico: stage business
el juglar: minstrel

el lapidario: lapidary
el lector ideal: ideal reader
el lector implícito: implied reader
la lectura: reading
la lectura apegada: close reading
la legibilidad: readability
la lengua: langue; language system
el letrado: literate, lettered
la letrilla: rondeau
el lexema: lexeme
la leyenda: legend
el libelo: lampoon
el libro de caballerías: book of knight-errantry
el libro de horas: Book of Hours
la lira: lira, a stanza of five lines, each of seven or eleven syllables
la literariedad/la literaturidad: literariness
la literatura comparada: comparative literature
la lítote: litotes
la loa (dramática): prologue
el logocentrismo: logocentrism
el lugar común: commonplace, cliché

el madrigal: madrigal
la máquina teatral: theater machinery
el marco: frame
la máscara: mask
la máxima: maxim
el mecenazgo: patronage, maecenatism
el melodrama: melodrama

el mester de clerecía: clerical verse

el mester de juglaría: minstrel verse

la metafísica de la presencia: metaphysics of presence

la metáfora: metaphor

el metalenguaje: metalanguage

el metateatro: metatheater

la metonimia: metonymy

la métrica: metrics

el milagro (dramático): miracle play

la mímesis/mimesis: mimesis

la mímica: mimicry

el mimo: mime

la mise en abîme: mise en abyme, the text embedded within the text; a textual part that duplicates the textual whole

el mito: mythos, myth

la modelización: construction of a model

la monografía: monograph, (term) paper

el monólogo: monologue, soliloquy

el motivo: motive, motif

la musa: muse

la narración: narration

el narrador: narrator

el narratario: narratee

la narratividad: study of narrative

la narratología: narratology, narrativics

el narrema: narreme, cardinal function; kernel, nucleus

el naturalismo: naturalism

el neoclasicismo: neoclassicism

el neologismo: neologism

el neorrealismo: neorealism

el nihilismo: nihilism

la novela: novel, romance

la novela corta: novelette, novella

la novela policial: detective novel

la obra abierta: open text

la obra cerrada: closed text

la obra de tesis: thesis play

la obra didáctica: didactic play

la octava: octave

la octavilla: octet

el octosílabo: octosyllable

la oda: ode

la oda sáfica: sapphic ode

la onomatopeya: onomatopoeia

la ópera: opera

la opereta: operetta

la oposición binaria: binary opposition

la oralidad: orality

el orientalismo: orientalism

la ostensión: ostension, showing

oxítono: oxytone

el palimpsesto: palimpsest

el palíndromo: palindrome

el panegírico: panegyric

el panfleto (Gallicism for *libelo*): pamphlet, lampoon

la pantomima: pantomime

el papel: part, role

la paradoja: paradox

la paráfrasis: paraphrase

el paralelismo: parallelism

la parodia: parody

paroxítono: paroxytone

la parte: casting

el pasquín: lampoon

el pastiche: pastiche, imitation

el pathos: pathos

el patriarcado: patriarchy

la payada: payada, improvised song of a traveling minstrel (from the Río de la Plata region)

el pentasílabo: pentasyllable

la perífrasis: periphrasis

el periodismo: journalism
la peripecia: peripety, peripeteia
el personaje: character
los personajes, redondos o planos: characters, round or flat
el petrarquismo: Petrarchism
el pícaro: picaro, a rogue or vagabond character
la pieza: play
la pieza en un acto: one-act play
el plagio: plagiarism
el pleonasmo: pleonasm
el poema: poem
la polifonía: polyphony
polisilábico: polysyllabic
la pornografía: pornography
el prefacio: preface, foreword
el presupuesto: presupposition
el primitivismo: primitivism
la (edición) princeps: first edition
el procedimiento: device, procedure
los procedimientos expresivos: expressive devices
el/la productor/a: manager, producer
la prosopopeya: prosopopeia
el/la protagonista: protagonist
el proverbio: proverb, saying
la proxémica: proxemics
el psicodrama: psychodrama
la puesta en escena: staging
el punto de vista: point of view
el purismo: purism

la quintilla: five-line stanza

el realismo: realism
el realismo mágico: magic(al) realism
el realismo socialista: socialist realism
la recepción: reception
el receptor: addressee

la redondilla: quatrain, made up of four syllables, rhyming in the pattern *a b b a*
el reestreno: revival
el referente: referent
el refrán: saying, proverb
el relato: narration, narrative
el relato enmarcado: embedding narrative
el reparto: cast
representación (artes de la): performing arts
la reseña: review
la retórica: rhetoric
la rima: rhyme
el ritmo: rhythm
el romancero: collection of Spanish *romances*
el rondó: rondo

el sainete: sainete, a short comedy
el salmo: psalm
la sátira: satire
la semiología teatral: semiology, semiotics
la semiosis: semiosis
la serranilla: serranilla, a lyric composition generally on a romantic theme
la sextina: sestina
la significación: meaning, sense
el significado: signified/signifie/ significatum
el significante: signifier/signifiant/ significans/significant
el signo: sign
el signo teatral: theatrical sign
el simbolismo: symbolism
el símil: simile
la sinalefa: synaloepha, synalepha
la sincronía: synchrony
la sinécdoque: synecdoche
la sinéresis: syneresis, synizesis

el sistema significante: signifying system

la situación de enunciación: enunciation situation

el soliloquio: soliloquy, monologue

el soneto: sonnet

el surrealismo: surrealism

la teatralidad: theatricality

el teatro burgués: bourgeois theater

el teatro callejero: street theater

el teatro de la crueldad: theater of cruelty

el teatro de tesis: thesis theater

el teatro en el teatro: play within a play

el teatro experimental: experimental theater

el teatro laboratorio: workshop theater

la teatrología: theater studies

la técnica teatral: theatrical technique

la telenovela: soap opera

el tema: theme

la teoría crítica: critical theory

el terceto: tercet

la tertulia: literary circle

el tetrasílabo: tetrasyllable

el texto dramático: dramatic text

el texto escribible: writerly text

el texto legible: readerly/*lisible*/ legible text

el texto principal / texto secundario: spoken text / stage directions

tónica (sílaba): accented (syllable)

el tono: tone

la torre de marfil: ivory tower

la tragedia: tragedy

la tragicomedia: tragicomedy

la trama: plot, scheme

el trisílabo: trisyllable

el tropo: trope, figure of speech

la unidad de acción: unity of action

la unidad de lugar: unity of space

la unidad de tiempo: unity of time

la utilería: props

el verismo: verism, a type of naturalistic realism

la verosimilitud: verisimilitude

la versificación: versification

el verso: verse, line

el verso blanco o suelto: blank verse

el verso libre: free verse

el vestuario: costumes

la vidalita: vidalita, a South American melancholic folk song

el villancico: Christmas carol

el villano: villein

la viñeta: vignette

el vodevil: vaudeville

la voz: voice

el yambo: iamb

la zarzuela: zarzuela, Spanish operetta having a spoken dialogue and usually a comic theme

el zéjel: zéjel, a medieval Spanish poetic composition of Mozarabic origin

LINGUISTIC TERMINOLOGY

el acento: accent (dialect)
el acento de intensidad: stress
el acto perlocucionario: perlocutionary act
el acto ilocutorio/ilocutivo: illocutionary act
el acto locutorio/locucionaro/locutivo: locutionary act
los actos de habla: speech acts
la actuación/ejecución: performance
la adquisición del lenguaje: acquisition of language
el afijo: affix
la africada: affricate
el agente: agent
el alfabeto fonético: phonetic alphabet
la aliteración: alliteration
el alófono: allophone
el alomorfo: allomorph
la alveolar: alveolar
la ambigüedad: ambiguity
la anomalía: anomaly
la antonimia: antonymy
la arbitrariedad: arbitrariness
el arcaísmo: archaism
el argumento: argument
la articulación: articulation
la aseveración/aserción: assertion
la asonancia: assonance

el aspecto: aspect
la aspiración: aspiration
el bilingüismo: bilingualism
el canal: channel
las categorías lingüísticas: linguistic categories
causativo: causative
la cesura: caesura
la clase natural: natural class
la cláusula: clause
code-switching: code switching
la cohesión: cohesion
la colocación: collocation
la competencia comunicativa: communicative competence
la competencia lingüística: linguistic competence
el complemento: complement
el componente gramatical: component of grammar
compuesto: compound
los conceptos nebulosos: fuzzy concepts
la consonante: consonant
el constituyente oracional: constituent of sentences
la constricción: constraint
el contenido: content
las convenciones lingüísticas: linguistic conventions

conversación, principios de la: conversational postulates

cooperación, principio de: cooperative principle

la coordinación: coordination

la cópula: copula

criolla, lengua / creole: creole language

deíctico: deictic

la deixis: deixis

la derivación: derivation

la desviación: deviance

el dialecto: dialect

la dicción: diction

la diglosia: diglossia

el diptongo: dipthong

el discurso: discourse

la distintividad: distinctiveness

la distribución complementaria: complementary distribution

el elemento lexical: lexical item

la entonación: intonation

el enunciado: utterance

la escritura: writing

el estilo indirecto libre: free indirect style

el estilo: style

la estructura arbórea: tree structure

la estructura profunda: deep structure

la estructura superficial: surface structure

la estructura subyacente: underlying structure

el eufemismo: euphemism

la expresión coloquial: colloquial expression

los factores contextuales: contextual factors

el fonema: phoneme

la fonética: phonetics

la fonética articulatoria: articulatory phonetics

el fono: phone

la fonología: phonology

la frase: phrase

la fricativa: fricative

la fuerza: force

las funciones del lenguaje: functions of language

el género: genre

la glotal: glottal

la gramática de casos: case grammar

la gramática prescriptiva: prescriptive grammar

la gramática generativa: generative grammar

gramaticalidad/agramaticalidad: grammaticality/ ungrammaticality

la hipercorrección: hypercorrection

la homonimia: homonymy

el icono/ícono: icon

la incrustación: embedding

la indeterminación semántica: vagueness

la inflexión: inflection

el innatismo: innateness

la innovación: innovation

la interdental: interdental

la isoglosa: isogloss

la jerga: jargon

la labial: labial

la labiodental: labiodental

las lenguas en contacto: contact languages

la lingua franca: lingua franca; common language

la líquida: liquid

los marcos de referencia: frames of reference
la metáfora: metaphor
el metalenguaje: metalanguage
el metro: meter
modal: modal
el morfema: morpheme

la nasal: nasal
la negación: negation
el neologismo: neologism
la nominalización: nominalization

la oración: sentence
la ortografía: spelling

la palabra: word
la palatal: palatal
el par mínimo: minimal pair
la paráfrasis: paraphrase
pasivo: passive
el performativo: performative
pidgin: pidgin language
el pie: foot (metrical)
la pragmática: pragmatics
el prefijo: prefix
el préstamo: borrowing
la presuposición: presupposition
la pronunciación: pronunciation
la psicolingüística: psycholinguistics

la raíz: root
los rasgos semánticos: semantic features
los rasgos: features
los rasgos distintivos/pertinentes: distinctive features
realizativo: performative
la recursividad: recursiveness
el referente: reference
reflexivo: reflexive
las reglas de estructura de frase: phrase structure rules

las reglas fonológicas: phonological rules
la restricción selectiva: selectional restrictions
la rima: rhyme
el ritmo: rhythm

la semántica generativa: generative semantics
la semántica: semantics
la semivocal: semivowel
el sentido (significado): sense
shifters/embragues: shifters
la sibilante: sibilant
el significado: meaning
el signo: sign
la sílaba: syllable
el símbolo: symbol
la sinonimia: synonymy
la sintaxis: syntax
la sociolingüística: sociolinguistics
el sonido: sound
la subordinación: subordination
el sufijo: suffix
el superestrato: superstrate
el sustrato: substrate

el tema: theme
el tópico: topic (of discourse)
la transformación: transformation

los universales lingüísticos: universals of language
el universo de discurso: universe of discourse

la variación regional: regional variation
la variación: variation
la velar: velar
el verso: verse
el vocabulario: vocabulary
la vocal: vowel

COMMON BIBLICAL ALLUSIONS AND REFERENCES

Abadón: Abbadon
Abel: Abel
Adán: Adam
Ahab: Ahab
ángel caído: fallen angel
Apocalipsis: Apocalypse
Apócrifos: Apocrypha
apóstol: apostle
Arca de la Alianza: Ark of the
    Covenant
arcángel: archangel
Armagedón: Armageddon
Arón: Aaron

Babel, la torre de: tower of Babel
Babilonia: Babylon
Barrabás: Barabbas
Belcebú/Beelzebú: Beelzebub
Betsabé: Bathsheba

Caifás: Caiaphas
Caín: Cain
Canaán: Canaan

Dalila: Delilah
David: David
Débora: Deborah

Edén, jardín del: Garden of Eden
Ester: Esther
Eva: Eve

fruto prohibido, el: forbidden fruit

Goliat: Goliath

Herodes Antipas: Herod Antipas
Herodes el Grande: Herod the
    Great

Isaac: Isaac
Isaías: Isaiah

Jericó, caída de: fall of Jericho
jinetes del Apocalipsis, los cuatro:
    four horsemen of the
    Apocalypse
Judas Iscariote: Judas Iscariot
Judas Macabeo: Judas Maccabaeus

Lázaro: Lazarus

Magos, los tres Reyes: Magi, the
    three Wise Men of the East
mandamientos, los diez: the Ten
    Commandments
María Magdalena: Mary
    Magdalene
Moisés: Moses
Monte de los Olivos: Mount of
    Olives
Monte Sinaí: Mount Sinai

Nabucodonosor: Nebuchadnezzar
    or Nabuchadrezzar
Noé: Noah
Noé, el arca de: Noah's ark

querubines: cherubims

resurrección de la carne, la: the
   resurrection of the dead

Sagrada Familia: Holy Family

Sagradas Escrituras: Holy
   Scriptures

Sagrado Corazón: Sacred Heart

samaritano, el buen: the good
   Samaritan

Trinidad, la: the Trinity

zarza ardiente: burning bush

COMMON CLASSICAL ALLUSIONS AND REFERENCES

Acates: Achates
Acteón: Actaeon
Adonis: Adonis
Afrodita: Aphrodite
Agamenón: Agamemnon
Alcestis: Alcestis
Alción: Halcyon
Amazonas: Amazons
ambrosía: ambrosia
Andrómaca: Andromache
Andrómeda: Andromeda
Anquises: Anchises
Anteo: Antaeus
Antígona: Antigone
Apolo: Apollo
Aqueronte: Acheron
Aquiles: Achilles
Arcadia: Arcadia
argonautas, los: Argonauts
Argos: Argus
Ariadna: Ariadne
Artemisa: Artemis
Asclepio: Asclepius
Atenea: Athena
Atlantes, los: Atlantis
Atlas: Atlas
Aurora: Aurora
Averno: Avernus
Ayax: Ajax

bacanal: Bacchanalia
Baco: Bacchus

Belerofonte: Bellerophon
Bóreas: Boreas

Cadmo: Cadmus
caduceo: caduceus
Calíope: Calliope
Calipso: Calypso
Caos: Chaos
Caronte: Charon
Casandra: Cassandra
Cástor y Pólux: Castor and Pollux
Céfiro: Zephyr
Centauros, los: Centaurs
Cerbero, can: Cerberus
Ceres: Ceres
Cibeles: Cybele
Cíclopes, los: Cyclopes
Circe: Circe
Clío: Clio
Clitemnestra: Clytemnestra
Coloso de Rodas: Colossus of
  Rhodes
cornucopia: Cornucopia
Creón/Creonte: Creon
Creta, laberinto de: labyrinth of
  Crete
Cronos: Cronos
Cumas, sibila de: Cumaean sibyl
Cupido: Cupid

Dafne: Daphne
Dafnis y Cloe: Daphnis and
  Chloe

Damocles, la espada de: sword of
   Damocles
Dánae: Danaë
Dédalo: Daedalus
Delfos, oráculo de: Delphic oracle
Deméter: Demeter
Diana: Diana
Dido: Dido
Dioniso: Dionysus
dríadas/dríades, las: dryads

Eco: Echo
Edipo: Oedipus
Electra: Electra
Elena de Troya: Helen of Troy
Eleusis, misterios de: Eleusinian
   Mysteries
Elíseo: Elysium
Elíseos, campos: Elysian Fields
Eneas: Aeneas
Eolo: Aeolus
Eos: Eos
Erebo/Érebo: Erebus
Erinias, las: Erinyes
Eros: Eros
Escila y Caribdis: Scylla and
   Charybdis
Esfinge, el enigma de la: The Rid-
   dle of the Sphinx
Eufrosine: Euphrosyne
Euménides, las: Eumenides
Eurídice: Eurydice
Europa: Europa
Euterpe: Euterpe

Faetón: Phaeton
Fauno: Faunus
Febo: Phoebe
Fedra: Phaedra
Fidias: Phidias
Furias, las: Furies

Galatea: Galatea
Ganimedes: Ganymede

Gea: Gaea
Gigantes, los: Giants
Gordiano, nudo: Gordian knot
Gorgonas, las: Gorgons
Gracias, las tres: Graces

Hades: Hades
hamadríades/hamadríadas, las:
   hamadryads
harpías: harpies
Hécate: Hecate
Héctor: Hector
Hécuba: Hecuba
Helicón: Helicon
Helio: Helios
Hera: Hera
Heracles: Heracles or Hercules
Hércules, los trabajos de: Labors
   of Heracles/Hercules
Hermes: Hermes
Hespérides, las: Hesperides
Hidra: Hydra
Himen: Hymen
Hiperión: Hyperion
Hipólita: Hippolyta; Hippolyte
Hipólito: Hippolytus

Ícaro: Icarus
Ifigenia: Iphigenia
Iris: Iris

Jacinto: Hyacinth
Jano: Janus
Jantipa: Xantippe
Jasón: Jason
Júpiter: Jupiter

Laocoonte: Laocoön
Layo: Laius
Leda: Leda
Liceo: Lyceum

manzana de la discordia: apple of
   discord
Marte: Mars

Mecenas: Maecenas
Medea: Medea
Medusa: Medusa
Melpómene: Melpomene
ménades, las: maenads
Menelao: Menelaus
Mercurio: Mercury
Midas: Midas
Minerva: Minerva
Minotauro: Minotaur
Mirmidones, los: Myrmidons
Morfeo: Morpheus
Musas, las: Muses

Narciso: Narcissus
Nausica: Nausicaä
Némesis: Nemesis
Neptuno: Neptune
Nereidas, las: Nereids
Nereo: Nereus
Néstor: Nestor
ninfa: nymph

Océano: Oceanus
Odiseo: Odysseus
Olimpo: Olympus
Orestes: Orestes
Orfeo: Orpheus
Órficos, misterios: Orphic Mysteries or Rites
Orión: Orion

Palas Atenea: Pallas Athena
Pan: Pan
Parcas, las: Parcae
Paris: Paris
Parnaso: Parnassus
Partenón: Parthenon
Pasífae: Pasiphaë
Patroclo: Patroclus
Pegaso: Pegasus
Penélope: Penelope
Perséfone: Persephone

Perseo: Perseus
Pléyades, las: Pleiades
Polifemo: Polyphemus
Poseidón: Poseidon
Príamo: Priam
Príapo: Priapus
Procrusto, el lecho de: Procrustean bed
Prometeo: Prometheus
Proserpina: Proserpina
Proteo: Proteus
Psique: Psyche

Quimera: Chimaera

Rea: Rhea
Rómulo y Remo: Romulus and Remus

sátiros, los: satyrs
Selene: Selene
sibilas, las: sibyls
sirenas, las: sirens
Sísifo: Sisyphus

Tais/Thais: Thaïs
Talía: Thalia
Tánatos: Thanatos
Tántalo: Tantalus
Telémaco: Telemachus
Terpsícore: Terpsichore
Teseo: Theseus
Tespis: Thespis
Tiresias: Tiresias
Titanes, los: Titans
Troya, caballo de: Trojan Horse

Ulises: Ulysses
Urano: Uranus

Venus: Venus
vestales, las: vestal virgins

Yocasta: Jocasta

Zeus: Zeus

COMMON LITERARY ALLUSIONS AND REFERENCES

Abelardo y Eloísa: Abélard and Héloïse
Aladino: Aladdin
Alí Babá: Ali Baba
Alicia en el país de las maravillas: Alice in Wonderland
Ariel: Ariel (character in *The Tempest*)
Arturo, rey: King Arthur
Atos, Portos y Aramís: Athos, Porthos, and Aramis (of *The Three Musketeers*)
Beatriz: Beatrice
bella y la bestia, la: Beauty and the Beast
Brave New World: Brave New World (the novel or the concept it spawned)
caballeros de la mesa redonda: Knights of the Round Table
Calibán: Caliban (character in *The Tempest*)
Ema Bovary: Emma Bovary
Eneida: Aeneid
Merlín: Merlin
Mil y una noches, las: Arabian Nights
Próspero: Prospero (character in *The Tempest*)

A DICTIONARY OF SPANISH GRAMMATICAL AND LEXICAL DOUBTS

Despite the enormous amount of interest in studying Spanish in the United States, the impressive numbers of native speakers residing in this country, and the increasing enrollments on all educational levels, there are few materials for the teaching of Spanish, beyond the many (often depressingly repetitive) first-year textbooks. While Spanish-English lexicography is solid and there are any number of reliable dictionaries, textbooks for the teaching of advanced grammar and guides for the formation of skills in composition in general and other forms of specialized writing are notably lacking. And there are virtually no accessible manuals of grammar. The Ramsey-Spaulding *Textbook of Modern Spanish,* originally prepared in the nineteenth century as a traditional rule-based teaching grammar and updated almost forty years ago, continues to be the only easily available U.S. publication. However, its traditional nature, the emphasis on examples drawn from nineteenth-century Spanish writers, and the overall prescriptive nature of its presentation makes it less than an ideal textbook for the American student. A recent reference grammar prepared in England and distributed by a small publisher in the United States is unreasonably priced for widespread classroom use (John Butt and Carmen Benjamin's *A New Reference Grammar of Modern Spanish*).

The present lexicon is inspired by, but is neither a translation of nor an adaptation of, Manuel Seco's *Diccionario de dudas,* a standard reference work in the Spanish-speaking world. Seco's work has three main disadvantages for the reader of the present volume: it is very expensive for the American user; it contains many flagrantly negative views of Latin American usages; and it is oriented toward the native speaker who has doubts about the structures of his or her own language. These doubts are quite frequently not the doubts native speakers of English have (either because they involve structures the nonnative speaker is not likely to use or because the English-language substratum eliminates them), and, not surprisingly, the nonnative speaker coming from English will have many doubts that do not occur to native speakers.

This work is organized in terms of the doubts of native speakers of English who are nonnative speakers of Spanish, with an extension also to native speakers of Spanish whose contact with English has created uncertainties in them with regard to Spanish. It is organized in a dictionary format with ample cross-referencing. Since the focus is on grammatical structures and lexical contrasts that native speakers of English have difficulty with, it does not duplicate the function of a standard dictionary, which users should have at their disposal in any event. An adequate bilingual dictionary, in addition to presenting language-to-language equivalencies, indicates the gender of nouns, provides models for the conjugation of regular, irregular, stem-changing, and defective verbs, and, if it is prepared in conformance with contemporary lexicological standards, provides additional information such as the prepositions governing verb + verb and noun + noun combinations. Because there are a number of dictionaries that fulfill these criteria, this manual does not duplicate that information.

This lexicon does, however, provide information that does not appear in dictionaries. This information includes ambivalences with respect to noun gender, verbs that fluctuate between being regular and irregular or that have alternate forms, divided opinion with regard to prepositional usage, and, more than anything else, detailed information about grammatical and lexical contrasts that require the sort of explanation that dictionaries cannot provide. Furthermore, our entries go into differences between dialects. While it would be impossible in a reference manual to describe usage in every one of the geographical, stylistic, generational, and social dialects of Spanish (parameters that would provide potentially for several dozen contrasts), we do attempt to record broad differences of usage so that the user will understand why apparently contradictory usages are encountered.

Spanish, like English, is a unique international language. While an international language like French or German has a closely circumscribed academic standard that characterizes to an enormously high degree the usage of all educated speakers (though less socially prestigious dialects do, of course, vary enormously), Spanish and English, despite a general consensus over what constitutes educated usage, reveal extremely flexible parameters for academic and educated speech and writing. Aside from obvious phonological divergences, the use of grammatical structures and lexical items varies enormously among individuals who have had the same type and level of formal education. The purpose of this repertoire is to account for the differences American users of Spanish are most likely to have about Spanish usage. Contact with authentic examples of the varieties of Spanish and the need to produce the language in ever more sophisticated contexts combine to make this sort of dictionary necessary. While information about doubts may be ferreted out of conventional grammars or clarified by consulting a source like Seco, in the former case it is embedded in topically oriented presentations and in the latter case it is presented (if a particular doubt of the nonnative speaker is even covered) from the perspective of the native speaker. This manual eschews grammar review and focuses its presentations on the needs of the English-language user of Spanish.

Material is presented in as nontechnical a way as possible, with little reference to grammatical terms beyond the most standard of grammatical categories. Nevertheless, it is assumed that the user has some sense of language structure and, in a few cases, may have to turn to a good English dictionary for the clarification of some of the more precise terms employed. Finally, we have attempted to clarify many of the distinctions with actual language examples.

A

*a.*1. Preposition of movement, accompanied by a noun phrase expressing destination or terminal place of action: *Van a México; Llegué a la estación.* It may be replaced by a locative adverb: *Allá van; Llegué ahí. A* is considered a weak or unmarked form; it may be replaced by more emphatic forms like *para, hacia,* or prepositional phrases like *con destino a, rumbo a.*

2. Preposition indicating relative location: *Ellos viven a dos cuadras de aquí; Se encuentra a la vuelta de la esquina.*

3. Preposition indicating point in time: *Llegarás a las ocho; Al día siguiente hubo un gran desfile; Murió al año de casarse.*

4. It is used to mark nonpronominal indirect objects: *Doy / Le doy el regalo a María.* (On the categories of indirect object, see *le*).

5. It is used to mark nonpronominal direct objects, typically human, animate, specific ones: *Observo a la gente sentada en la plaza.* Often it is used with nonhuman, inanimate, specific objects when those objects are viewed with human qualities and, especially, when they are used with verbs that are considered paradigmatically human: *El niño besó al perrito.*

The *a* marker may occur with inanimate nouns that are abstractions or that are in some way hypostasized: *Defendemos a la patria; Se considera a la libertad el valor democrático fundamental.* Conversely, the *a* may be suppressed with a direct object in a syntagm in order to avoid confusion with the homonymously marked indirect object: *Recomiendo (a) María a Juan.* It may be found sporadically not to occur with certain verbs: *Vi mucha gente en la estación.* It never occurs with direct objects of the impersonal verb *haber: Había diez personas en la sala.* With unspecified, indeterminate direct objects, *a* is not used: *Necesitamos una criada para esta casa.*

6. Specific verbs that require *a* before infinitive complements are listed individually in this guide.

7. Constructions like *¡A trabajar!* may be considered apocopes of head verbs that are either explicit or implied commands: *Vamos a trabajar.*

8. The preposition *a* is used in numerous manner adverb constructions: *a la mexicana; a diario; a veces.* It is often combined with plural nouns, either masculine (*a puñados*) or feminine (*a escondidas*). It is also found in neuter constructions: *a lo profesor.* Neuter constructions may function as adjectival phrases, especially when proper names are involved: *Pronunció un discurso a lo Lincoln.*

9. The construction *a no ser por* is synonymous with *si no fuera por: A no ser por la lluvia haría calor = Si no fuera por la lluvia haría calor.* This synonymy also occurs with impersonal constructions with indicative cause-and-effect meanings: *A decir verdad, eso es una estupidez = Si se dice la verdad, eso es una estupidez.* These latter tend to be fixed phrases like *a decir verdad, a juzgar por.* The use of *al* rather than *a* in these constructions is considered substandard.

10. In a construction like *Este es el trabajo a discutir,* the *a* is equivalent to *que hay que discutir* or *que será discutido.* Compare with *por* 4.

11. Instrumental prepositional phrases: *olla a presión, motor a reacción, cocina a gas, radio a pilas.* These same constructions may also appear with other prepositions like *con* or *de.* Even though it is frequent, this use of *a* is considered a French importation.

abajo. 1. Locative adverb used with either stative or motion verbs: *Está abajo; Se dirigió abajo.*

2. With motion verbs it may be combined with prepositions to form more precise adverbial phrases: *Va hacia abajo; Subió desde abajo.*

3. *Abajo* may appear as a noun modifier with the sense of *en la dirección de abajo: Cuesta abajo en mi rodada.* Typically, the nouns with which it is thus used indicate the path of a directional movement.

4. *De arriba abajo* is preferred to *de arriba a abajo.*

5. In its contrast with *debajo* (q.v.), *abajo* indicates absolute position,

while the former is relative or relational, comparing the position of one thing with reference (if only implied) to something else: *Tu libro está debajo,* i.e., *en posición inferior con respecto a los libros de los que estamos hablando.* In this sense, it would be equivalent to English "on the bottom" or "underneath."

6. *Abajo de* is considered a regional, colloquial, or substandard synonym of *debajo de* or *bajo: Encontró el zapato abajo de la mesa.*

7. *Abajo de* is a synonym of *menos de* in expressions of approximate quantity: *Le calculo abajo de cincuenta años.*

8. Note the interjection *¡Abajo X!,* equivalent to English "Down with X!"

abertura. *Abertura* describes physical opening: *Hay una pequeña abertura en la tapa. Apertura* describes the process executed by the verb *abrir: Mañana habrá un acto de apertura para inaugurar (poner en marcha) el Congreso.* Both nouns are used interchangeably to describe the quality of the adjective *abierto* in its meaning of "openness of character," although *abertura* is preferred: *Con la abertura de sus intenciones convencía a todos.*

abogado. *Abogada* is now in general use as the feminine form, although *la abogado* and *la mujer abogado* may be found.

abolir. Defective verb: only first- and second-person plural forms are used in the present indicative: *abolimos, abolís.* It is not used in the present subjunctive.

abrir. *Abierto* is the past participle.

absorto. Used as an adjective derived from *absorber: Ando absorto en mis problemas.* The past participle of *absorber* is regular: *absorbido.*

abusar. The use of *abusar* as a transitive verb without the verbal preposition *de* is considered a calque from English: *Es un padre que abusa a sus hijos;* the most standard wording would be *Es un padre que abusa de sus hijos.* This use also provides a derived adjective: *El problema de las mujeres abusadas es escandaloso.* The Peninsular Spanish equivalents are *mujeres golpeadas, mujeres maltratadas.*

acá. *Acá* and *aquí* (q.v.) are synonymous for many speakers, with the preference for one or the other being based on dialect.

acabar. In the sense of "to have just": *Acabas de decirlo.* In the sense of "to end up doing": *Acabé por odiarlo.* In the sense of "to finish off, to do away with": *Acabemos con nuestros problemas. Acabar de* is also used as a so-called dative absolute: *Acabada de comer, ella se echó a descansar.*

académico. The feminine noun in the sense of a professional person is *académica*, although *la mujer académico* may be found.

acaecer. Used only in the third-person singular, specifically as an impersonal verb.

acaso. 1. Like *tal vez* and *quizá(s)*, *acaso* is normally used with verbs in the subjunctive: *Acaso la lluvia salve la cosecha.* Its use with the indicative indicates a certainty only slightly attenuated by the meaning of the word itself.

2. *Acaso* as a modal adverb has the meaning of *por casualidad,* but its use is archaic or literary: *Si acaso me buscas, me vas a encontrar enseguida.* The same is also true of *por si acaso.* This latter structure is an adverbial phrase when the verb is omitted: *Llevemos paraguas por si acaso = por si acaso llueve.*

3. In interrogatives and with a sarcastic or ironic implication, it is used with the indicative: *¿Acaso no sabes ese asunto?*

4. In some dialects, *acaso* is synonymous with the conjunction *si*.

accesible. Although it is possible to distinguish between *accesible* (= *de acceso/entrada posible*) and *asequible* (= *lo que se puede conseguir*), colloquial usage tends to extend *accesible* to cover the latter.

acerca de. It is considered substandard to use this preposition without *de.*

acontecer. Defective verb used only in third-person singular or plural.

acordar. *Acordar* in the senses of "strike an accord" and "accord to" is not universally accepted, although it tends to prevail in Latin America.

acordarse. 1. Occasionally, uses are found without the linking preposition *de,* especially before the conjunction *que.* By extension, examples of usage with direct object pronouns are found: *Me lo acordé* instead of *Me acordé de ese asunto.*

2. The probably now little used *acordársele a uno algo* is equivalent to *hacerle a uno acordarse de algo* or *recordárselo.* This construction may also mean *ponerse de acuerdo en algo para beneficio de uno: Se le acordó/ concedió a Pérez una pensión vitalicia.*

acostar. There is a regular verb *acostar* that means *acercar a la costa; acostar,* however, in the sense of "to go/put to bed," is stem-changing.

acostumbrar. As a synonym of *soler,* this verb does not customarily employ a linking preposition: *Acostumbrábamos recorrer librerías los sábados por la tarde.* However, it is common to find *a* used as a linking preposition: *Acostumbrábamos a recorrer librerías los sábados por la tarde.*

acrópolis. While this noun is usally feminine, masculine uses, considered substandard, may be found.

actor. The feminine is *actriz* in the theatrical sense, but *actora* in the legal sense.

actual. This adjective is not a cognate of English *actual* (which, in Spanish, is translated as *real* or *verdadero*). Rather, it means "current" or "at this time."

acuerdo. 1. *Estar de acuerdo con alguien en/sobre/para algo.*

2. *De acuerdo a* may be found as a synonym of the more traditional *de acuerdo con.*

acullá. Occurs only as a literary form in conjunction with and as an intensifier of *allá.*

adecuar. The stem *u* is usually atonic: *yo adecuo.* However, tonic forms may be found: *yo adecúo.*

adelante. 1. As a locative adverb, it is used with motion verbs: *Pasaron adelante.* It may be combined with prepositions to form more precise adverbial phrases: *Va hacia adelante; Se dirigió para adelante.*

2. *Adelante* may appear as a noun modifier with the sense of *en la dirección de adelante: Siguió camino adelante.* Typically, the nouns with which it is thus used indicate the path of a directional movement.

3. As a locative adverb expressing specific or resulting static position, *delante* is used: *Estamos delante en la fila; Él se puso delante de todos. Delante* and *adelante* are often used interchangeably.

adentro. 1. As a locative adverb, it is used with both stative and motion verbs: *Él está adentro, Él va adentro.* However, it is usually considered more appropriate to use *dentro* in stative constructions: *El abrigo está dentro.*

2. *Adentro* may appear as a noun modifier with the sense of *hacia adentro: Caminó bosque adentro.* Typically, the nouns with which it is thus used indicate the part of a directional movement.

3. *Adentro* and *dentro* are both used to indicate the interior part of something: *La sala de (a)dentro. Adentro* in this case is preferred in Latin America. Followed by the preposition *de,* the same alternation may be found, although *dentro* is more common: *Se oyó un ruido dentro de la caja.* By contrast, with possessives, *adentro* predominates: *Hay una gran confusión adentro mío.*

adherir. This verb is usually reflexive when its meaning is literal; however, it may appear nonreflexively in the sense of supporting or backing an issue or a cause: *Todos adherimos a la causa de los derechos humanos.*

adjunto. When used as a noun modifier, it is variable: *La carta adjunta, los documentos adjuntos.* It may be used as an adverb, in which case it is invariable: *Adjunto envío los documentos solicitados.*

admirarse. If used as a nonreflexive, the linking preposition *de* is not used: *Admiro tus intenciones; Me admiro de tus intenciones.*

adonde. Written customarily as one word, although by analogy with *de donde, a donde* may be found. *Adonde,* used with verbs of motion, is not to be confused with the combination of the independent preposition *a* followed by the stative conjunction *donde: Llegaron a donde están las ruinas = Llegaron donde están las ruinas.*

adónde. This is the interrogative form for *adonde,* and like the latter is used only with motion verbs.

adondequiera. The relative *que* normally accompanies *adondequiera: Te encontraré adondequiera que estés.*

adquirir. Objects indicating source appear with either *de* or *a: Adquirí la casa de/a Juan.*

advertir. Used with the linking preposition *de* in the sense of "call someone's attention to something": *Te advierto de los peligros de hacer eso.* With the meaning of "notice," it carries no linking preposition: *Advirtieron la mala situación.*

aferrar. This verb in its contemporary usage is regular, although premodern irregular forms may be found.

afiliar. The stem *i* is atonic: *yo afilio;* however, examples may be found where it is tonic: *yo afilío.*

afuera. This adverb is used with verbs of motion to indicate goal of movement: *Salieron afuera.* It is also used with stative verbs to indicate the location of something: *Afuera hay mucha gente.* With stative verbs, the distinction between *fuera* and *afuera* is that the former indicates specific location outside as opposed to inside, while the latter indicates a vague location outside rather than inside, here as the consequence of a verb of motion describing movement away from here: *En este momento, María está fuera en el patio; Él viajó y va a estar afuera por una semana.* The corresponding preposition of *fuera* is *fuera de: María está fuera de la casa, en el patio. Afuera* may be found replacing *fuera* in these examples; compare with *dentro* and *adentro.* It may be combined with prepositions: *de afuera, hacia afuera, para afuera.*

agarrar. The affective construction *agarrar y* is limited to colloquial Argentine Spanish; compare with *ir y* and, in Peninsular Spanish, *coger y: Agarro y le digo la verdad.*

agredir. Defective verb; only the forms in which the stem *i* is retained are used, although other forms may occasionally be found: *agrede, agreden.*

agresivo. This adjective and its companion noun, *agresividad,* have not yet been naturalized in Spanish with the meaning of "emphatically assertive."

aguafuerte. This noun is masculine when referring to a type of graphic art; its plural is *aguafuertes,* as in *Los aguafuertes porteños* by Roberto Arlt. When used to refer to a chemical substance, it is feminine and may be written as one word or two; when written as two words, both formants are marked for the plural: *aguafuerte/aguafuertes; agua fuerte/ aguas fuertes.* Note that the feminine *el* and *un* would be used in the singular.

aguamarina. The feminine articles *la* and *una* are used with this noun.

aguamiel. In general usage, this noun is feminine, although examples of it as masculine are to be found.

aguanieve. It may also appear as *agua nieve.* This noun is feminine, and the feminine *el* and *un* are used with it, although *la* and *una* may be found.

ahí. 1. Adverb of location typically used to specify the place of the second person: *Ahí donde tú estás;* it may also be used to indicate movement toward the place of the second person: *Ahí voy.* This specification of place may range from precise to vague, the latter case often signaled by an accompanying preposition: *Hay mucha gente por ahí.*

2. The colloquial pronunciation of *ahí* as the restressed bisyllabic [ái] is to be noted, especially in the phrase *por ahí.*

3. Like many location adverbs, *ahí* may also have a metaphoric temporal meaning: *Ahí por el siglo quince. Ahí* in a temporal sense may be synonymous with *ahora (mismo),* particularly in Central America.

4. Whereas *ahí* is associated with the place of the second person, *allí,* at least in a contrastive pairing, refers to the third person. However, in noncontrastive contexts and in some colloquial registers, *ahí* and *allí* may be used synonymously to refer to the place of the second person. With *ahí* there is no contrast like *aquí/acá; allí/allá.*

aire-acondicionado. As a compound adjective, this form is a direct calque of English "air-conditioned": *casas aire-acondicionadas. Climatizado* would appear to be the more generalized Spanish form. Note that the compound noun *aire acondicionado,* by contrast, is in general use: *Este edificio tiene aire acondicionado,* although one could equally prefer *Este edificio está climatizado.*

al. 1. a + el.

2. *Cuando* followed by a conjugated verb may be replaced by *al* plus the corresponding infinitive: *Cuando llegué . . . = Al llegar . . .*

alante. Colloquial form of *adelante.*

álbum. The plural is *álbumes,* although *álbunes* is widely found.

alcalde. The feminine is *alcaldesa.*

alegrarse. In colloquial speech, the preposition *de* is often omitted before a following verb or subordinate clause introduced by *que: Me alegro que vengas.* Note that when the verb is nonreflexive with a following infinitive or clause that is the subject, *de* is never used: *Me alegra saber que has venido; Me alegra que hayas venido.* The subordinate clause that is either the subject of *alegrar* or the object of *alegrarse de que* is typically in the subjunctive.

alerta. This adverb is in the process of being construed as an adjective. Thus the traditional adverbial use, *Los hombres están alerta a los problemas,* alternates with a still rather uncommon masculine form: *Los hombres están alertos a los problemas.* As an adjective it is anomalous in that it may customarily have an invariable plural: *Los más alertas ya lo saben.*

algo. In addition to being an indefinite pronoun, it also functions as an adverbial modifier of adjectives, the former as in *Algo interesante ha sucedido,* the latter as in *Ese es un tema algo interesante.*

alguien. Although *alguien* is an indefinite pronoun, *alguien* is preceded by the definite marker *a: Busco a alguien que lo sepa.*

algún. Like *un, algún* occurs both before immediately following masculine nouns and before immediately following feminine nouns beginning with a stressed *á: Algún libro/Algún águila.*

alguno. When it is used as a postpositioned adjective, its force is negative, rather than positive, as it is when prepositioned: *Algún libro; Libro alguno = Ningún libro.*

alicate. The singular form coexists alongside the plural *alicates* with a unitary meaning.

alinear. The academic conjugation along the lines of *yo alineo* coexists with the colloquial *yo alíneo.* Moreover, the subjunctive, in order to avoid the double occurrence of *e,* may occur as *que yo alinie.*

allá. Adverb of location typically used to specify the place of the third person. Often used synonymously with *allí,* although in some dialects the two are distinguished on the basis of close correspondence to the place of the third person (*allí*) and an imprecise, sort of "fourth-person" place

(*allá*); hence the reasonableness of the combination *allá lejos*, but not
*allí lejos,[1] and of qualifiers like *más, menos allá*.

allende. Strictly literary in use, when accompanied by the added preposition *de*, it means *además de*; with no connecting preposition, it has the
locative meaning *más allá de*.

allí. See *allá*.

alma. This feminine noun takes the immediately preceding feminine articles *el* and *un*.

alrededor. Acceptable but infrequent is the transcription as two words, *al
rededor*.

alta. This feminine noun takes the immediately preceding feminine articles *el* and *un*: *Le dieron el alta en el hospital*. The feminine adjective
alta takes the feminine articles *la* and *una*: *Me preocupa la alta tarifa de
los servicios*. Examples are found of the treatment of the noun *alta* as
masculine and of the use with the feminine adjective of the articles *el* and
un.

altavoz. This noun is masculine.

alto. 1. Both *más alto* and *superior* are used as the superlative of *alto* in a
spatial sense, but only *superior* is used in a qualitative sense: *el piso superior / el piso más alto; de alta calidad / de calidad superior*.
    2. Used before a noun, *alto* means "high" in the sense of "important";
used following a noun it means "tall."

ambidextro. This is academically the recognized form, although *ambi-
diestro* is frequently found as an influence of *diestro*.

americano. See *estadounidense*.

amoblar. *Amueblar* is generally preferred.

amor. The linking preposition *a* is more frequent than *de: amor al arte*.

andar. 1. Regular preterite and imperfect/future subjunctive forms may
be found: e.g., *andamos* for *anduvimos*, etc.
    2. *Andar* + present participle is a progressive form indicating continu-
ity of an action; the meaning of *andar* may be literal or emphatic for *estar*:
Anduve perdiendo el tiempo hasta que me decidí a entrar.

anochecer. Normally used only in the third-person singular to refer to the
time of day; in the sense of where one is when night falls, it is used with
all persons.

---

[1] Asterisks signify forms or constructions not recognized as grammatical by prevailing standards of academic, educated, and literary usage.

ante. 1. Preposition used with verbs of either state or motion: *Quedó ante el cuadro* / *Pasó ante todos.* Most often it is used with verbs not to describe movement, but to indicate the place from which an action takes place: *Habló ante la clase.*

2. It is also used with the sense of "with respect to" or "in view of": *Ante semejante escándalo, hay que tomar medidas.*

anteriormente a. Used as a synonym of *antes de.*

antes. 1. When used with a following clause, the linking preposition *de* often disappears in colloquial speech: *Antes (de) que terminemos . . .*

2. It may be used as an invariable quasi adjective: *siglos antes.*

3. *Antes que* + noun/verb has the meaning of "instead of": *Antes que un abrigo, puedes comprarte zapatos.*

antinomia. *Antinomía* is considered incorrect.

antípoda. Although it may frequently be found used in the feminine, the correct form is considered to be masculine, as in *estar en los antípodas* = "diametrically opposed."

antojarse. Used only with a dative of interest: *Se me antojó un helado de chocolate.*

aparte. 1. Used as an invariable quasi adjective: *en un lugar aparte; chistes aparte.*

2. The preposition *aparte de* may be found without the connective *de,* although it is more frequently accompanied by it.

apellidos. The plural form of last names used in a generic sense is formed in accord with the rules for forming plurals of common nouns in Spanish: *Ellos son los nuevos Cervantes de la novela española.* When speaking of the members of a family defined by its last name, the name may remain in the singular but preceded by the plural article, or the name may be pluralized according to the rule for forming plurals of common nouns in Spanish: *Los Oropesa(s) viven en la casa de al lado.*

apéndice. Although it can be found as a feminine noun, especially in its anatomical sense, it is customarily masculine in gender.

apendicitis. Although sometimes found as a masculine noun, it is customarily feminine in gender.

apercibirse. Used with linking preposition *de,* it has the sense of "to realize"; with *contra,* it carries the sense of "be prepared."

apertura. See *abertura.*

apetecer. This verb may occur transitively, or intransitively with a dative of interest: *Me apetecen unas uvas.*

apocalipsis. As the name of one of the books of the Bible, it is masculine; as a common noun it is also masculine, although feminine examples, by false analogy with *génesis* (q.v.), may be found.

apócope. This noun is feminine, although masculine uses are found.

apoderar. Used with the linking preposition *a* in the sense of "empower"; with *de* in the sense of "take over."

apostar. Used with the linking preposition *a* in the sense of "to place a bet," it is irregular: *te apuesto lo que quieras. Apostar,* with the meaning of "to post," is regular.

apóstrofe. This noun is used interchangeably as masculine or feminine, with a preference for masculine. It should not be confused with *apóstrofo.*

apotema. Despite its Greek ending, this noun is feminine.

apoteosis. This noun is feminine, although masculine examples are found.

aprender. Although the typical pattern is *aprender algo de alguien, a alguien* may also be found.

aprendiz. The feminine form is *aprendiza.*

apretar. This verb, while normally stem-changing, may also be found conjugated as regular.

apropiarse. The direct object may or may not be preceded by a connective *de.*

aprovechar. There is no connective preposition before a following direct object with the meaning of "to take advantage": *Aprovecharemos la oportunidad para dar nuestra opinión.* However, *de* is used with the meaning of "profit from": *Se aprovechó de su dinero.*

apto. The negative is *poco/no apto* or *inepto.*

aquel. Demonstrative usually referring to the third person; see *este.* The feminine is *aquella,* and the masculine and feminine plurals are, respectively, *aquellos* and *aquellas.* When these demonstratives are used as pronouns, the *e* carries a written accent except when followed by *que. Aquello* is the corresponding neuter pronoun. Although the feminine form immediately preceding a noun beginning with a tonic *a* is customarily *aquella,* by analogy with *el,* one may occasional find *aquel* used: *aquel águila* versus *aquella águila.*

aquí. 1. Adverb of place indicating the space of the first person; see also *acá.*

2. Although *estar* is used with location adverbs, the phrase *ser aquí* occurs with the meaning of "this is the place; here it is"; *aquí* functions as the subject of *ser* and usually no other noun occurs.

árbitro. The feminine form is *árbitra,* although the noun is sometimes used as invariable with regard to gender.

armazón. This noun may be either masculine or feminine, although some uses distinguish between a feminine meaning ("rigging," "armature") and a masculine meaning ("skeleton").

aroma. As a feminine noun, it is the flower of the *aromo* tree; as a masculine noun, it is the cognate of the English word aroma.

arquitecto. The feminine noun is *arquitecta.*

arrasar. This verb may or may not be used with a connective *con* preceding the object noun; note the idiomatic expression *arrasarse los ojos en lágrimas.*

arrascar. Variant of *rascar;* the latter is generally preferred.

arreglo. *Con arreglo a = según, de acuerdo con.*

arrendar. The subject of this verb is customarily the person who provides a property through a rental agreement (the *arrendatario*), although in some dialects the subject may be the person who acquires the property (the *inquilino,* from *alquilar,* more customarily).

arriba. 1. This locative adverb may be used with stative and motion verbs: *El está arriba / El vino arriba.*

2. The specific scope of this adverb may vary considerably between dialects, which is also true of its companion preposition, *arriba de.* Some usages distinguish between *arriba* to indicate motion and *encima* to indicate stative location, but the distinction is neutralized in favor of location in an example like *Lo puso arriba del escritorio.* Strictly as a locative adverb, *arriba* may signal an absolute higher position, while *encima* is more relative, as in *Vivo arriba* and *Vivo encima,* the former indicating on the topmost floor, the latter only at least one floor above. However, this distinction may also be neutralized in actual usage.

3. *Arriba* may appear as a noun modifier with the sense of *en la dirección de arriba: Corrió cuesta arriba.* Typically, the nouns with which it is thus used indicate the path of a directional movement.

4. *Arriba de* may be used as a synonym of *más allá de: Arriba de cien personas llegaron a la función.*

arribista. The French-based spelling *arrivista* is considered incorrect.

arte. This noun may be found used as either masculine or feminine. However, as a singular noun indicating art in general or the art of something, it is customarily masculine. As a plural noun referring to "the arts"—i.e., the totality of artistic manifestations and practices—it is customarily feminine, especially when referring to an institution: *El Palacio de Bellas Artes.* The phrase or title *Arte poética,* translated from the Latin, is typically feminine. Note that, as a noun beginning with a tonic *a,* when *arte* is feminine it takes the immediately preceding feminine *el.*

asá. Affective counterpart of *así* used only in fixed phrases like *así y asá.*

asaz. Literary equivalent of *bastante* used as a degree modifier of adjectives; sometimes used with a connective *de* before the following adjective.

asegurarse. Asegurarse de que is followed by the indicative in the sense of ascertaining that something is certain; it is followed by the subjunctive when it means "to make sure of" or "ensure" an outcome.

así. 1. The reduplicated *así, así* is equivalent to English "not very well": *¿Cómo te va? Así, así.*

2. *así de* followed by an adjective is equivalent to English "this" plus an adjective to indicate relative description; in spoken Spanish, the phrase is often accompanied by a descriptive gesture. *Así* and *de* may also be separated by other syntactic material: *Así estamos de felices.*

3. *Así* is followed by the subjunctive when it is used as a synonym of the concessive *aunque.*

4. *Así que* is a temporal conjunction, synonymous with *tan pronto como,* and is followed by the indicative.

5. The preceding *así que* should not be confused with the homonymous connective expression equivalent to English "therefore": *Eso no me interesa, así que deja de molestarme con ello. Así es que* may be found with the same meaning.

6. *Así mismo* means both "by the same token" and "also." *Asimismo* may also be found as an alternative spelling for *así mismo* in the sense of *también.*

7. *Así pues* is equivalent to English "therefore, as a consequence."

8. Followed by a subjunctive verb, *así* is synonymous with *ojalá: Así seas feliz.*

asistente. The feminine of this noun is *asistenta* when it refers to a type of servant underling; otherwise, it is customarily invariable with respect to gender.

asolar. Stem-changing with the meaning of "knock to the ground." This verb is regular when its meaning is "parched by the sun." However, both verbs may be found used with regular conjugations.

asumir. *Asumir* with the meaning of English "assume," "take on (proportions)," as well as synonymous with *suponer* and *presumir*, is usually rejected as inappropriate, being limited in meaning to "assume (a position, a responsibility)."

atañer. Defective verb used only in the third person.

atardecer. Impersonal verb used only in the third person singular.

atender. The connecting preposition *a* is used when the verb means "pay heed to, answer," but is not used when the sense is "attend to, deal with."

atento. The linking preposition *a* is used in the sense of "listening carefully"; *con* is used in the sense of "respectfully attentive toward."

aterrar. Stem-changing when related to *tierra* with the meaning of "to land"; regular as the causative verb of *terror.*

atestar. Although usually used as a regular verb, *atestar* with the meaning of "to jamb full of" may also be found with stem-changing forms; as a synonym of *testimoniar,* it is always regular.

atorar. The verb is regular in the sense of "act stubborn, get jambed"; stem-changing when it is the factive verb related to *tuero,* "large piece of kindling."

atracar. The only connecting preposition when the meaning is "to assault" is the personal *a; en* is used when the meaning is "to dock." *Atracarse de algo = comer algo hasta hartarse.*

atraer. Preterite and imperfect subjunctive forms like *atrayó, atrayera* may also be found rather than the more standard *atrajo, atrajera.*

atrás. 1. Locative adverb used with verbs of both motion and state: *Pasó atrás; El hombre estaba atrás.*

2. Like other locative adverbs, it also has a figurative temporal meaning: *Lo conozco de muchos años atrás.*

3. In stative constructions *atrás* tends to be underspecified or absolute in meaning, while *detrás* signifies position relative to something else: *Él viene atrás; Ella está detrás de mí en la cola.* In this sort of constrast, *atrás* may carry a degree modifier, which would be unusual for *detrás: Nosotros terminamos tan atrás en el estadio que no vimos nada.* Nevertheless, *atrás* and *detrás* manifest some interchangeability of usage. *Detrás* is not used as a locative adverb with motion verbs. In a sentence like *Caminó detrás mío* the meaning is *Caminó, estando detrás mío.* The construction *detrás de mí* is more academic.

4. *Detrás de* is the customary preposition form, although *atrás de* may be found.

atronar. Although usually a stem-changing verb, it may occasionally be found as a regular verb.

aun/aún. *Aun* is synonymous with *inclusive/incluso. Aún* is synonymous with *todavía.* However, often in utterance-initial position *aún* is pronounced as though it did not carry a written accent.

aun cuando. Concessive conjunction followed by the subjunctive: *Aun cuando estudie toda la noche, no aprobará el examen.*

aunque. 1. Followed by the indicative with the meaning of "despite the fact that" (i.e., conceding a reality); followed by the subjunctive with the meaning of "even though" or "if the case were" (i.e., rejecting as inapplicable or merely hypothetical a circumstance): *Aunque Juan es hombre, suscribe los derechos de la mujer; Aunque Juan sea hombre, suscribe los derechos de la mujer.* The first example implies the speaker's objection to the proposition; the second, a presumed objection by the hearer.

2. *Aunque* may be used as a synonym of *pero,* in which case it is only used with indicative verbs.

Austria. The feminine *el* is used with the immediately following noun.

austriaco. This form alternates with *austríaco.*

auto-. This prefix is often added to reflexive verbs, as well as to their derived nouns, to underscore the agentive role of the subject: *Él se eliminó del concurso* can mean both "He took himself out of the contest" and "He ended up eliminated from the contest by not doing well," etc., but *Él se autoeliminó del concurso* can only have the first meaning.

autodidacto. The feminine form is *autodidacta,* which is often found used as an invariable noun with respect to gender.

auxiliar. The stem *i* may be either tonic or atonic, although it is generally the latter: *yo auxilio.*

avemaría. The immediately preceding singular article is the feminine *el.*

avenida. The name designation following this noun may or may not be introduced by *de;* prevailing contemporary usage is to suppress the *de: Avenida de Mayo = Avenida Mayo.*

avestruz. Although customarily masculine, usages as feminine may be found.

-avo. The suffix may be added to any cardinal number to form an ordinal: *el treceavo capítulo.* This form, considered substandard when written but marginally acceptable when spoken, is, however, widely extended and replaces the traditional compound *decimotercero.*

ayudante. This noun is invariable with regard to gender in its general meaning as the agentive of *ayudar; ayudanta*, however, exists as the feminine assistant of a shopkeeper or artisan.

ayudar. Usage varies in Latin America, probably along dialect lines, as to whether personal objects are direct or indirect: *Lo ayudé* versus *le ayudé*. Direct usage predominates in the Southern Cone, indirect usage elsewhere.

azúcar. Although customarily masculine, this noun may also be found in feminine constructions, with the article *la* or the feminine *el* (despite the fact that it does not begin with a tonic *a*): *el azúcar morena*. In the plural, it appears only as a masculine noun.

B

bajo. 1. The preposition *bajo* alternates with the stronger form *debajo de* in locative constructions. In figurative uses, only *bajo* (or less frequently, *bajo de*) appears: *Yo trabajo bajo sus órdenes.*
　2. The adjective *bajo* has as a comparative both *inferior* and *más bajo*, while *más bajo* is the only comparative for the adverb *bajo*. With a comparative term, the construction is *inferior a*, but *más bajo que. Bajísimo* and *ínfimo* both exist as the superlative form of *bajo*, although the former tends to prevail colloquially. *Ínfimo* is used only as the superlative of *inferior*.
　3. There is a Latin American usage, considered substandard, whereby *bajo* is also used as synonymous with *de acuerdo a* and similar constructions: *Bajo tu criterio, somos todos ladrones.*

balbucir. *Balbucir* and *balbucear* are synonyms, although the latter predominates in current usage, especially since the former is a defective verb (it has no forms for the first-person present indicative or the present subjunctive).

baño. The cooking phrase (equivalent to English "double boiler") is both *baño de María* and *baño María*, with the latter more prevalent.

base. *En base a* and *a base de* are often used synonymously, although the first more properly means *basándose en*, while the second refers to the basic constitutive element of something: *En base a [= sobre la base de] su declaración, fue declarado culpable; Hecho a base de cacao.*

bendecido. This form is the past participle of the verb *bendecir*, and is used in compound tenses or as an adjective indicating the result of an action: *Esta agua ha sido bendecida. Es agua bendecida. Bendito* is a strictly adjectival form and may be used ironically as well, in a fashion similiar to English "blessèd." Thus, *agua bendecida* = *agua bendita*, but also *estos benditos impuestos.*

bien. Used as an adjective in fixed phrases, like *gente bien* and *niño bien,* the form is invariable for number and gender.

billón. The sum of 1,000,000,000 is expressed in Spanish as *mil millones. Billón* means a million millions (1,000,000,000,000).

blandir. It is used with the same restrictions as *abolir.*

brevedad. *Con la mayor brevedad* alternates with *a la mayor brevedad,* with the former being considered more standard.

bueno. The reduced form *buen* is used before immediately following masculine singular nouns. It is considered substandard to use the reduced form before feminine nouns beginning with stressed *(h)a.* Note, however, the fixed form *en buen hora* and the saying *A buen hambre no hay pan duro.* The comparative is *mejor,* with *más bueno* being considered colloquial or even substandard. The preferred superlative is *buenísimo,* with *bonísimo* and *óptimo* occurring only in highly formal usage. As an interjection, *¡Bueno!* may be articulated as *bué* and written as *¡Bueh!*

C

caballo. The feminine is *yegua.*

cabe. This preposition exists only in literary contexts, with the meaning of *junto a* or *cerca de.*

caber. Used as an impersonal verb, its meaning is *ser posible: Cabe decir que hoy hace calor.*

cacique. The feminine is *cacica.*

cada. *Cada cual* is synonymous with *cada uno,* but tends to be used only with persons, as is *cada quien,* a construction prevalent only in Latin American Spanish. *Cada que,* with the meaning of *siempre que,* only occurs with a nonfuture iterative meaning, and therefore is followed only by the indicative.

caer. *Caerle a uno mal/bien que* is a colloquial expression equivalent to *parecerle a uno mal/bien que.*

calle. The name designation following this noun may or may not be introduced by *de;* prevailing contemporary usage is to suppress the *de.*

calor. Although there exist some regional uses in the feminine, the masculine gender is generalized for this noun.

camino. Although examples exist of *camino a*, the generalized use is *camino de*, in the sense of "on one's way to/toward."

candidato. The feminine is *candidata.*

cansar. *Cansarse*, with the meaning of *ponerse cansado*, is considered substandard when employed without the *se* particle.

cantante. Although the generalized feminine form is also *cantante*, the form *cantatriz* also exists.

caparazón. Used as both feminine and masculine, with a tendency toward the feminine predominating.

capaz. *Capaz que*, in the sense of *a lo mejor*, is almost universally used with an introductory verb and in the indicative: *Capaz que nos vemos mañana.* Used with the verb *ser*, there may be greater reason for the sub-junctive to appear, by conformity with *es probable/posible que: Es capaz que nos veamos mañana*, although this usage is infrequent.

cara. *Cara a* is a synonym of *ante*; it may be found also as *de cara al*, although this usage is considered substandard.

carácter. The plural is *caracteres.*

caradura. This noun is masculine or feminine, depending on the gender of the referent. As a noun referring to the quality or state of being a *caradura*, it is written either as *caradura* or as *cara dura* and is feminine.

caries. The form *carie* as the singular, though widely used, is considered substandard.

casa. Both *ir a casa de alguien* and *ir en casa de alguien* are recognized constructions, although the former tends to predominate.

caso. *En caso de que* is followed by the subjunctive; omission of the *de* is considered substandard. *Caso de que* is synonymous with *en caso de que.*

cassette. This noun appears as both masculine and feminine; in the more assimilated Spanish form *casete*, it is treated as a masculine noun.

causa. Although the construction *a causa de* predominates, the synonym *por causa de* may be found.

causar. *Causar que* is followed by the subjunctive.

cerca. Both *cerca de* and *cerca a* occur, with the former being the domi-nant form.

chance. Used as both a masculine and feminine noun, with the latter dominating: *tener chance = tener suerte/oportunidad*; this use is usually considered substandard. *Chanza* also occurs in some dialects, although in general in Spanish this word means "joke" or "witticism."

ciento. This number appears in the reduced form *cien* when preceding an immediately following noun, masculine or feminine. In compound numerical formations, however, it is not reduced: *doscientas personas.* When used as a freestanding noun, *cien* is also used: *Había más de cien.* In the expression equivalent to English "one hundred percent," the following three variants are found, from the most prevalent to the least used: *cien por ciento, cien por cien, ciento por ciento.* In percentage expressions, *ciento* is used: *cuatro por ciento.*

cierto. 1. Used before a noun, *cierto* means "certain" in the sense of "some ones"; used following a noun it means "certain" in the sense of "true."

2. *Es cierto que* is followed by the indicative, but *no es cierto que* is followed by the subjunctive.

circunscribir. Although the generalized past participle is *circunscrito,* the form used in Argentina is *circunscripto.*

ciudad. Names of cities in Spanish are generally masculine if ending in *o,* feminine if ending in *a;* the masculine predominates for other terminations. Moreover, there are a number of established variants, like *la Toledo histórica, el Málaga antiguo.* Adjectives tend to agree accordingly, although forms like *todo, medio, un, propio, mismo* occur predominantly in the masculine, regardless of the gender of the city. Needless to say, a certain amount of variation exists with names like *Nueva York.*

claro. As used in an impersonal construction, *claro* may be introduced by either *ser* or *estar,* with the latter being more emphatic. An additional affective feature of this item is the possibility of inverting the verb-adjective order for greater emphasis. Note the following ascendant degree of affective utterance: *Es claro que lo tenemos que hacer, Está claro que lo tenemos que hacer, Claro es que lo tenemos que hacer, Claro está que lo tenemos que hacer.*

cliente. The feminine is *clienta,* although *la cliente* is considered the academic form.

coger. The widespread use of this verb with sexual connotations in Latin America has meant its displacement from its "dictionary meaning" by synonyms like *tomar* and *agarrar.* In Argentina, in order to stress the sexual connotation, the spelling is frequently *cojer.*

coliflor. Although this noun appears as both masculine and feminine, the latter is considered the more academically acceptable gender.

color. Although this noun appears as both masculine and feminine, the former is considered the more acceptable gender. The phrases *a color* and *en colores* are synonymous. Although basic color adjectives agree in number and gender with the nouns they modify, some color adjectives are common (e.g., *azul*) and there are a number of derived adjectives that lack plurals, typically nouns used in a color sense: *dos camisas naranja*. Frequently, the phrase *de color de, de color, color de,* or just *color* is used with such terms. In the case of compound adjectives, whether or not basic color terms are involved, there is no agreement in either number or gender; again the phrase *(de) color (de)* may be used: *dos corbatas ([de] color [de]) gris perla*. The notion of a color, when used as a noun, is prefixed by the neuter article *lo;* when various shades are spoken of, the masculine article is used: *los azules, el azul que se usó aquí.*

comediante. The feminine form is *comedianta.*

cometa. As a masculine noun it refers to the astronomical phenomenon; as a feminine form it means *mordida, soborno.*

como. 1. *Como para* alternates with *para* in expressions following *suficiente* and *bastante: Había suficientes estudiantes (como) para ofrecer dos clases.* The use of *para* alone is considered more academic.

2. Like other question words, *cómo* retains the written accent when it appears in implied and indirect questions: *Dígame cómo son las cosas.* As a conjunction, it is followed by the indicative when referring to a specific or definite proposition, but by the subjunctive when the proposition it states is unspecific or nondefinite: *Lo haré como (ya) me dijiste, Lo haré como me digas, así que dígame de una vez.* In cause-and-effect utterances where *como* is synonymous with *si*, it is followed by the subjunctive: *Como sigas diciendo esas cosas, te vas a meter en líos.* Both forms, *como quiera* and *comoquiera* are found as equivalents to English "however." *Comoquiera/como quiera que* is followed by the subjunctive.

competir. *Competir* and *competer* are two separate verbs. The first is fully conjugated and means "to compete," while *competer* is impersonal, meaning "it is appropriate that": *Compete que discutamos el asunto.* It is also equivalent to "be someone's business": *Este asunto no te compete.*

computadora. Alongside this form used most commonly in Latin America, there exists *computador*, preferred in Spain, where *ordenador* is also used.

comunicar. In Spain, with reference to telephone calls, *comunicar* means that the line is busy, while in Latin America it refers to the fact that the other phone is ringing but has not yet answered (*Me estoy comunicando* *con la oficina)*; in Latin America, "busy" in relation to the phone is *ocupado.*

con. The use of *con* as synonymous with *en casa de* is considered a rural usage found in Latin America: *Vamos a comer con los vecinos* = *Vamos a comer en casa de los vecinos.*

con que. As an adverbial conjunction, it is used with the subjunctive in the sense of "as long as," "provided that": *Con que vengas temprano, será suficiente.*

conforme. Followed by the subjunctive if the reference is to an unspecified or nondefinite proposition, by the indicative if the proposition is stating a specific or definite proposition. *Conforme a* is used before nouns: *Conforme al manual, ese verbo lleva subjuntivo.* Estar *conforme con* is equivalent to English "to be in agreement with": *Estoy conforme con mi suerte* ("I accept my fate").

conque. *Conque* is to be distinguished from *con que* (preposition + relative pronoun, followed by the indicative). The former is roughly equivalent to English "So, then": *¡Conque tienes novio!*

consejero. The feminine is *consejera.*

considerar. *Considerar que* is followed by the indicative as a statement of fact, although negations of such statements of fact take the subjunctive: *Consideramos que él es bonito; No consideramos que él sea bonito.* Considerar *que* is followed by the subjunctive to introduce a hypothetical fact: *Consideremos que ellos aparezcan sin haber sido invitados, ¿qué hacemos?* A negation of such a statement would also take the subjunctive.

consistir. *Consistir en* is the standard construction; *consistir de* and *consistir a* are considered substandard.

contactar. Although *contactar con alguien* exists, perhaps by English influence, *contactar a alguien* has become prevalent.

contento. *Estar contento de que* is normally followed by the subjunctive, although if taken as a simple assertion without affective coloring, the indicative may occur.

continuar. *Continuar* + present participle describes the duration or repetition of an action presented as beginning in the past and ongoing from the point of reference of the utterance. *Seguir* may also be used in such constructions.

conveniente. *Ser conveniente que* is followed by the subjunctive.

convenir. *Convenir que* is followed by the subjunctive. Note that this construction is impersonal and is synonymous with *ser conveniente que: Conviene que confirmes tus reservas con anticipación.*

convidar. *Convidar a que* is followed by the subjunctive.

correr. This verb may appear as a transitive, in the sense of "to chase"; as an intransitive, in the sense of "to run"; and as an intransitive with the *se* particle, in the sense of "to move over" or "to scoot over." *Correrse* in Spain also has a sexual connotation.

coste. *Coste* and *costo,* as in *el costo de la vida,* are generally synonyms; the latter is the term found in economic contexts, while *coste* has a more concrete monetary meaning.

creer. *Creer que* is followed by the indicative, while negative *no creer que* is followed by the subjunctive. Note that *creer que* may occur with the subjunctive in a noncategorical assertion or with the implication of reservations: *Creo que pueda ser posible. No creer que* may appear followed by the indicative if the truth-value of the assertion is presupposed and emphasis is on the act of nonbelieving: *Yo no creo que eso debe ser así.* In questions, *no creer que* is followed by the indicative: *¿No crees que es más que suficiente?*

cual. Concerning the uses of *el cual,* etc., see *que. Cual* in place of *como* is highly formal: *Lo hizo cual le habían señalado.* Like other question words, *cuál* retains the written accent in implied and indirect questions: *Dime cuál es la respuesta. ¿Cuál es?* + noun asks for a selection between possible items, while *¿Qué es?* + noun asks for a definition of that noun. Immediately preceding a noun *qué* is the academically preferred form, although *cuál* is frequently found.

cualquiera. Before following nouns, with or without intervening modifiers, the reduced form *cualquier* is used. The plural of *cualquiera* is *cualesquiera,* and *cualesquier* is the reduced form; *cualquieras* is considered substandard.

cuán. In literary use, it appears as a question word for an adjective or adverb; *cuán* alternates with *qué tan: ¿Cuán/qué tan ancho es?*

cuando. *Cuando* is followed by the subjunctive when its reference is to the future, but the indicative in iterative utterances. Future iterative combinations are signaled by the subjunctive. *Cuándo* in implied or indirect questions retains the written accent: *Dime cuándo piensas hacerlo.*

cuanto. *Cuanto* may be a synonym of *todo lo que: Dame cuanto tengas = Dame todo lo que tengas.* By the general pattern of adjectival clauses, it is followed by the indicative if the proposition is specific and definite, but by the subjunctive if it is unspecific or nondefinite. *Cuánto* in implied or indirect questions retains the written accent: *Quiero saber cuánto vale. En cuanto* (= *tan pronto como*) is followed by the subjunctive when it has a future meaning, and by the indicative when it refers to a habitual present: *En cuanto llega, comienza a gritarme.*

culpa. *No es (mi, etc.) culpa que* is followed by the subjunctive.

cumpleaños. This noun is used as a singular masculine; plural agreement with possessives, modifiers, and verbs is considered substandard.

cumplir. This is one of several major verbs in Spanish in which there is a tendency to suppress a prepositional connector, which in this case is customarily *con: Cumplió con su deber* versus *Cumplió su deber.*

cúyo. *Cúyo* is not ordinarily used as a question word, the form *de quién* being preferred.

D

dado. The conjunction *dado que* is regularly followed by the indicative when it has a causal or concessive meaning: *Dado que piensas así, cambiaré de idea.* As a conditional conjunction (only used literarily), even though followed by the subjunctive, it refers to a real condition: *Dado que llueva, iré.*

dar. As this is one of the basic inventory verbs in Spanish, there are numerous fixed expressions and constructions with various prepositions and accompanying parts of speech: *Te doy mi palabra de que llegaremos a tiempo; Les daba igual venir a cada uno; Me da vergüenza verte así. Dar examen* refers to the activity of the student, while *tomar examen* is what the teacher does. However, the influence of English may serve to reverse the usage.

de. 1. Expresses origin or source, including possession; "noun$_2$ (*Juan*) possesses noun$_1$ (*cabeza*)": *la cabeza de Juan.*

    2. The direct objects of nominalizations of active verbs are usually preceded by *de.* Compare *Reseñé el libro* and *Escribí una reseña del libro.* However, *de* in these cases may be replaced by *a* to stress the verb–direct object relationship, especially in nominalized forms: *una reseña al libro de Borges.*

    3. Many adverbial phrases of manner are formed with *de: Ella lo dijo de corrido; Lo dijo de repente.*

4. *De* introduces a passive agent when the meaning of the verb is more durative than perfective: *Es una persona venerada de todos = Goza de la veneración de todos / Todos lo veneran.* Colloquially, the *por* used with active verbs with perfective meanings tends to replace *de* in these sentences: *Es una persona venerada por todos.*

5. Used to express negative appositional meanings: *El estúpido de Pedro = Pedro es un estúpido.* Sentences in which the *de* can also be construed as possessive lead to legendary ironic and jocular ambiguities: *El asno de Sancho Panza = El asno del que Sancho Panza es dueño* or *Sancho Panza es un asno.*

6. Typically in Río de la Plata dialects, *de* may appear as an adjectival degree modifier synonymous with *muy: La fiesta estuvo de fabulosa.*

7. *De* + infinitive is equivalent to *si* plus a hypothetical or contrary-to-fact subjunctive: *De saberlo = Si lo hubiera sabido.* Often the verb may also be supressed when *de* is accompanied by *no* or predicately correlated pronouns: *de no = si no* + verb; *Yo de no ser ella = Si yo no fuera ella.*

8. The connective *de* is frequently omitted with conjunctions like *antes de que*, factive constructions like *el hecho de que*, predicate adjective constructions like *estar cierto de que*, and middle verb constructions like *darse cuenta de que* and *alegrarse de que.* Conversely, it is often inserted as a connective with impersonal verbs and before *que* introducing a dependent noun clause; the latter is frequent in the Andean area: *No le interesa de venir; Me dijo de que lo sabía.* Both of these intrusive uses of *de* are regularly condemned by the academic standard.

9. In some dialects, *de* may replace *a* to indicate the goal of the verb *ir* and its close synonyms: *Voy del médico.*

10. *De a* is a frequent compound preposition in certain fixed expressions: *de a caballo; a caballo* is considered more standard. *De a de veras* is a notable colloquialism for *en realidad, de veras.*

de ahí que. This conjunction, and its less frequent companion *de allí que*, are customarily followed by the subjunctive. On occasion, however, usages will be found with the indicative, indicating a strong assertive proposition, especially as the conclusion of an argument: . . . *De ahí que estás totalmente equivocado.*

debajo. Although *debajo* may be found, like other locatives, with possessive pronouns (e.g., *debajo nuestro*), it normally occurs with the preposition *de* to form a locative preposition. Compare *debajo* with *abajo* and *bajo.*

deber. Some speakers regularly confuse pairs like *deber* + verb (= obligation) and *deber de* + verb (= probability): *Él debe venir mañana* (= *Él está obligado a venir mañana / Es necesario que venga mañana*) versus

Él debe de venir mañana (= *A lo mejor él viene mañana*). For some speakers, the distinction is resolved in favor of *deber* + verb; for others, it is in favor of *deber de* + verb. Note that the synonymy between *deber* (obligation) and *tener que* is not necessarily acceptable in all dialects, the preference being for construing *tener que* as only referring to necessity.

debido. *Debido a* is equivalent to English "due to," "by virtue of the fact that." It is not recognized by all dialects.

decidirse. *Decidir* + verb is synonymous with *decidirse a* + verb.

decir. 1. As this is one of the basic inventory verbs in Spanish, there are numerous fixed expressions and constructions with various prepositions and accompanying parts of speech.

2. *Decir que* followed by the indicative transmits information; *decir que* followed by the subjunctive transmits an imperative. This distinction tends to be lost with *no decir que*, and *No dijo que viniera mañana* alternates with *No dijo que vendría mañana* as the negative of *Dijo que vendría mañana*. *Decir de* + infinitive, recorded in some dialects, alternates with the subjunctive construction: *Te dije de hablarle* = *Te dije que le hablaras*. In many dialects, principally those of the Andean region, *decir de que* in both senses is common.

decodificar. Synonymous with *descodificar.* Both verbs have respective nominal derivations, like *decodificación* versus *descodificación.*

decreto-ley. The plural is *decretos-leyes.*

deformar. Infrequent synonyms are *desformar* and *disformar.* This synonymy extends to derived forms, e.g., *deforme* versus *disforme.*

dejar. 1. When the subject of a dependent-clause verb is moved forward as an object of *dejar*, it appears as a direct object: *Dejé que ella volviera* = *La dejé volver.*

2. *Dejar saber* as a synonym of *informar* or *hacer saber* is considered an English calque and is not recognized in all dialects.

del. Portmanteau for *de* + *el.* In premodern texts *dél* may be found for *de* + *él*, a combination that extends to *de* plus other third-person pronouns.

delante. Locative used with stative verbs: *No hay nada delante.* The corresponding adverb used with motion verbs is *adelante.* Used in combination with *de* as a preposition: *Se portó muy mal delante de mí.* Like other locative prepositions, it may also occur with possessives: *Se portó muy mal delante mío.* However, there are many who consider such a use substandard, especially when written.

delegado. The feminine is *delegada.*

delinear. By analogy with *línea,* the present indicative forms of this verb may occur with an antepenultimate stress: *yo delíneo.* However, the preferred stress would be in terms of a regular -*ar* verb: *yo delineo.*

delta. The Greek letter is feminine; the geographic configuration is masculine.

demoníaco. Demoniaco is equally acceptable.

denegrir. Defective verb used only in forms retaining the stem *i.*

dentro. Locative adverb used with stative verbs: *El está dentro.* The form used with motion verbs is *adentro.* In some dialects, *adentro* is used synonymously with *dentro.* The corresponding prepositional form is *dentro de.*

dependiente. The feminine noun is *dependienta;* the adjective is invariable.

derecho. The linking preposition is either *a* or *de; a* may be preferred with the nominalization of an action verb: *Nos negaron nuestro derecho a la crítica / a criticar.*

derredor. Literary synonym of *alrededor;* note the prepositional construction *en derredor de.*

derrocar. In current usage, this verb is regular; earlier irregular forms followed the pattern of *recordar.*

desandar. Conjugated like *andar,* including the occasional regular preterite and imperfect subjunctive.

desayunar. This verb may either be intransitive or transitive; often transitive objects are preceded by + *con: Desayuné una hamburguesa; Desayuné con una hamburguesa.*

descodificar. See *decodificar.*

descontado. Dar algo por descontado is equivalent to the English "to take something for granted"; *descontado* is invariable.

descuidarse. The reflexive form plus preposition alternates with a nonreflexive form with a direct object noun without connecting preposition: *Descuidó su trabajo; Se descuidó en el / del trabajo.*

desde. 1. *Desde que* is followed by the indicative, in both its temporal and its causal meanings.

   2. *Desde ya* = *seguro; sin lugar a dudas.*

   3. *Desde hace* = English "for" + period of time: *Desde hace dos años vivo en los Estados Unidos.*

desiderátum. The plural is either invariable or it is *desiderata.*

despacio. In addition to being synonymous with *lentamente,* in a sentence like *Yo hablo despacio,* it is in some dialects synonymous with *suave* or *callado.*

después. *Después de que* is followed by the subjunctive if future time from the point of view of the main verb is referred to, and the indicative in other cases; it frequently occurs without the preposition *de.* The prepositional form *después de* noun/verb is synonymous with *tras* noun/verb.

detrás. Locative adverb used with stative verbs to indicative relative position: *Se quedó detrás.* Therefore, for purposes of relative comparison, it is usually used with an accompanying prepositional phrase or, in some dialects, possessive: *Se quedó detrás de mí/mío.* With action verbs, the meaning is to assume this relative position: *Él pasó detrás de mí.* Compare *atrás* for nonrelative position. *Detrás de* alternates synonymously with *tras,* although the latter does not appear with possessives in place of the prepositional phrase: *detrás de él / detrás suyo* versus *tras él.*

devenir. The noun or adjective complement may occur with or without a connective *en: Mis ideas han devenido (en) vanas ilusiones.*

devolver. *Devolverse* may be found as a regional synonym for *volver(se).*

diablo. The feminine form is either *diabla* or *diablesa.*

diario. As a synonym for *diariamente, a diario* may be truncated to *diario* in some Latin American dialects.

dibujante. The feminine form is either *dibujante* or *dibujanta.*

dichoso. Used before a noun, it means "damned/darned"; used following a noun it means "lucky."

diestro. The superlative is either *destrísimo* or *diestrísimo.*

diferente. Used before a noun, *diferente* means "various"; used following a noun it means "different." See also *distinto.*

dignarse. Although this verb may appear with the linking preposition *a* or *de,* most frequently no connective is used: *Nos dignamos reconocer su presencia.*

dimitir. May be found without the connective *de: Dimitió su cargo.* In some dialects, *de* is replaced by *a: Dimitió a su cargo.* Also found with a direct personal object as an ironic synonym of *despedir/destituir: Me dimitieron.*

dinamo. Generally feminine, although may be found as masculine; *dínamo* may also be found, particularly as a masculine noun.

diputado. *Diputado al/en el Congreso por Catamarca.* *Diputada* is the feminine form.

director. As a noun, the feminine is *directora;* as an adjective, it is *directriz.* *Directriz,* as a feminine noun, exists as a synonym of *norma.*

disfrutar. This is one of several major verbs in Spanish in which there is a tendency to suppress a prepositional connector, which in this case is customarily *de: Disfrutó de la primavera* versus *Disfrutó la primavera.*

dispensar. Transitive when it is a synonym of *dar: El jefe dispensa favores.* It is used with a connective preposition *de* when it means "do without/dispense with/excused from": *Está dispensado de venir a clase. Dispensar por* = "excuse (someone) for": *Dispénseme por haber llegado tarde.*

distinto. Used with either *a* or *de* as connective preposition: *distinto a/de los otros.* Note that *distinto,* like English "distinct," means "having separate existence," while *diferente,* like "different," means substantially different. Thus, for example, two pennies are distinct one from another, while a penny and a quarter are different (as well as distinct). *Diferente* may also use either *a* or *de.*

divergir. Although often found conjugated in the preterite and the imperfect subjunctive on the model of *sentir,* this verb is regular.

divertir. Often found conjugated as a regular verb in the preterite and imperfect subjunctive.

divertirse. The construction with the linking preposition *en* + infinitive verb is more frequently replaced by a progressive one: *Yo me divierto estudiando.*

dizque. Also written as *diz que: Dizque la casa tiene ocho habitaciones* = *Se dice que la casa tiene ocho habitaciones.*

doble. Used as an adverb replacing *doblemente,* the article is optional: *Tenemos que trabajar (el) doble.*

doblez. The masculine noun is synonymous with *pliegue* and *dobladillo;* the feminine noun is synonymous with *decepción* and *mala fe.*

doctor. The feminine form is *doctora.*

dolor. By extension of the construction *ataque a, dolor a* may be found.

doméstico. The use of this adjective as synonymous with *nacional,* especially in the phrase *vuelo doméstico,* is often considered an Anglicism.

donde. 1. Locative adverb and conjunction; its interrogative form, implied or when used as part of a question, is *dónde: No sé dónde estamos.* Through the influence of its synonymous form *en el lugar que, en donde* may be found.

    2. Following a personal noun, it has the meaning of *en la casa de* or *en el lugar de: Nos conocimos donde Juan.*

    3. Often used colloquially as a synonym of *cuando.*

    4. *Donde* followed by the subjunctive is a colloquial variant of *si* in cause-and-effect sentences.

dondequiera. Adverb meaning *en cualquier sitio;* it may also be used as a conjunction with *que,* which is, however, often omitted: *dondequiera (que) vayas.*

doquier. Also *doquiera;* literary synonym of *dondequiera: Ellos van doquier(a).* When used as a conjunction it is rarely followed by *que. Por doquier* is another literary synonym.

dormir. Various colloquial variants are found, like irregular preterite forms *durmiste* and *durmimos* and regular subjunctive forms like *dormamos* and *dormáis.*

dote. Although found used as both a masculine and a feminine noun in the sense of "dowry," it is more commonly feminine; as a plural noun meaning "qualities," it is only feminine.

dudar. When followed by a subordinate clause, academic use prefers the *que* to be preceded by *de,* although the latter is frequently omitted colloquially. Subordinate clauses with *dudar* take the subjunctive; with *no dudar,* the indicative. The opposite distribution may be found for affective or emphatic purposes: *Dudo que mañana es apropriado para hacerlo | No dudo que él sea la persona idónea. Dudar de* followed by a neuter pronoun frequently loses the *de,* thus allowing for preverbal pronominalization: *Dudo eso que me has dicho = Lo dudo.*

duermevela. Occurs as both a feminine and a masculine noun, although its second constituent usually dictates its identification as feminine.

dulzura. The synonym *dulzor* is often limited to describing a physical property or sensation, in which case *dulzura* may be reserved for affective meanings.

durar. In time constructions the preposition may be omitted: *La función duró (por) cinco horas.*

E

e. Replaces the conjunction *y* before words beginning with *(h)i-* or words (typically of non-Spanish extraction) beginning with *y* + consonant. Note that this excludes the combination *hi* + vowel (most frequently, *e*) and *y* + vowel.

echar. *Echar* is frequently used in colloquial Spanish American speech, followed by a nominalized past participle, as an emphatic or affective construction roughly synonymous with the root verb of the nominalized past participle: *Voy a echar una mirada al libro = Voy a mirar el libro.*

-ecito. This variant of the diminuative suffix *-ito* is used with monosyllabic words ending in a consonant (*red/redecita*), with polysyllabic words ending in unstressed *-ia, -io, -ua* (*lengua/lengüecita;* there are some exceptions: *agua/agüita*), and polysyllabic words ending in *-e* (*baile/bailecito*).

editorial. As a noun meaning publishing company, it is feminine. As a noun meaning a text of journalistic opinion, it is masculine.

educativo. This adjectival form of *educación* is academically preferable to the English-inspired *educacional*. *Educativo* refers to whatever educates; *educacional* to everything connected with education as a social institution.

el. 1. Masculine definite article; feminine definite article used with immediately following feminine nouns beginning with stressed *(h)a-*. Exceptions are women's names (*La Ana*), some place names (*La Haya*), and the letters of the alphabet, *la a* and *la hache*.

2. The use of the article before first names is considered rustic and, in some countries, pejorative. The article is also used in some formal contexts before last names, and there are a number of literary and cultural figures where this usage is standard: *el Petrarca, la Pardo Bazán.*

3. Certain geographic entities may frequently be preceded by the article, although in most cases it is optional: *(la) Argentina, (el) Brazil, (el) Uruguay, (los) Estados Unidos.*

4. The use of the article with nominalized infinitives serves an emphatic function; therefore, it is frequently used when infinitives are followed by a limiting or defining modifier or modifying phrase: *El decirlo así me parece una tontería.*

él. 1. Third person masculine pronoun; *ella* is the feminine form. The corresponding plurals are *ellos* and *ellas*. As with other subject pronouns in Spanish, these are used only for purposes of emphasis, contrast, or to avoid ambiguity. Since the third person covers a large scope of meaning, accordingly its pronouns are more likely to occur than those of the first and second person. It should be noted that dialects are likely to vary as to the circumstances in which the third person is considered to be required explicitly.

2. The verbally affixed reflexive form of the masculine and feminine, singular and plural, is *se* (q.v.); the reflexive prepositional form is *sí*, although with *con* it is *consigo*. The use of *él*, etc., with *con* is considered substandard.

3. See *le* for the various direct and indirect object pronoun patterns of *él*.

el que. As the conjunction introducing a dependent noun clause, it is followed by the subjunctive: *El que no haya terminado me sorprende* (or: *Me sorprende el que no haya terminado*). *El hecho de que* as a synonymous conjunction may take the indicative in assertive contexts, although the subjunctive is far more common even when a matter of fact is being stated. When *que* is used instead of *el que* to introduce a dependent noun clause, it always takes the subjunctive: *Que sea así, no me sorprende.*

elegido. Past participle of the verb *elegir: Estas son las prendas elegidas por el cliente.* When used adjectivally with persons, especially to designate the result of formally voting, the form *electo* is preferred: *El presidente electo presta juramento mañana.*

élite. This French loanword is pronounced with the final vowel silent and with stress on the *i*; the written plural *s* is also silent. However, the word has been incorporated into Spanish by either pronouncing it as written, with all three written vowels pronounced and with stress on the initial *e*; in this case, the pluralizing *s* is pronounced. Alternately, it is written *elite*, with all three vowels pronounced and with the *i* stressed; the pluralizing *s* is pronounced. This third variant is preferred. In all three cases the noun is feminine.

ella. See *él*.

ello. This neuter third-person subject pronoun is used to refer to underspecified nouns (adequate specification of which would result in the choice between a masculine or feminine, singular or plural pronoun) or to verbal clauses treated as subjects. Like other third-person subject pronouns, it only appears in cases of emphasis, contrast, or to avoid ambiguity. Even at that, *ello* tends to appear rather infrequently, being replaced by neuter demonstratives like *esto, eso,* or *aquello.* The verbally affixed forms are *lo* and *le.*

embajador. The feminine form is *embajadora.*

embarazada. *La mujer está embarazada de cuatro meses.*

embargo. *Sin embargo* and *en cambio* are not synonymous. The former introduces a reservation, while the latter proposes an alternative (and is therefore synonymous with *por el contrario*).

emborrachar. *Me emborraché con/de vino.*

embriagar. *Se embriagaron con/de vino. Se embriagaron de felicidad.*

embutir. *Nos sentimos embutidos de comida. Embutieron el relleno en el colchón.*

empezar. *empezar a* + infinitive means to begin an action; *empezar por* + infinitive or a noun means to undertake a global action by beginning with a specific one contained within it.

en. 1. Locative or temporal preposition expressing place or time frame within which an entity is found or takes place. Like all of the basic prepositions, it covers a range of locative and temporal meanings and may be replaced, for greater precision or emphasis, with more specific synonyms: *El libro está en la mesa* versus *El libro está encima de la mesa. El libro está en el cajón* versus *El libro está dentro del cajón. Eso pasó en febrero* versus *Eso pasó durante (el mes de) febrero.*

2. With many motion verbs *en* indicates where an action took place, while *a* indicates the goal of the action; in actual usage, it may be difficult to make such a distinction: *Se sentó en la mesa* versus *Se sentó a la mesa. Entré en la sala* versus *Entré a la sala.*

3. Followed by a gerund, *en* indicates an action from which a subsequent one follows: *En diciendo eso, me di cuenta de mi ignorancia del tema.* This construction rarely appears in colloquial speech, being replaced by *al* + infinitive or a similar synonymous construction.

4. An enormous range of manner, instrumental, and partitive constructions are based on *en* + noun. Rarely does the article appear with the accompanying noun, except for emphasis or to indicate that the noun refers to a specific entity rather than the general concept: *Viajar en auto* versus *Viajar en el auto (de uno, etc.).*

5. *En la mañana*, etc., is a frequent Latin American variant of the peninsular *por la mañana. De mañana*, etc., is also a Latin American variant.

encantar. As a direct object verb, *encantar* means "to bewitch": *La bruja lo encantó, convirtiéndolo en una estatua de sal.* As an indirect object verb, *encantar* means "to be enchanted by/thrilled with": *Le encantan las cuecas chilenas.*

encima de. 1. As a more emphatic variant of locative *en*, this preposition varies in usage with respect to whether it specifics in physical contact with/on top of or whether it refers to spatial position over. In the latter case and with a motion verb it may be preceded by *por: Pasamos por encima del cañón.*

2. As a manner preposition, it is synonymous with *además de.*

3. Like other "strong" prepositions, *de* + pronoun may be replaced in some dialects by a possessive: *encima de nosotros* versus *encima nuestro.* Because the root noun is the feminine *cima,* agreement may additionally be in the feminine: *encima nuestra.*

enema. Although a feminine noun, by analogy with other masculine words ending in *-ma,* masculine agreement may be found. There is an archaic *el enema* used to refer to certain types of herbal applications to stop the flow of blood from a wound.

enfermar. As an intransitive verb, it tends to be reflexive in Latin American usage and nonreflexive in Spain: *(me) enfermé del hígado.*

enfrente. Locative adverb indicating in an opposite and facing position with respect to the utterer's point of reference; *enfrente de* is the corresponding preposition. By contrast, *frente de* or *frente a* (there is no corresponding adverb form) indicates "facing on" without respect to utterance point of reference. Like all so-called "strong" prepositions, *enfrente de* + pronoun may be found as *enfrente* + possessive.

enhorabuena. May be found written as three separate words, *en hora buena.* When construed as one word, it carries one tonic accent.

enojarse. *Se enojó con/contra su amigo. Se enojó de lo que dijo.*

enojoso. Followed by the preposition *a,* the adjective means a burden, "producing *enojo*"; with *en* it refers to the quality of the noun modified, "annoying."

enseguida. Also written as two words, *en seguida.*

entrambos. Strictly literary variant of *ambos,* with corresponding feminine form, *entrambas.*

entrar. For difference between *entrar a* and *entrar en,* see *en.*

entre. 1. Unlike the other prepositions, *entre* is followed by the nominative pronoun: *entre tú y yo.* Although in a reflexive or reciprocal construction, the pronoun would academically be *sí,* the influence of the nominative pattern often results in a nonreflexive usage: *Juan y Pedro pelearon entre ellos* versus *Juan y Pedro pelearon entre sí.*

2. *Entre* may also be a synonym of *dentro de.*

3. *Entre* may be a synonym of the adverbial conjunction *cuanto: Entre más hablo, menos me prestan atención.*

4. *Entre que* is a synonym of *mientras* + indicative.

entremeterse. The form *entrometerse* is also found.

entrenar. As an intransitive verb it is preferably reflexive.

entretanto. As an adverb or adverbial conjunction, also written as two words, *entre tanto.* As a noun, it is written as a single word.

entretenerse. A following verb may be either a gerund or *en* + infinitive: *Me entretuve leyendo* or *Me entretuve en leer.*

entusiasta. The noun form is strictly *entusiasta;* the corresponding adjective may be *entusiasta* or *entusiástico.* The manner adverb is *entusiásticamente.*

enzima. Variable with respect to gender, although the feminine form tends to prevail.

epifonema. This rhetorical term is predominantly feminine, although analogy with the masculine *fonema* may produce masculine forms.

errar. Although customarily stem-changing, in its meaning of "cometer errores," with respect to forms accentuated on the first syllable (*yo yerro* versus *nosotros erramos*), this verb is often treated (typically in Argentina) as completely regular: *yo erro.* In its meaning of "andar errante" it is customarily regular.

escribir. Although the past participle is *escrito,* note should be taken of the ironic expression *leído y escribido;* the first component may also be pronounced *leido.*

esculpir. *Uno esculpe a cincel en mármol.*

escurrirse. The connecting preposition may be either *de, entre,* or the combination *de entre: Se me escurrió de entre las manos.*

ese. 1. This demonstrative is often used to signal pejorativeness: *esa idea tuya.* Although, by analogy with feminine *el, ese* may appear with feminine nouns beginning with tonic *a, esa* is the academically preferred form: *esa arma.*

2. As a demonstrative pronoun, it may or may not carry a written accent. The neuter pronoun *eso* never carries a written accent.

3. *Ese,* etc., may frequently replace the more properly third-person demonstrative *aquel,* etc., especially in Latin America.

esfinge. Gender varies, but feminine is now preferred.

esforzado. In Spanish, this adjective is synonymous with *valiente,* although English influence has also given it a meaning equivalent to the latter's "forced." *A la fuerza* may, however, be preferred in the latter sense.

esforzar. *Nosotros nos esforzamos en/por comprender.*

eslogan. This adaptation of English "slogan" alternates with the Spanish calque *slogan,* masculine in gender, and the academically preferred *lema,* also masculine.

espalda. *A espaldas de* = "behind someone's back"; *De espaldas a* = "with one's back toward/backing onto/into." The latter also means "by opposition to."

español. Although *español* and *castellano* are considered to be synonyms with reference to the "Spanish language," the former more properly refers to a group of dialects, the historically dominant and official one of which is the dialect of Castile, *castellano.* Therefore, *castellano* is frequently used, especially in Latin America, to refer to the Spanish language and to the academic subject based on it (roughly like English Comp.). Although *castellano* now includes innumerable elements drawn from the other Spanish peninsular dialects and non-Spanish languages (including the Latin American indigenous languages), it continues to be a preferred, if rather imprecise, designation in many areas of the Spanish-speaking world. Note that *castellano* (or *español*) is juxtaposed to the two other official Romance languages of the Iberian Peninsula, *portugués* (and its dialect in Spain, *gallego*) and *catalán.*

espécimen. The plural is *especímenes.* By back formation, the incorrect singular *especimen* is found.

esperar. 1. *Esperar que* has the meaning of "hope/expect." In the past tense, it is always used with the subjunctive, present or past, depending on the pragmatic relationship of the dependent verb: present if the action is conceived of as not yet having occurred; otherwise past: *Esperábamos que salieran nuestros números en la lotería.* By the same token, used in the present or the future, it would normally be followed by a present subjunctive. However, a future tense may occur if the dependent verb is considered posterior to the main verb, *esperar,* and the sense of the latter is more "expect/presume" than "hope": *Espero que saldrá bien en el examen.*

2. *Esperar a que* has the meaning of "wait (until)" and is always followed by the subjunctive, past or present: *Esperaba a que viniera a verme.*

3. The impersonal construction *ser de esperar que* is always followed by the subjunctive: *Era de esperar que actuaras así.*

esperma. *La esperma* = *cera derretida; el esperma* is what is found in semen.

espúreo. Hypercorrect form of the academically preferred *espurio.*

Estados Unidos. This noun is treated as masculine singular if used without an article, but as masculine plural if the article is present: *Estados Unidos considera que ése es un tema discutible. Los Estados Unidos han decidido combatir las drogas en todos los frentes posibles.* The academically preferred abbreviation is *EE.UU.*, although *USA* (pronounced *usa*) is frequent. *USA* is treated as a masculine singular: *USA invadió Panamá en 1989. EUA* also exists as a purely written abbreviation.

estadounidense. Although this noun is a logical derivative of *Estados Unidos, (norte)americano* is preferred almost universally. *Norteamericano* tends to be used in Mexico, Central America, and some countries of the northern tier of South America, while *americano* is preferred in Spain, the Caribbean, and most of South America, sometimes with an ironic overtone.

estándar. Alternates with the incorporated English *standard*. The latter tends to be invariable, while *estándar* has the plural *estándares. Estandardizar* and *estandardización* are used as derivates of either adjectival form, although *estandarizar* and *estandarización* are preferred.

estar. 1. Basic locative verb, used with predicate adverbs to indicate location.

2. Used with most adjectives to focalize a quality, whether temporary, recently permanent, or notable from the perspective of the speaker: *Estás muy bonita ahora que te pusiste ese vestido. Mi padre está muerto desde hace varios años. Este paisaje está precioso.*

3. In command forms, *estar* may occur reflexively to emphasize a change in condition being demanded: *Nene, estate quieto de una vez.* In other constructions, *estarse* may be synonymous with *mantenerse* or *quedarse,* with either adverbial or adjectival predicates.

4. *Estar de más que* is always followed by the subjunctive; the written form *estar demás* is considered academically incorrect.

5. *estar al* may be found in some countries as a substitute for *estar por* in the sense of "to be about to."

6. *Estar* plus a predicate noun is rare, although some adjectives which also double as noun forms, typically items indicating nationality, may occur with *estar* to indicate an unusual condition or appearance: *Con ese sombrero de charro, estás mexicanísimo.*

7. *Estar* + present particle is used to express progressive tenses. Note that, in general terms, only verbs whose subjects are the direct agent of an action are used in the progressive: *Escribo una carta / Estoy escribiendo una carta.* This restriction also extends to intransitive verbs like *ir, venir,* and *volver.* Combinations like *estoy siendo, estoy yendo, estoy volviendo* are usually considered ungrammatical. Non-action or stative verbs like *saber, tener, conocer* normally do not appear in the progressive either.

este. See comments with respect to *ese. Este* generally signals what belongs to the scope of the first person. When it is used emphatically, its meaning is either positive or negative (as opposed to the emphatic negative *ese*): *la niña esta* versus *la niña esa.*

estrés. Incorporated Spanish version of English *stress.* The adjectival form, corresponding to "(all) stressed out" is *estresado. Estresante,* in the sense of "producing stress," also exists.

estudiante. This invariable adjective/noun also has a colloquial feminine form, *estudianta.*

excepto. This preposition is followed by the nominative pronomial forms: *excepto tú.*

exclusive. Adverb that is used following a noun, in the singular, to indicate the exclusion of that item: *Todos, Juan y María exclusive, se decidieron por el vino.*

exento. Used exclusively with *estar: Está exento de hacer la tarea.*

exiliar. This word is the preferred academic form, not the frequently encountered *exilar;* compare also the derived nouns *exiliado* and *exilado.*

explotar. There are two homophonous verbs, meaning "to exploit" and "to explode." In the former case the nominalization is *explotación,* while in the latter it is *explosión.*

F

faltar. The distinction between *faltar* and *hacer falta* is "to lack, be missing, not to have" versus "to need, to be necessary for one to." In terms of corresponding English constructions, the role of the subject and object pronouns in Spanish is reversed: *Me faltan cinco hojas* = "I'm missing five pages." *Me hacen falta tus consejos* = "I need your (words of) advice."

fecha. In date constructions, *(estar) a* introduces a day of the month specified by number; *en* introduces the month or the year: *Estamos a cinco de mayo. Estamos en mayo. Estamos en 1999.* The following are all acceptable equivalents for a date like "May 27, 1990," in descending order of formality: *27 de mayo de 1990; 27 de mayo, 1990; 27-V-90; 27-5-90; 27/V/90; 27/5/90; 27 mayo 1990; Mayo 27, 1990.* Note that the first day of the month is written as *1º de mayo. En* is not used to introduce a day-of-the-month construction: *Se celebra la Declaración de la República Argentina el 9 de julio.*

felicitaciones. This expression is used to congratulate someone upon learning of good fortune or success; *felicidades* is a wish that someone will have good fortune and is, therefore, often used, like *suerte* and other similar phrases, as a parting formula.

fiel. The superlative of *fiel* is *fidelísimo.*

film. The plural of this English word incorporated into Spanish is *films* or *filmes.* The singular *filme* also exists, although *film* seems to be preferred. The word, as in English, refers to either the industry (in which case it is synonymous with *cine*) or to a specific title (in which case it is synonymous with *película*). The word has provided derivations like *filmar, filmación,* etc.

filólogo. The feminine is *filóloga.*

filósofo. The feminine is *filósofa.*

fin. The conjunction *a fin de que* is always followed by the subjunctive. *Con el fin de que* is a synonym of *a fin de que,* and both have preposition forms, *a fin de* and *con el fin de.*

físico. The feminine is *física.*

flor. In the pseudoadjectival compound *flor de,* meaning something like the English emphatic "real," *flor* agrees with the object of its preposition: *una flor de casa, un flor de coche.* Similar construction like *pedazo de* and *mar de* are invariable; note that the latter expressions always uses *mar* in the feminine: *la mar de inteligentes.*

fluido. Past participle of *fluir; fluido* = "fluid," both as a noun and as an adjective; it may also mean "fluent": *El habla fluido el español.* Note that *fluente* with the meaning of English "fluent" is not used. The forms *flúido* (noun and adjective) and *flúidamente* are considered substandard.

folklore. The final *e* may or may not be pronounced in the singular, but in the plural it is. The variants *folclore* and *folclor* are found, and the variation is retained in derivations: *folklórico* and *folclórico.*

fotógrafo. The feminine is *fotógrafa.*

frente. 1. This noun is feminine when it means "forehead," masculine when it means the "front" (of a building, a military zone).

2. *Frente a* is synonymous with locative *ante* and *enfrente de,* indicating a position opposite to the pragmatic point of reference in an utterance or alongside it; cf. English "in front of" and "facing." Like *ante,* it may have a metaphorical meaning, in the sense of "in the face of (such events, etc.)," whereas *enfrente de* is strictly literal.

3. *frente a frente* means "face to face," while *frente con frente* or *frente por frente* means "opposite each other, facing each other."

frijol. This generalized Latin American form alternates with *fríjol* and *fréjol*, the latter commonly found in the Andean region.

frío. The superlative is either *frigidísimo* or *friísimo*, with the latter tending to be more prevalent.

fuera. The distinction between *fuera* and *afuera* is that the latter is used in stative constructions (*En el verano, me gusta estar afuera en el jardín*). However, one may also find *fuera* used in such stative constructions: *En el verano, me gusta estar fuera en el jardín*. In active constructions, *afuera* is used to indicate movement from one place to another: *Todos salimos afuera para ver las nubes. Fuera,* by contrast, is used to indicate movement from one locale to another: *Juan no está en la ciudad. Salió fuera: está en el campo.* Thus, *fuera* is also used in the stative equivalent: *El está fuera, en el campo.* Thus, the following distinction is usually maintained: *El está afuera* = "He's outside," while *El está fuera* = "He's out of town." However, particularly in Latin America, the distinction tends to be lost in favor of *afuera*.

fuerte. The superlative may be either *fortísimo* or *fuertísimo*, with the latter prevailing colloquially.

funcionario. The feminine is *funcionaria*.

G

génesis. Masculine as the title of a book of the Bible; feminine in its general meaning of "origin."

gente. In some dialects of Spanish, notably Mexican, *gente* is used as a count noun, synonymous with *persona: Muchas gentes piensan así.* In general, however, *gente* is only a mass noun, referring to a group of people. As a consequence, it agrees with a verb in the singular. Note, however, the general Spanish use of set phrases like *buena gente, mala gente* to refer to a specific person: *El es buena gente.* This phrase remains singular even in a plural construction: *Ellos son mala gente.* This lexical item often presents problems of agreement, being grammatically singular and feminine, but semantically plural and common: *La gente está entusiasmada con el proyecto* preserves the sense of a collective singular, but *Hay gente como ellos que no sabe(n) cuidar sus propios intereses* may split between a collective singular and the specification of a plurality. A solution would be to use some other plural item like *personas* or *individuos* in place of *gente.*

geógrafo. The feminine is *geógrafa.*

geólogo. The feminine is *geóloga.*

grande. 1. Directly preceding a noun, the singular form of this adjective, which is both masculine and feminine, is *gran;* the plural is *grandes.* There are exceptions having to do with fixed phrases like *un grande hombre* and the use of the nonreduced form before nouns beginning with *e* (now rare): *grande esperanza;* this latter use may also be found extending to other nouns beginning with a vowel: *grande ilusión. Grande,* however, does not reduce to *gran* when directly preceded itself by *más* or *menos: la más grande fiesta del año.*

2. *Grande* used in a prenominal position tends to refer to "great" in the sense of character (person) or quality (object or idea), while *grande* in a postnominal position tends to refer to size. This distinction, however, may be altered by stylistic considerations.

3. The comparative of *grande* is either *mayor* or *más grande,* with the latter prevailing colloquially. Often, the different meanings of *grande* on the basis of position are maintained by using *mayor* for *grande* in the sense of quality and *más grande* in the sense of size. These comments extend also to *menor* versus *menos grande. Mayor* and *menor* are the preferred forms in comparative utterances involving size, etc., followed by *que: Tú padre es mayor que el mío.*

gratis. Used either as an invariable adjective or as an adverb: *libros gratis, viajar gratis.*

grosso modo. This adverb phrase, meaning "in general terms," is often found preceded by the preposition *a,* but it is unnecessary: *Podemos decir, (a) grosso modo, que hay doscientas personas interesadas en el tema.*

guarda. The feminine noun is the nominalization of the verb *guardar.* The person who performs the action is *el guarda* or *la guarda,* depending on the real-person referent. The feminine form *guardesa* also exists. In the case of compound nouns built on the verb *guardar,* the second element may be singular or plural: *el guardabosque, el guardacostas.* If it is singular, it carries the plural marker: *el guardapolvo, los guardapolvos.*

guardia. The feminine noun refers to the body of guards: *la Guardia Civil.* The person who serves in such a body is *el guardia* or *la guardia* (also *mujer guardia*), depending on the real-person referent.

guía. The feminine noun refers to a book or manual that provides guidance, etc. The person who serves as a guide is *el guía* or *la guía,* depending on the real-person referent.

gustar. 1. With the meaning of "to like," in terms of corresponding English constructions, the role of the subject and object pronouns in Spanish is reversed: *Me gustan esos zapatos* = "I like those shoes." Reference is usually made to English "to appeal to" and "to be pleasing to" as English constructions where the subject and object pronouns match those of Spanish *gustar: Me gustas tú* = "You appeal to me" or "You are pleasing to me." However, English "to find pleasing" orders the pronouns like "to like," but with the possibility of echoing the subject pronoun as an object pronoun to match the Spanish object pronoun: *Nos gusta el panorama* = "We find the view pleasing (to us)."

2. *Gustar de* means "to enjoy," and the subject and object pronouns match the corresponding English ones: *Gustamos de hablar francés* = "We enjoy speaking French."

gusto. The formula *mucho gusto en conocerlo* may also be found with the preposition *de*, which is considered substandard. The use of *de* may be an extension from other social formulas: *encantado de conocerlo, me alegro de conocerlo, tengo el gusto de conocerlo.*

H

h. As all letters are feminine, the name of this letter, *hache*, is also feminine. However, unlike other feminine nouns beginning with a stressed *(h)a*, the immediately preceding articles are *la* and *una*, rather than the feminine *el* and *un.*

haber. 1. As an impersonal verb followed by *que*, with the meaning of "one must/should," all forms are third-person singular, and the present indicative is *hay: Hay que estudiar duro, Había que estudiar duro.*

2. As an impersonal verb followed by a noun, with the meaning of "there is/are," all forms are third-person singular, and the present indicative is *hay: Hay mucha gente aquí, Hay muchas personas aquí, Había mucha gente aquí, Había muchas personas aquí.* However, in the nonpresent indicative forms, it is quite common to encounter plural agreement: *Habían muchas personas aquí.* This agreement is, however, considered substandard.

3. As a personal verb followed by *de*, with the meaning of obligation, there is full agreement with the subject: *Hemos de salir temprano.*

4. *Haber* plus past participle forms the present perfect, also called the *pasado definido* (also, *pretérito perfecto, antepresente, pretérito perfecto actual*) because it refers to a definitive and immediately past event from the point of view of the speaker: *He hablado hoy con Juan.* By contrast, the preterite, in addition to being called the *pretérito*, is also called the *pasado indefinido* because it may refer to the entire range of past time and

not just the immediate past. This distinction is, however, lost in some dialects. Perhaps by French influence, Peninsular Spanish uses the present perfect to cover past references that would in the majority of dialects be covered by the preterite: *Hemos viajado a Italia hace seis meses.* By contrast, some Latin American dialects expand the range of the preterite and use it rather than the present perfect to refer to the immediate past: *Hablé hoy con Juan.* (Note: Spanish also follows the common practice in historical, literary, and other formal texts of using the simple present tense to narrate past events: *Después del golpe militar de 1976, Ferrari deja el país por razones políticas y se traslada a San Pablo, Brasil.*)

hacer. 1. *Hacerse* + noun means "to become" as the result of a conscious effort and with the connotation of something lasting: *Juan se hizo médico. Hacerse* + definite article + noun/adjective is equivalent to "to play (the part of)": *Me hice el distraído para no tener que escuchar sus tonterías.*

2. *Hacer* + point/period in time, with the meaning of "ago," may appear before or after the verb phrase; note the presence of *que* in the former: *Hace un año que vino = Vino hace un año.*

3. Used with a tense that is identical to that of *hacer,* the utterance is equivalent to English "for + time period" expressions: *Hace cinco semanas que está aquí* = "He's been here for five weeks." *Hacía cinco semanas que estaba aquí* = "He'd been here for five years." This expression may also be captured with *desde hacer,* equivalent to English "since": *Está aquí desde hace cinco semanas.* The period expression may also appear first: *Desde hace cinco semanas está aquí.*

4. In weather expressions, *hacer* is used only in the third-person singular, and there is no agreement with a following plural: *Ayer hizo treinta grados.*

hallar. Colloquially, *hallar* (which is often restricted to meaning "to find" as the result of a deliberating quest) is treated as synonymous with *encontrar* (which is often restricted to meaning "to find" in the sense of a chance encounter). Concomitantly, *encontrar* may be used in the restricted sense of *hallar.*

hambre. While this noun is feminine and takes the feminine *el* and *un* as immediately preceding articles, it is frequently treated as masculine, with corresponding adjectival agreement: *Tengo un hambre canino.* This agreement is, however, considered substandard.

harina. This noun is feminine, and since it does not begin with a stressed *(h)a,* the use of the feminine *el* or *un* is unjustified, despite sporadic occurrences.

hasta. 1. As an adverb of quantity placed before a lexical item, *hasta* is synonymous with *incluso* and *aun.*

2. *Hasta que* is followed by the subjunctive when its pragmatic meaning is subsequent to the main verb, but followed by the indicative when its pragmatic meaning is anterior to or correlative with the main verb: *Me quedo hasta que él venga; Me quedé hasta que él vino.* The particle *no* often occurs with the subordinate verb when the main verb is negative; this particle is empty in the sense that it does not signal a negative meaning: *No iré a trabajar hasta que (no) esté recuperado.*

3. With temporal expressions, in some Latin American dialects, *hasta* is equivalent to *solamente* or *no antes: Él llega hasta el lunes = Sólo él llega el lunes. Recién* may be found with this usage in other dialects: *Recién él llega el lunes.*

haz. The feminine noun means "surface" or "face," while the masculine noun means "bundle." In the former case, the feminine articles *el* and *un* are used: *El haz brillosa del disco* versus *El haz abultado de leña.* Confusion between the two nouns is frequent, with conflicting agreements.

he. This independent verb, which occurs only in this form, is used with an accompanying pronoun or noun/noun clause, and often with a locative adverb, with a sense equivalent to English "behold": *He aquí los frutos de su labor.* It is historically related to the verb *haber,* although it is not, as is often assumed, its imperative, which is *habe.*

henchir. This verb means "to stuff," while *hinchar* means "to (cause to) swell."

hender. The form *hendir* is now preferred.

heredar. This verb is both intransitive, in the sense of "to inherit," and transitive, in the sense of "to will/leave as an inheritance." In the latter case, the person receiving the inheritance is an indirect object, while what is inherited is a direct object: *Su padre le heredó la fábrica.*

herpe. Used as both masculine and feminine, although the masculine gender tends to prevail. Usually used in the plural, *los herpes,* while *el herpes* may also be found.

hijodalgo. Variant of *hidalgo.* While the latter forms its plural as *hidalgos* (and *hidalga* becomes *hidalgas*), *hijodalgo* has *hijosdalgo* as the plural and the corresponding *hijadalgo* and *hijasdalgo* in the feminine.

hincha. In some dialects, the word for "sports fan." The form is the same for both masculine and feminine, *el hincha/la hincha* and the plural is *hinchas.* The fans as a group are the *hinchada,* and the verb *hinchar* is used in the sense of "cheerleading/cheering on."

hipérbole. Now customarily used as a feminine noun, it presents premodern uses as a masculine noun.

hirviendo. The present participle of *hervir,* it is one of the few that can be used as an adjectival gerund: *agua hirviendo, aceite hirviendo.* Compare *casa ardiendo* and *hombres trabajando* as other such combinations. With other verbs a clause is the standard construction: *Había gente que estaba gritando* versus *Había gente gritando.* The latter is considered substandard and the result of the influence of English; *Había gente que gritaba* is more standard.

historiar. This verb occurs in conjugations both with a tonic and an atonic stem *i: yo historio* versus *yo historío;* the first stress pattern is the predominant one.

honor. The prevalent construction is *en honor de;* the phrase *en honor a la verdad* is a fixed construction.

huésped. Although the feminine form *huéspeda* exists, *huésped* may also be used as a feminine noun.

I

ibero. Both *ibero* and *íbero* exist, although the former is preferred.

icono. Both *icono* and *ícono* exist, although the latter is preferred.

ignorar. The usual meaning of this verb is *desconocer* or *no saber.* However, the influence of English has created the meaning equivalent to "to ignore," which is considered substandard for *no hacerle caso a alguien.*

imperativo. 1. As substitutes for the command forms, both the future and the present indicative are found, the latter as a polite question: *¿Me acercas la silla, por favor?* In the case of the future, the sense tends to be authoritarian, much like English "you shall": *En lo sucesivo, tú sabrás hacerme caso.*

2. In the case of the positive *vosotros* form, substandard usage may substitute the infinitive: *venir* versus *venid, callaros* versus *callaos.*

imposible. *Ser imposible que* is always followed by a subjunctive verb.

imprimir. Both *impreso* and *imprimido* exist as past participles, with the latter preferred in Latin America. *Impreso* is also a noun meaning a pamphlet or handbill.

inclusive. This adverb is used at the end of a list to stress the inclusion of the last member: *de lunes a viernes inclusive.* Since it is an adverb, an agreement is incorrect.

incluso. Used before a verb to mean the same thing as *hasta, también, aun*, roughly equivalent to English "(you can) even."

incluyendo. By English influence, this participle is used to further specify an inclusionary listing: *Trabajo todos los días, incluyendo el domingo.* Academic usage would prefer *hasta* or *entre ellos* (in which *ellos* refers to *días*).

individua. As the feminine *individuo*, this noun has a strictly negative meaning. Compare *tipa* (from *tipo*) in some Latin American dialects, and the pejorative *tía* in general.

infinitivo. 1. The use of a nominalized infinitive in place of the corresponding nominalization stresses, as in English, the active or performative nature of the verb as opposed to the static nature of the nominalization. The article may or may not be used if the infinitive is unmodified, but is always used if modification is present: *(El) cantar es una linda actividad* versus *El canto es un fenómeno lindo; El diario ir y venir de la gente me molesta.*

2. *Al* + infinitive = *Cuando* + conjugated verb: *Al llegar el Director, le informaré sobre el asunto* = *Cuando llegue el Director, le informaré sobre el asunto.*

3. *A* + infinitive = *si* + present indicative: *A decir verdad, no tengo la solución* = *Si te digo la verdad, no tengo la solución.*

4. *A no* + infinitive = *si no* + imperfect subjunctive: *A no haber un problema, podríamos seguir con el negocio* = *Si no hubiera un problema, podríamos seguir con el negocio.*

5. *De* + infinitive = *si* + present indicative: *De haber algún problema, te llamo* = *Si hay algún problema, te llamo.*

6. *De no* + infinitive = *si no* + imperfect subjunctive: *De no haber un problema, podríamos seguir con el negocio* = *Si no hubiera un problema, podríamos seguir con el negocio.*

7. *Con* + infinitive = *Aunque* + indicative or subjunctive: *Con ser domingo, pienso trabajar igual* = *Aunque sea domingo, pienso trabajar igual.*

influenciar. This verb is considered an English-based substitute for *influir en.*

informar. This is one of several major verbs in Spanish in which there is a tendency to suppress a prepositional connector, which in this case is customarily *de*, although *sobre* is also used: *Informaron de la decisión de la comisión* versus *Informaron la decisión de la comisión.*

ingeniero. The feminine form is *ingeniera.*

inscribir. In general the past participle is *inscrito*; in Argentina, it is *inscripto.*

inserto. This is strictly an adjectival form, although it may alternate with the past participle *insertado.*

íntegro. This adjective is used to indicate that something is complete; *integral* indicates that something goes toward making a phonemenon complete.

interesar. *Me intereso en algo* means that I am interested in something and that something sparks my interest; in the latter case, one might also say *Me interesa algo.* These meanings correlate with *Estoy interesado en algo. Me intereso en algo* may also mean that I have interests (i.e., commercial ones) in something, which correlates with *Soy un interesado en algo.* However, *ser un interesado* has a certain pejorative meaning, indicating that the person is not completely impartial.

ir. 1. As a nonreflexive, this verb indicates movement or procedure toward undertaking something (*vamos a pescar*), while *irse* indicates, with an emphatic connotation, departing for the purpose of undertaking something (*nos vamos a pescar*). *Ir y* + verb indicates emphasis vis-à-vis the second verb: *Voy y le digo* = "I up and tell him." This usage is considered colloquial.

2. *Ir* + gerund describes an ongoing action from the point of reference of the present of the utterance in relation to the future.

J

juez. The feminine is either *jueza* or *juez,* with the latter preferred.

junto. The preposition is either *junto a* or *junto de,* although the former predominates.

L

la. Direct object pronoun, third-person singular. The use of *la* as an indirect object pronoun, third-person singular or plural, is considered substandard, although its use is understandable, since, unlike *le,* which is either masculine or feminine, *la* underscores the fact that a feminine object is involved: *La di (a ella) el libro. La* can also be found where a plural indirect object pronoun would be expected, since indirect object *le* often is invariable regarding number in colloquial and substandard usage. By contrast, as a direct object pronoun, a logically singular *la* may attract the indirect object plural marker blocked by the use of *se* in place of *le* before *la: La libreta se las di a ellas.*

lástima. *Ser una lástima que* ordinarily is followed by the subjunctive when the dependent verb has a future meaning, but the indicative when it has a present meaning, although the subjunctive may also be found in constructions with a present meaning: *Lástima que (hoy) sea lunes. Lástima que* ordinarily takes only the indicative.

laxo. *Laxo* means "lax" or "relaxed," while *laso* means "tired" or "lazy."

le. Indirect object pronoun, masculine and singular; often invariable regarding singular and plural, especially if its referent is an abstract noun: *Le tengo miedo a los exámenes.* In academic Peninsular Spanish, *le*, with its corresponding plural form, *les*, is used as the direct object pronoun for human and animate nouns. In colloquial usage in some Spanish dialects, it may also be used as the direct object pronoun for inanimate nouns, although this usage is considered substandard; the preferred inanimate direct object pronoun is *lo*. In most Spanish American dialects (with the exception of the so-called conservative ones—e.g., Mexico and the Andean region), *le* is exclusively the indirect object pronoun, while *lo* is exclusively the direct object pronoun (see under *la* for feminine third-person pronoun usage). However, it should be noted that there is a discrepancy between what is considered a direct object pronoun and what is considered an indirect object pronoun. For example, a verb like *ayudar*, along with most verbs in which a direct, explicit action is not involved, may be construed in some dialects as demanding a direct object pronoun (*Lo ayudo [a Juan]*), while in others as demanding an indirect object pronoun (*Le ayudo [a Juan]*). By the same token *Le ayudo (a Juan)* may be interpreted as involving a *le* that is a direct object pronoun or involving a *le* that is an indirect object pronoun. A verb like *dar* involves only an indirect object pronoun, for the person affected by or receiving the action of giving, while a verb like *ver* involves only a direct object pronoun, for the person who is seen. In the case of *dar, le* is only an indirect object pronoun as the recipient of the action, while in the case of *ver, le* is only a direct object pronoun as the person being seen.

lejano. *Lejano de* is the preferred construction; *lejano a* is considered substandard.

lejos. *Lejos de* is the preferred construction, although *de* + personal pronoun may alternate with a possessive (e.g., *lejos nuestro*), which is considered substandard.

lente. This noun is feminine in the singular, with the meaning of "lens," while it is masculine in the plural, meaning a "pair of eyeglasses."

lento. The adverb form *lento* may substitute for *lentamente*.

llamado. In the sense of "telephone call." Both *llamado* and *llamada* are correct, although the masculine tends to prevail and is the only form used in the general sense of the nominalization of *llamar.*

lleno. This adjective is always used with *estar,* except in the fixed use in the "Ave María": *llena eres de gracia.*

llover. As the verb "to rain," *llover,* like all weather verbs, is conjugated only in the third-person singular. However, *lloverse,* which means to leak in some dialects, is fully conjugated, according to its subject. *Llover,* as a transitive verb meaning "to rain (down)"—e.g., blows—is also fully conjugated, according to its subject.

lo. See *le* for direct object third-person pronoun usage. *Lo* also may be used as an invariable neuter article before any adjective to indicate the abstract quality of that adjective: *lo bello = la belleza.*

M

mal. *Mal* is both an adjective and an adverb. As an adverb used with active verbs, it alternates with *bien,* and other degree adverbs, to indicate how well something is performed. With *estar,* the adverb *mal* alternates with *bien* to describe how someone feels; *estar* may alternate, in turn, with other roughly synonymous verbs like *sentir* and *encontrarse. Mal* as an adjective is the shortened form of *malo* used before an immediately following noun, and in this usage alternates with *buen/bueno.* Used as a degree adverb with certain adjectives, it has come to constitute a single-word compound: *mal pensado = malpensado;* the same is also true of the adjective *mal* and certain nouns: *un mal entendido = un malentendido,* as well as of certain verbal combinations: *maldecir.* The comparative form of *mal* is *peor,* as either the adverb or the adjective. Note that there is also a masculine *mal.*

maldecido. *Maldecido* is the past participle of *maldecir,* while *maldito* is the accompanying adjectival form.

malo. Used with *ser, malo* indicates quality of character; used with *estar, malo* indicates health. The comparative form of *malo* is *peor* in both senses.

mandar. There are two separate verbal constructions, *mandar* + verb, which means to "order," and *mandar a* + verb, which means to "send (someone) to do something." The two constructions are frequently confused.

manera. Since *de* is the preposition used with *manera* (*de una manera,* etc.), appositional clauses would logically use *de: la manera de que lo hice.* However, it is not unusual to find *en* used in this construction rather than *de. De* is always used followed by an infinitive: *La manera de hacer algo. De manera que* is followed by the indicative in the sense of a consequence, by the subjunctive in the sense of purpose.

mano. The diminutive of *la mano* is both *manita* and *manito,* both treated as feminine. *Mano* is also the shortened form of *hermano* in Mexico and other regions; in this case it is masculine and only *manito* exists as the diminutive.

mañana. This noun is masculine in the sense of "tomorrow," but feminine in the sense of "morning."

mar. In most uses, this noun is masculine. However, *la mar* exists, both as a poetic or archaic form in fixed expressions, and in the expression *la mar de,* meaning "a lot of/many": *Había la mar de libros encima de su mesa.*

maratón. Although found as both a masculine and a feminine noun, the former predominates as the standard form.

margen. Although found as both a masculine and a feminine noun, the former predominates with the meaning of "margin" in the context of measurements and layouts; *la margen* may be found as a synonym of *la orilla.*

más. *Más de* indicates the upper limit of the same thing in quantitative terms: *más de diez muertos,* while *más que* indicates a contrast between two things: *Se trata de amor, más que de cariño* (the *de* here is an obligatory particle of *tratarse*). *Más que* may involve comparisons between two entities, vis-à-vis the same adjective or adverb: *Ellos son más respetuosos que ustedes; Él canta más desafinado que María.*

me. In the co-occurrence of *me* and *te,* the order *te me* is admissable, but *me te* is not: *Te me fuiste,* but not **Me te fui.*

medialuna. The plural is normally *medialunas,* although *medias lunas* may be found as a hypercorrection.

médico. The feminine is *médica.*

medio. Used before a noun or adjective, it means "half": *medio inútil, medio albañil.* In this case it is invariable in form: *medio estudiantes.* Used following a noun it means "mediocre": *un trabajo medio.* In expressions like *el hombre medio* or *el consumidor medio,* it means "ordinary."

mejora. Although *mejora* and *mejoría* may be used as synonyms, the latter is specifically a medical improvement, while *mejora* is equivalent to English "betterment."

menester. The literary construction *es menester que* takes the subjunctive. As an adjective, it is invariable in number and gender: *Las medidas que es menester tomar.*

menos. The distinction between *menos de* and *menos que* parallels that of *más de* and *más que.*

mero. *Mero* is used in Mexico as an adjective meaning *mismo*, especially with pronouns (*yo mero*), as a degree adverb meaning something equivalent to English "truly" (*mero bueno*), or as an adverb meaning *casi* (*mero me morí*).

México. Although usage in Spain prefers *Méjico* and its derivations, official Mexican usage is *México*, with corresponding derivations.

mientras. *Mientras* (usually without a connecting *que*) introduces a clause in the indicative and signifies "while (at the same time, in the same sense)." *Mientras* is a conjunction that introduces an indicative that correlates with the main verb ("while along with"): *Mientras estoy en casa, veo televisión. Mientras que* (and the *que* is usually used) is used with a subjunctive to capture the sense of "as long as," "(not) until": *No seré feliz mientras él viva/no haya muerto.*

ministro. The feminine is *ministra*, although constructions like *la Primer Ministro* may be found.

mismo. *Mismo* is used in two emphatic ways: 1. It is used with the reflexive pronouns to underscore identity: *Se vio a sí mismo en el espejo* = He saw himself (not someone else) in the mirror.

2. It is used with subjects to stress identity: *Unamuno mismo lo dijo* = Unamuno himself said that.

3. Used before a noun, *mismo* means "same"; used following a noun it means "oneself."

modelo. The feminine form is *la modelo.*

modo. *De modo que* parallels *de manera que* in the opposition between indicative and subjunctive in the following verb.

molestar. In some usages, *molestar* takes an indirect object in the sense of "to annoy," and a direct object in the sense of "to sexually molest." This pattern has yet to be standardized. Compare the construction *Le molestaba su forma de mirar* and *Él la molestaba con su forma de mirar.*

morir. Although normally intransitive, with or without the emphatic *se*, the past participle *muerto* often alternates with *matado* in passive sentences: *Cinco hombres fueron matados/muertos por la guerrilla*, although the corresponding active would only be *Mataron a cinco hombres.*

motor. The feminine of this adjective is *motriz*, although the less accepted *motora* may be found. *Motriz* used as a masculine adjective is considered substandard.

muy. As the degree adverb form of *mucho*, *muy* is used before adverbs and adjectives. In some dialects, there is an augmentative, *muy mucho: Me gusta muy mucho.*

N

nacer. The passive construction *fue nacido*, etc., although found, followed by a place and/or a date, is considered a calque of English *was born. Nació*, etc., is the standard form.

nada. Like all negatives, *nada* placed before a verb or other form being negated is not followed by *no*, although when placed after the form being negated, that form is preceded by *no: No importa nada = Nada importa.* As a noun, *nada* is feminine.

nadie. Like all negatives, *nadie* as a preverbal subject is not followed by *no*, although when placed postverbally, the verb is preceded by *no: No vino nadie = Nadie vino.*

necesario. *Ser necesario que* is followed by the subjunctive.

necesitar. *Necesitar que* is followed by the subjunctive.

negar. *Negar que* is followed by the subjunctive, while *No negar que* is followed by the indicative. In strong assertions, the reverse distribution of indicative/subjunctive may be found, but it is not the predominant usage. In these latter cases, the strong assertion may involved echoing a prior assertion: *¿Usted dice que ellos vinieron? Pues, yo niego que vinieron.*

ni bien. As a synonym of *cuando* and *tan pronto como*, *ni bien* is followed by the subjunctive when it refers to a future event and by the indicative when it refers to the past or an iterative present.

ninguno. 1. Parelleling *alguno*, *ninguno* is reduced to *ningún* before and immediately following masculine nouns. Although the reduced form may also be found before feminine nouns beginning with stressed *(h)a*, it is considered substandard.

2. Like all negatives, *ninguno* placed before a verb or other form being negated is not followed by *no;* however, when it appears following the verb or form being negated, the latter is preceded by *no: No lo dijo ninguno de ellos = Ninguno de ellos lo dijo.*

3. When used as a negative adjective, *ninguno* precedes the noun, but *alguno* is preferred in a postnominal position: *No hay ninguna razón para decir eso = No hay razón alguna para decir eso.*

4. In constructions like *ninguno de nosotros* verb agreement may be in the third-person singular or in the first-person plural, even when *de nosotros* is suppressed: *Ninguno vamos.*

no. The customary prenominal equivalent of the English prefix *non* in Spanish is *no,* which may or may not be followed by a hyphen: *el no-sexismo = el no sexismo.* The latter tends to predominate.

nomás. This form alternates with *no más* as a synonym for *solamente.*

nominar. This verb and its nominalizations, *nominado* and *nominación,* are considered calques of English "to nominate" and "nominee/nomination." *Proponer como candidato* is the more academic verbal construction, with *candidato* and *la candidatura* matching the two nominalizations. Note that the verb form *candidatear* also exists.

nos. The standard first-person plural appears as *los* in some dialects, notably substandard Chilean Spanish.

nosotros. The feminine is *nosotras.* When used as the so-called royal we, verb and object or reflexive pronoun agreement is plural, and adjectival agreement is also plural: *Nosotros estamos contentos de saberlo.* However, if the archaic subject pronoun *nos* is used, adjectival agreement is singular: *Nos estamos contento de saberlo.*

notable. *Es notable que* is followed by the subjunctive.

nuevo. 1. The superlative is both *novísimo* and *nuevísimo,* although the latter is considered colloquial.

2. Used before a noun, *nuevo* means "another"; used following a noun it means "new."

O

o. The conjunction *o* changes to *u* before words beginning with *(h)o.*

obligatorio. *Ser obligatorio que* is followed by the subjunctive.

obvio. *Ser obvio que* is followed by the indicative; when negated, it is followed by the subjunctive.

ocurrir. A distinction is maintained between *ocurrirme*, etc., "to happen to me," and *ocurrírseme*, etc., "to occur to me."

oficial. The feminine is both *oficial* and *oficiala*, the latter with reference to someone who practices an *oficio*, the former in the sense of a "public official."

oír. 1. Historically, written usage has varied with respect to the *í*; it is now standard to use the accent mark. Note that, alongside the standard second-person singular imperative *oye*, there is a colloquial form, *oyes*.
  2. When followed by a verb that expresses an action "heard," the verb appears as a gerund if the action is ongoing, but as an infinitive if it is perfective (compare: *La oí gritando* versus *La oí gritar*). This pattern extends to other perception verbs like *ver, sentir, encontrar, escuchar,* and *mirar.*

ojalá. Meaning *Dios quiera que* in Arabic, this construction is always followed by the subjunctive. In some dialects, it may appear as *ojalá que* or as *ojalá y que.*

olvidar. There are various, basically synonymous, syntactic constructions involving *olvidar.* The verb may or may not be used reflexively and may or may not have a connecting preposition *de.* Standard usage tends to prefer *olvidarse de* and *olvidar: Olvidé el libro* = *Me olvidé del libro.* Note that these two constructions are ambiguous with respect to whether the forgetting was deliberate or not. As with other such ambiguous verbs, Spanish uses the so-called "*se* for unplanned occurrences" to make explicit the nondeliberate nature of the forgetting: *Se me olvidó el libro.*

ómnibus. The plural is *ómnibus.*

oponer. *Oponerse a que* is followed by the subjunctive.

orden. The noun is feminine in the sense of "order = command" or a religious order; masculine in the sense of "order = arrangement." The phrase *orden del día* is both masculine and feminine, according to which of these senses it matches: "password" (feminine) versus "agenda" (masculine).

otro. 1. In reciprocal constructions, such as *Se saludaron uno a otro*, the singular indicates that two individuals were involved (regardless of gender distribution, although if two women were involved, *una a otra* would occur). *Se saludaron unos a otros* indicates that more than two individuals were involved. *Se saludaron el uno al otro* and *Se saludaron los unos a los otros* are simply more emphatic in regard to the reciprocity of action.
  2. The combination *un otro* is considered substandard, as in *Un otro hombre* rather than *Otro hombre.*
  3. *Otro* as a feminine form preceding nouns beginning with stressed *(h)a* (by analogy with feminine *el* and *un*) is considered substandard.

P

pa. Sometimes written *pa'*, this is a colloquial variant of *para*.

padecer. This is one of several major verbs in Spanish in which there is a tendency to suppress a prepositional connector, which in this case is customarily *de: Padece de asma* versus *Padece asma*.

pago. In some dialects, this adjective alternates with the past participle *pagado: La cuenta está pagada/paga*.

pantalón. This noun is used in both the singular and the plural as equivalent to the English "pair of pants."

papá. Three diminutives exist for this noun: *papito, papacito,* and *papaíto,* the first two being the most common in Latin America.

par. Although this noun is masculine, note should be taken of the fixed expression *a la par de,* "on the same level as."

para. 1. Alternates with *a* as the more emphatic partner (cf. also *hasta*) to indicate the direction toward and the indirect noun complement of a verb. This latter use also includes benefactive meanings: *Lo hice para Juan.* In time expressions, *para* indicates an approximate point in the future: *Lo tendremos listo para el martes.*

2. In its contrasting uses with *por* as an equivalent for English "for," *para* is the goal or purpose for/toward which an action is oriented, while *por* expresses the anterior cause or motivation for/because of which an action takes place; in this distribution, *por* also indicates the path of an action: *Lo arrojé para el arco* (direction toward) versus *Lo arrojé por el arco* (path through); *Lo hice para Juan* (toward benefiting him) versus *Lo hice por Juan* (on account of him/his need/his motivation).

3. Either *por* or *para* is used with *estar* to express English "to be about to."

4. *Para con* is a compound preposition used with personal objects to express an attitude or a feeling toward them: *Usted es siempre muy gentil para con nosotros.*

5. In time expressions, *para* is used to indicate minutes before the hour: *Faltan diez minutos para las cuatro.* This usage is, however, considered by some an English calque, preferring instead *Son las cuatro menos diez.*

pariente. The feminine is *parienta,* although *pariente* may be found.

pasable. This adjective is used to indicate something like English "okay."

pasible de. This adjective is used to indicate that someone or something is "susceptible" to an accusation or criticism.

pegar. When used with a direct object, this verb means "to glue," "to stick to": *Lo pegué en la pared.* Used with an indirect object, it means "to hit": *Le pegué duramente.*

pena. *No valer la pena que* is followed by the subjunctive.

pensar. *Pensar que* is usually followed by the indicative, and *no pensar que* by the subjunctive. In cases of strong assertion, however, the usage may be reversed. The construction *pensar de que* is considered substandard. In some dialects, *pienso que* is more frequent than *creo que* to express an opinion, as in *pienso que sí. Pensar* + infinitive = "to plan, to intend." *Pensar de* is followed by the subject of an opinion or feeling: *¿Qué piensas de este libro?*, while *pensar en* is followed by the subject of someone's thoughts: *Estoy pensando en ellos.*

pequeño. The comparative of this adjective is *menor*, although *más pequeño* is quite frequent.

perder. Used reflexively, this verb is equivalent to English "to miss": *Me perdí el programa de ayer.* Like a number of verbs, *perder* is ambiguous as to the deliberateness or nondeliberateness of an action: *Perdí la moneda.* The so-called *"se* for unplanned occurrences" is used to underscore the nondeliberateness of the act of losing: *Se me perdió la moneda.*

permitir. When the subject of a dependent clause used with *permitir* is moved forward, it appears as an indirect object: *Permití que ella volviera* = *Le permití volver.*

pero. *Pero* can be used to correlate two actions, when the first is negative and the second is additional to the first or is in spite of the first: *No quise hacerlo pero lo hice igual.* In cases where two actions are contrasted such that the second replaces the first, *sino que* is used: *No lo vi, sino que lo oí.* The same contrast exists with nonclauses: *Decepcionado, pero no triste* versus *No contento sino triste.*

pesar. *A pesar de que* is followed by the indicative when it asserts a fact, by the subjunctive when it states a circumstance or condition that is not necessarily a confirmed fact: *A pesar de que todos somos seres humanos, a veces nos comportamos como animales* versus *A pesar de que sean las diez, no tenemos que comer en seguida* (it may or may not actually be 10 P.M.).

pese. *Pese a que* is a more literary variant of *a pesar de que.*

pie. Both *a pie juntillas* and *a pies juntillas* exist with the meaning of "without a doubt"; the expression usually occurs with *creer* or a similar verb: *Creíamos a pie juntillas todo lo que nos decía.* The form *a pie juntillo* also exists.

pinza. Used in both the singular and the plural as equivalent to English "pliers."

placer. Archaic synonym of *gustar* in the sense of *to be pleasing: Me place que hayas venido.*

pluscafé. In the sense of an "afterdinner drink" (in reality, a postcoffee liqueur), this is an erroneous version of the French *pousse-café* (literally, "coffee chaser").

pobre. Used before a noun, it means "pitiful"; used following a noun it means "poor/not rich": *Un pobre hombre* versus *Un hombre pobre.*

poco. *un poco de.* Presumably this would be an invariant form: *un poco de amor, un poco de alegría.* However, colloquially *poco* may show agreement with the object of the following preposition, as in the famous song lyric *una poca de gracia.*

poder. 1. The more academic *no poder menos de* alternates with the colloquial *no poder menos que.*

2. *Puede ser que* is followed by the subjunctive. However, in some dialects, notably in Chile, the phrase is *pueda ser que* followed by the indicative.

podrir. This infinitive form alternates with *pudrir.* The past participle is *podrido,* but *pudr-* is the root used in the various conjugations: *pudre, pudría, pudriera,* etc.

poeta. Although the feminine *poetisa* exists, the latter is now used pejoratively, while *la poeta* is the preferred neutral feminine form.

por. 1. For the contrasts with *para,* see the latter.

2. *Por* is used to mark the agent of passive constructions, although only with active verbs. In constructions where the meaning is stative, *por* alternates with *de: Viene acompañada por/de muchas amigas.*

3. The construction *por* + adjective + *que,* in the sense of the English "no matter how + adjective," the following verb is in the subjunctive: *Por malos que sean, después de todo son seres humanos.* This construction also combines with adverbs: *Por bien que cante, no es una estrella.*

4. In a construction like *Este es el trabajo por discutir* (cf. *a* 10.), the preposition implies that the discussion is still pending.

5. *Por mucho/más que* is usually followed by the subjunctive; however, the indicative may be found as a strong assertion, particularly in the preterite: *Por mucho que estudie, nunca lo va a entender* versus *Por mucho que estudió, no pudo aprobar el examen.* The latter asserts that he did, in fact, study hard.

porque. This causal conjunction is written as one word in declarative statements, but as two words, with an accent on *qué*, in questions: *¿Por qué viniste? Porque no tuve otra cosa que hacer.* Like other question words, *por qué* also occurs in indirect or implied questions: *No sé por qué lo dijo así.* The noun *el porqué*, "the reason why," is written as one word. Note that in Spanish, as an exception to a previous statement, where English would use "Why (not)?," Spanish uses *porque no;* equivalent to the meaning of "just because" is either *porque no* or *porque sí*, depending on whether the statement referred to is, respectively, negative or positive: *¿Por qué lo dices? Porque sí | ¿Por qué no vienes? Porque no.*

pos. This written form is often found as a transcription of the colloquial Mexican pronunciation of *pues*.

pos-. Both *pos-* and *post-* are found as prefixes. It is customary to use the former, which is preferred, without a hyphen, while *post-* often occurs followed by a hyphen, although not necessarily: *posmodernismo* and *postmodernismo*.

posible. *Ser posible que* is followed by the subjunctive.

preciso. *Ser preciso que* is followed by the subjunctive.

preferible. *Ser preferible que* is followed by the subjunctive.

preferir. This verb cannot be negated; rather, the negative scope is attributed to its dependent phrase or clause: *Prefiero no decírtelo.*

prescindible. *Ser (im)prescindible que* is followed by the subjunctive.

prescribir. The generalized past participle is *prescrito;* in Argentina, *prescripto* predominates.

presentar. In the meaning of "to introduce someone to someone else," in order to avoid ambiguity between the person being introduced and the person making the acquaintance, the personal *a* may be omitted before the person being introduced: *Presenté (a) Juan a María.*

presidente. The feminine is *presidenta*.

prestar. Spanish does not have a single-word equivalent of "to borrow." *Pedir prestado* is used to request to borrow, *tomar prestado* is used for the act of borrowing, and *tener prestado* is the result of the borrowing, equivalent to "to have on loan." Following the same pattern, *prestar* alternates with *dar prestado* for the act of lending: *Le pedí prestado el libro, Lo tomé prestado, Me lo dio prestado = Me lo prestó, Lo tengo prestado.*

pretencioso. *Ser pretencioso que* is followed by the subjunctive.

primero. The form used before masculine singular nouns is *primer.* It is considered substandard to use *primer* as a feminine form. In dates, *primero* is the only cardinal number used: *el primero de junio,* but *el dos de junio, el tres de junio,* etc. The first is written as *1º de junio.*

prístino. This form is preferred over *pristino.*

probable. *Ser probable que* is followed by the subjunctive.

problema. *Ser un problema que* is followed by the subjunctive.

pronto. *Tan pronto como* is followed by the subjunctive when it refers to the future; by the indicative with other temporal references.

propio. Used before a noun, it typically means "own"; used following a noun it means "just/appropriate," although these distinctions may often be lost in actual use: *Conduzco un coche propio = Conduzco mi propio coche.* However, *Esa no es conducta propia de un profesor.*

proponer. This verb is followed by the indicative when a general fact is being asserted (*Propuso que la tierra se movía alrededor del sol*), but by the subjunctive when something is being hypothesized or given as a desirable suggestion (*Propuso que la reunión se realizara a las diez de la manana*).

proscribir. The past participle is generally *proscrito;* however, in Argentina *proscripto* is used.

prueba. For most dialects, *tomar una prueba* is what the teacher does, *dar una prueba* is what the student does. The same pattern applies to similar words, e.g., *examen.* By influence of English "to take an exam" and "to give an examen," usage is sometimes found reversed. *Sufrir una prueba/un examen* applies to what students do.

psicología. In this and other words with the same prefix, the *p* is now only articulated in hypercorrect pronunciations.

pudrir. See *podrir.*

puente. Generally, this noun is masculine, although it may be found treated as feminine.

puesto. *Puesto que* is followed by the indicative.

puro. In the sense of "one and the same," *puro* is only found in Latin America: *la pura verdad.* Note that this is a strictly prenominal meaning. In postnominal position, *puro* in all dialects means "pure": *Es agua pura.* In general usage, *puro* as a prenominal adjective means *solamente: Ese vino es pura agua.*

pus. This noun is generally masculine, and feminine uses are considered substandard.

Q

que. 1. As with other question words, in indirect or implied questions, *qué* is distinguished from *que: Me dijo que me preocupaban las cosas; Me pregunté qué me preocupaba.*

2. Although dependent clauses are routinely introduced by *que* (unless they are introduced by a question word or one of the few conjunctions, like *cuando,* that do not include *que*), *rogar* often is not: *Les rogamos tengan a bien permanecer sentados.* Such a usage, however, is strictly formal and formulaic.

3. *Que* may be omitted in a dependent clause that contains a subsequent dependent clause: *Me dijo que el asunto que habían tratado era delicado = Me dijo el asunto que habían tratado era delicado.*

4. Prepositional particles accompanying dependent verbs appear before the conjunction *que: El asunto de que hablábamos.*

5. The dependent conjunction *que* may or may not appear without the article; however, the article appears for emphasis or in order to avoid ambiguity: *Los temas del día de los que hablábamos* versus *Los temas del día del que hablábamos.* In the first case, the dependent clause is specified as modifying *temas;* in the second case, *día.*

6. *El que,* etc., is more properly restrictive and alternates with *el cual,* which is generally nonrestrictive. Note that in *el que,* the article carries the phrase stress, while in *el cual,* the conjunction carries the phrase stress. However, with prepositions of more than two syllables, typically compound ones, *el cual* tends to be used to the exclusion of *el que: La fiesta durante la cual te conocí, fue un gran acontecimiento. Durante la que* may, however, be found.

quedar. 1. In general terms, *quedarse* is used in a literal sense of "remaining behind," "staying in a place," while *quedar* covers the equivalent of English "to end up," "to be left over," "to remain more of": *Me quedé seis meses en México; Quedan seis temas que tratar.* However, *quedar,* especially when used with adjectives and other descriptive words to describe "ending up/remaining in a state" may, like other such combinations, carry an emphatic *se: El muy cretino se quedó babeando; Me quede sorprendida de los resultados del examen.*

2. *Quedar en* means "to agree to."

3. *Quedarse con* means "to retain," "to keep." In colloquial usage, however, the preposition may disappear and a direct object pronoun may be used: *Me quedé con los libros = Me quedé los libros, = Me los quedé.*

quien. This conjunction is used only to refer to people (rarely personalized animals). It may alternate with *el que* or *el cual*. In nonrestrictive contexts *quien* is usually replaced by *que* unless accompanied by a preposition, in which case either *quien* is retained or *el que* or *el cual* is used: *La persona de quien hablaba* = *La persona de la que hablaba; María, quien es mi hermana, viene hoy* = *María, que es mi hermana, viene hoy*. Like other question words, *quién* may appear in indirect or implied questions: *Quiero saber de quién estás hablando*. Note that both *quien* and *quién* have plural forms, *quienes* and *quiénes*.

quitar. There is considerable dialect variation between *quitar* and *sacar* in the sense of "to remove clothing," with *quitar* being considered more formal. This variation also extends to numerous metaphorical expressions involving *quitar* and *sacar: quitar años de encima* versus *sacar años de encima*, in the sense of "suddenly looking years younger."

quizás. Both *quizá* and *quizás* occur, with the former being the more literary one. Either may be followed by either the indicative or the subjunctive, depending on the degree of implied assertion being made: the greater the assertion, the more likely the indicative. However, normally, the subjunctive is found.

R

radio. Although universally feminine with the meaning of "radio communications," there is dialect variation with respect to the designation for the apparatus. In Mexico and northern Latin America, *el radio* prevails, while *la radio* prevails in Spain and the Southern Cone.

rápido. The adverb form *rápido* may substitute for *rápidamente*.

recién. In some dialects, the adverb *recién* + conjugated verb replaces the more standard *acabar de* + infinitive: *Recién llegamos de Buenos Aires* = *Acabamos de llegar de Buenos Aires*. *Recién* also appears before past participles with a meaning equivalent to English "just." When used with an adverb, it has the meaning of "not before/until": *Recién ahora lo pude hacer*.

recordar. This verb is synonymous with *acordarse de*. Frequently, the two verbs are crossed syntactically, with the latter occurring without the *de* and *recordar* occurring reflexively, with or without *de*. Both of these usages are considered substandard. Note that there is a use of *recordar* that is not synonymous with *acordarse de*, which is *asemejarse a: Esta casa recuerda/se asemeja a la casa de mis abuelos*.

régimen. The plural is *regímenes.*

reír. The differentiation between *reír* and *reírse* is vague. *Reirse de algo/ alguien* seems to prevail, especially with emphasis on the inchoative nature of the action "burst out laughing." *Reír,* by contrast, is used to indicate the ongoing or imperfective nature of the action "to go on laughing," and it tends to be intransitive. There is a transitive use, however, in the sense of "laugh along with": *Juan ríe las gracias del jefe.* Note that, although historically the use of the written accent has varied, *reír* now always carries a written accent on the infinitive and derived forms. Also, the preterite, *rió,* carries a written accent to indicate that the form is pronounced as two syllables.

reloj. Although the *j* is only pronounced in hypercorrect speech, the plural is *relojes,* with the *j* being pronounced. The form *relós* and its pronunciation, although reasonable on the basis of the singular form, is considered substandard.

reo. The feminine noun is *la reo,* although *rea* exists as a feminine adjective.

reóstato. The form *reostato* is considered substandard.

reserva. In the sense of English "tourist/travel reservation," *reserva* alternates with the English calque *reservación.*

resfrío. Both *resfrío* and *resfriado* exist as equivalents of English "head cold."

respecto. The three constructions, *respecto a, con respecto a,* and *respecto de* are all synonymous equivalents of English "with respect/regard to."

restaurant. This French word exists in Spanish in several forms. Spelled as in French, it is pronounced, and also may be spelled, as *restorán,* with the plural *restoranes.* It is also spelled, and pronounced accordingly, as *restaurante,* with the plural *restaurantes.* The spelling *restaurant* has as its plural *restaurants.*

rogar. Frequently, in fixed expressions, this verb occurs without a dependent clause *que: Rogamos al señor cliente revise la cuenta antes de efectuar el pago correspondiente.*

S

saber. In some dialects, notably Mexican, *No saber si* is followed by the subjunctive; dominant usage takes the indicative. *No saber que,* by contrast, universally takes the subjunctive, while *saber que* takes the indicative. *No saber qué* takes the indicative: *No sabe qué pasó con el dinero.*

sacar. Concerning confusion between *sacar* and *quitar*, see the latter.

salir. *Salir con que* takes the indicative.

salvo. *Salvo que* takes the subjunctive.

santo. As part of a saint's name, the reduced form *San* is used before masculine names; the full form is retained before names beginning with *To-* and *Do-*, typically *Santo Domingo* and *Santo Tomás.* By contrast, the adjective *santo* is not reduced: *Lo llamamos el santo David porque es tan bueno.*

sastre. The feminine is predominantly *sastra*, although *sastresa* exists; cf. *modista.*

satisfacer. The preferred academic root for the preterite and the imperfect/future subjunctive is *satisfic-: satisficiera.* Forms like *satisfaciera* are considered substandard.

se. 1. This participle is one of the most distinguishing characteristics of Spanish and generates some of its most complex syntactic patterns. One of its primary uses is to signal third-person direct and indirect objects that are either reflexive or reciprocal (plural only): *Juan me ve a mí* versus *Juan se ve a sí mismo; Ellos se miran a sí mismos en el espejo* versus *Ellos se miran unos a otros en el espejo.*

2. *Se* also appears as an integral part of some verbs, particularly intransitive ones; often two verbs are distinguished from each other by the presence or absence of this particle, e.g., *ir* versus *irse.*

3. Reflexive *se*, along with the other reflexive pronouns, is used for unstressed possession: *Me toqué la cara con la mano* (for emphatic purposes, the possessive may be used, without the reflexive pronoun, but only infrequently). Note that some spontaneous actions of the body take neither the possessive nor the reflexive: *Abrí los ojos, Levanté la mano, Estiré la pierna;* the implication being that they predominantly occur with reference to one's own body.

4. *Se* may occur as an emphatic particle with a range of transitive action verbs and certain intransitive verbs of existence or state. For example, *Juan murió el año pasado* states the facts of his death; *Se murió de cáncer* gives emphasis to the process of dying. In the case of transitive action verbs, the *se* underscores the completion or the exaggeration of the process: *Comí todo el chocolate* states a neutral fact; *Me comí todo el chocolate* stresses the outrageousness of having done so. In English, a separate verb would be used, usually with an accompanying particle: "I

wolfed all the chocolate *down."* Emphatic *se* may also occur in commands with intransitive verbs of motion: *Súbase a la silla.* This *se* may also have an inchoative meaning; again English would use either a separate verb and/or a verbal particle: *Nos dormimos en seguida* ("we *fell* right asleep") *y dormimos cuatro horas* ("and we slept four hours"). *Caer* versus *caerse* matches English "to fall" versus "to fall down."

5. The most complex use of *se* is as a "dummy" subject, filling the gap left by an unspecified real subject. In English, empty "they" or "you" may be used, along with "one" and similar forms, including an agentless passive. When *se* is used in Spanish, it immediately precedes the verb, and negatives or other particles precede it: *No se ve nada* versus *Juan no ve nada.* Routinely, the direct object of a transitive verb in such a construction determines the verb agreement: *Se ve basura por todas partes, Se ven desperdicios por todas partes.* Infrequently, a plural direct object may not trigger plural verb agreement: *Se vende cosas lindas en aquella tienda.* However, if the direct object is preceded by the personal *a* (i.e., typically, a human noun), agreement is always singular: *Se saluda a la persona, Se saluda a las personas.* In generic statements involving human direct objects where the personal *a* is absent, a plural direct object may signal plural verb agreement: *Se solicitan vendedores.* A substitute for the dummy *se* may be an empty third-person plural: *Se dice siempre la verdad = Dicen siempre la verdad.* *Uno* may also be used as a formal empty subject.

6. *Se* also occurs as a substitute for indirect object *le(s)* in contact with the third-person direct object pronouns: *Se lo dijimos a Juan.*

7. In some colloquial usages, notably in Argentina, *se* that is part of an imperative may carry the plural marker: standard *Siéntense* versus both *Siéntensen* and *Siéntesen.*

seguida. Both *enseguida* and *en seguida* exist.

seguir. *Seguir* + gerund describes the duration or repetition of an action begun in the past but ongoing at the point of reference of the utterance. *Continuar* may also be used in such constructions.

según. Like *entre,* this preposition takes subjective pronouns: *según yo.* *Según que* takes the indicative in asserting a correlated adverb clause, the subjunctive in asserting a determining condition. *Según y como,* like *como,* takes the indicative if the condition has been specified, but the subjunctive if it has yet to be specified.

seguro. *Estar seguro de que* takes the indicative; *no estar seguro de que* takes the subjunctive. The preposition *de* is often omitted in colloquial speech.

semejante. Used before a noun, it means "such a"; used following a noun, it means "similar."

sendos. Used only in the plural, with a feminine form, *sendas*, to indicate "one for each one": *Nos dieron sendas infracciones* ("we each got a ticket").

sentir. *Sentir que* is followed by either the indicative or the subjunctive, depending on whether an assertion of fact is being made (indicative) or whether a statement of feeling is being made. *Siento que no pudieron venir* would be roughly equivalent to English "I regret they weren't able to come," while *Siento que no lo hayas podido hacer* would correspond roughly to "I am (truly) sorry you were not able to do it."

septiembre. The form *setiembre* is also used, the first being considered the most academic. The same is true of *séptimo* versus *sétimo*.

ser. 1. *Ser* + an unmodified human noun usually is unaccompanied by an article: *Él es profesor.* The definite article will appear if the noun is modified: *Él es el profesor que te dije.* The indefinite article carries with it a negative connotation: *Él es un ladrón.*

2. *Ser* is used to introduce predicate adjectives that are unmarked with respect to their predicating function: *Ella es alta.* If, however, the predicating function is marked by virtue of representing a modification the speaker wishes to stress or some other sort of perceived uniqueness, *estar* replaces *ser*: *La casa está muy bonita con todos los arreglos que has hecho.* There is a regular pattern of alternation between *ser* and *estar* with a large nucleus of adjectives. In some cases the meaning is "permanent" versus "transitory" (e.g., *feliz*), while in other cases different semantic notions are involved (e.g., *ser vivo* means "to be crafty," while *estar vivo* means "to be alive"). Note, however, that some adjectives can only be used with *estar* (e.g., *muerto, lleno,* and *vacío*), while others can typically only be used with *ser* (e.g., adjectives of nationality or origin). Predominantly, adjectives based on past participles use *estar*, although those that have achieved a semantic status independent of their verbal origin occur with *ser* and enter into the *ser* versus *estar* alternation. It should be noted that there is considerable dialect variation concerning some items.

3. *Ser de* indicates origin. Compare *estar de*, which means "to play the part of."

4. *Ser* + past particle (+ agent) is the standard passive construction in Spanish and predominantly involves transitive action verbs. The state resulting from the passive is expressed with *estar*, without the agent: *La puerta es abierta por la criada; La puerta está abierta.*

servir. This verb, like *ayudar*, is ambiguous as to whether it takes a direct or an indirect object. Dialect variation is one factor (in Mexico, it tends to take an indirect object, while in Argentina, it tends to take a direct object). The more active and transitive the verb is felt to be, the more likely a direct object will appear.

si. There are basically three types of "if" sentences in Spanish.

1. Statements of cause-and-effect use the indicative and may appear in any tense, in conformance with the real-world time referent. However, customarily such utterances occur in the present tense as "timeless" statements about the world and human events: *Si llueve, uso paraguas; Si tengo hambre, como algo; Si uno tiene sueño, se acuesta;* etc.

2. Statements of a hypothetical nature or that express contrary-to-fact conditions make use of the present subjunctive if their real-world reference is present, and the pluperfect subjunctive if their real-world reference is past: *Si viviéramos en Suecia, hablaríamos sueco y no español; Si la semana tuviera ocho días, tendríamos uno más de descanso; Si el Cid no hubiera sido buen vasallo, no habría asumido las dimensiones de un héroe.*

3. Polite statements of condition may use either the present indicative or the imperfect subjunctive in the *si* clause and either the present indicative, the future, or the conditional in the result clause: *Si tiene/tuviera tiempo, llámenos.* Mixing of present and past forms is common, and typically these sentences involve a limited range of verbs in the *si* clause, those that serve to express an oblique command: *Si fuera/es usted tan amable de darme su tarjeta, lo anuncio/anunciaré al Gerente; Si usted quisiera acompañarme, lo llevaría a su despacho.*

4. In a few expressions like *saber si* the present subjunctive may occur.

5. The particle *si* occurs to make a positive assertion about a verb: *Pero si lo creo.* It may also occur emphatically (*Él sí viene*), in which case an accent is used.

6. The imperfect indicative often replaces the conditional in contrary-to-fact sentences: *Si tuviera el tiempo, lo haría/hacía en seguida.*

siempre. *Siempre que* may take either the indicative or the subjunctive, although the former predominates in a temporal sense, while the subjunctive is used excusively in a conditional sense. *Siempre y cuando* is followed by the subjunctive. Note that *siempre y cuando que* may also be found.

simple. Used before a noun, it means "mere" for both people and things. Used following a noun referring to a person it means "simple minded": *Juan es una persona simple = Juan es una persona tonta.* Used following a noun referring to a thing, it means "not complex": *Quiero un arreglo simple* = I'm looking for a simple arrangement.

sinfín. This masculine noun means "an infinitive amount," and there is a corresponding adjectival phrase, written as two words, *sin fin.*

sino. See *pero* regarding contrasts. Substandard usage often writes *si no* ("otherwise") as *sino: Hay que trabajar—si no nos morimos de hambre.*

siquiera. Used as a conjunction synonymous with *aunque,* it is followed by the subjunctive.

sirviente. The feminine is *sirvienta.*

solo. The adjective *solo* is distinguished from the adverb, a synonym of *solamente,* by a written accent on the latter, *sólo.* However, in many written usages, there is a growing tendency for the adverb to appear without the accent. Note that in the construction *no solo . . . sino* the written accent virtually never appears.

sonreír. The alternation between *sonreírse* and *sonreír* parallels *reírse* and *reír.*

sorprendente. *Ser sorprendente que* is followed by the subjunctive.

sosia. This noun in the singular also appears as *sosias* (considered acceptable) and as *sosía* and *sosías* (considered substandard).

sospechoso. *Ser sospechoso que* is followed by the subjunctive.

su. It is considered substandard, and probably an English influence, to use contrastive stress with this and other possessive pronouns: *Ese es su libro.* More standard would be *Ese libro es de usted.*

sufrir. This is one of several major verbs in Spanish in which there is a tendency to suppress a prepositional connector, which in this case is customarily *de: Sufre de asma.* versus *Sufre asma.*

suponer. This verb is followed by the indicative in the sense of "to suppose = guess": *Supongo que lo tendremos listo a tiempo.* It is followed by the subjunctive in the sense of "to suppose = hypothesize": *Suponemos que dos y dos no sean cuatro.* When used in a direct or indirect command, "suppose that, let us suppose that," it is followed by the subjunctive.

suscribir. The generalized past participle is *suscrito,* although in Argentina it is *subscripto. Suscribir* is now preferred over *subscribir.*

T

tal. *Con tal de que* is followed by the subjunctive.

tal vez. Frequently, this form is encountered written as a single word, *talvez.* It is followed predominantly by the subjunctive, although the indicative may be found in a context asserting the factuality of the statement.

tanto. The reduced form *tan* is used as an adverb modifying adjectives, with the exception of adjectives like *mayor, peor, mejor,* where the unreduced form occurs. *En tanto que* is considered a French construction for the more preferred *en cuanto que,* with the sense of "with respect to."

temer. This verb is followed by the indicative when asserting a fact, with the English sense of "I am afraid = I suspect," but by the subjunctive when stating an emotional or psychological reaction to what is being asserted, equivalent to the English sense of "I fear = I am concerned." The indicative use predominates, and it is often accompanied by the emphatic *se: Me temo que vamos a tener que suspender la función.* Another feature of *temer* is that an indirect object *le* often remains invariable: *Le tememos todos a los fantasmas. Tener miedo de* is synonymous with *temer* and shares with it the same syntactic features, with the exception of the emphatic *se.*

temor. The preposition used to introduce a noun complement is either *de* or *a,* with the latter being preferred.

tenaza. This noun is both singular and plural as an equivalent to English "pincers."

tener. 1. *Tener que* is followed by an infinitive to express obligation and, in some dialects, a condition or probability. In truncated expressions the *que* may be retained as a dangling preposition: *¿Tienes que verlo? Sí, tengo que.* However, a more academic standard would not provide for this truncation, requiring the second verb to be echoed with the dummy *hacer: Sí, tengo que hacerlo.*

2. *Tener* + past participle is used in place of *haber* perfect constructions in order to underscore the perfective nature of the action: *He estudiado dos lecciones* versus *Tengo estudiadas dos lecciones.* Note that in the *tener* construction, the past participle agrees with the direct object, although constructions, considered substandard, are found in which agreement does not take place.

3. There is a growing present progressive use of *tener* in so-called idiomatic expression to indicate "beginning to": *Tengo hambre* ("I'm hungry") versus *Estoy teniendo hambre* ("I'm starting to get hungry").

4. *Tener a* is equivalent to an *estar* construction with reference to a second person implicated in the state: *Tengo a dos hijos en cama = Dos de mis hijos están en/guardan cama.*

tercero. This cardinal number has the same morphological pattern as *primero.*

terminal. Usage varies with respect to gender, although *la terminal* tends to be used to indicate a terminal in the sense of the completion point of a transportation system, while *el terminal* is used in the context of electrical and electronic instruments.

terminar. *Terminar de* indicates the cessation of an action; *terminar por* indicates the initiation of an action, in the sense of English "to end up doing something."

termostato. Both *termostato* and *termóstato* are acceptable variants.

testigo. The feminine is *la testigo.*

tiempo. *Es tiempo de que* is followed by the subjunctive. The *de* is often omitted.

tigre. There are four feminine forms: *el tigre hembra, la tigre, la tigra,* and *la tigresa.*

tijera. Both *tijera* and *tijeras* are used in the sense of English "scissors," although the plural predominates.

tilde. In the sense of a diacritical mark, this noun is both masculine and feminine.

tirar. *Tirar* + direct object means "to throw," while *tirar de* means to "pull (on/at)."

todo. 1. *Todo* plus a singular noun alternates with *todos los* and a plural noun in the sense of a whole class: *Todo ciudadano debe respetar las leyes = Todos los ciudadanos deben respetar las leyes.*

2. *Todo* when it appears with the feminine article *el* often appears as *todo* rather than the academically standard *toda.* Its use with following adjectives is frequently ambiguous. If modifying an adjective, it should be treated as an invariable degree adverb (*Estamos todo (= completamente) furiosos*), but as an agreeing adjective when it is a count word (*Estamos todos [= cada uno de nosotros] furiosos*).

transcribir. The generalized past participle is *transcrito;* however, in Argentina it is *transcripto.*

tratar. *Tratar de* means "to deal with something"; followed by a verb, it means "to try/attempt to." *Se trata de* is a common construction, with *se* serving as a dummy subject. The use of *se* with *tratar de* when an actual subject is present is syntactically incorrect: *Este es el libro que te dije. Trata [el libro] de Madrid. Tratar con* means "to have dealings with" and is not synonymous with *tratar de.*

triste. Used before a noun it means "unimportant"; used following a noun it means "sad."

tú. There is a colloquial, unspecified or empty use of second-person singular pronouns, roughly equivalent to English *you* in an impersonal sense: *En este lugar te tratan como la nada.* More formal would be *En este lugar lo tratan a uno como la nada.* Note that, in reality, the *ellos* form here is also an unspecified or empty referent.

U

u. The conjunction *o* appears as *u* before nouns beginning with *(h)o.* Used between numbers, it customarily carries a written accent in order for it not to be confused with the number 0: *3 ó 4 ejemplos.*

un. 1. Before immediately following feminine nouns beginning with stressed *(h)a,* the feminine article *un* is used. Followed by an incorrectly construed masculine adjective preceding a feminine noun beginning with *(h)a,* the masculine *un* will appear. Therefore, a construction like *un buen arma* would, in academically standard usage, be *una buena arma.*

2. The use of the indefinite article before unmodified predicate nominals provides a negative connotation: *Ella es una antipática.* The use of the article in imitation of the customary use of the indefinite article with predicate nominals in English is considered substandard.

único. Used before a noun, it means "only/sole"; used following a noun it means "unique."

uno. 1. This pronoun functions both as an unspecified or dummy subject pronoun, in which case it alternates with *se* or the third-person plural, and as a displaced first-person pronoun: *Uno tiene que cuidar sus intereses = Yo tengo que cuidar mis intereses.* In the former usage, a feminine subject would use *una,* although *uno* may also be used unvaryingly, giving rise to an internally contradictory utterance like *uno está encinta* instead of *una está encinta = Yo estoy encinta.*

2. A construction like *uno de los que* provides agreement vacillation, with the subsequent verb agreeing either with *uno* or with *los que.* In reality, agreement should be on the basis of which one of the two pronouns is being referred to or focused on by the verb.

usted. The abbreviation is written either as *Ud.* or *Vd.,* and the full form may or may not be capitalized: *usted* versus *Usted.* In some dialects, since the pronoun is formal and an honorific, it appears used more than actual syntax would call for—i.e., it receives a certain usage of emphasis, since, in reality, it would only need be used, like *tú,* in contexts where emphasis, contrast, or the need to avoid ambiguity were present. Although the object pronouns and the possessives match those of *él* or *ella*, depending on the gender of the referent, there does exist in some dialects of Latin America a possessive use of *vuestro* instead of *su* when *ustedes* is the plural of *tú*. This *vuestro* contrasts with the *vuestro* that accompanies the use in Latin America of *vosotros* as a hyperformal pronoun.

V

varices. Both *varices* and *várices* are found, although the former tends to prevail.

varios. Used before a noun, it means "various/several"; used following a noun it means "miscellaneous." Note that this form is used only in the plural.

venir. 1. The use of *venir* as a passive replacement for *ser* occurs in utterances that describe an action previous to the present point of reference: *Cuando la compramos, la casa ya venía pintada* = *La casa ya había sido pintada anteriormente.*
    2. *Venir de* is considered a French-inspired substitute for *acabar de.*
    3. *Venir* + present participle is used to describe an ongoing action originating in the past from the point of reference of the utterance and is often accompanied by temporal phrases that describe the past-present relationship: *Viene estudiando latín desde su juventud.*

ver. Often, the human direct objects, except for individuals identified by name, of this verb are not introduced by the so-called personal *a: Vi mucha gente en el partido, Vi a Juan.*

ves. The use of *ves,* in place of *ve* as a second-personal singular familiar imperative of *ir,* is considered substandard.

vez. *Una vez que* functions like *cuando,* in that the subjunctive is used with future reference, the indicative when the meaning is coordinate or iterative.

vía crucis. Despite the feminine head noun, this phrase is masculine in Spanish.

víctima. This noun is always feminine, regardless of the gender of the real-life referent. Often a masculine or feminine noun is introduced to allow for adjectives that match the real-life gender: *La víctima fue una mujer descuidada, La víctima fue un hombre honrado.*

viejo. Used before a noun, it means "former" or "long-standing"; used following a noun it means "elderly."

visible. Used with *ser*, this adjective means "visible" or "able to be perceived with the eyes"; used with *estar* it means "presentable" or "able to be seen for reasons of decency."

vislumbre. Although customarily feminine, this noun also can be found in the masculine.

vos. 1. *Vos* is the archaic singular of *vosotros*, used, however, as a formal or honorific form; verb agreement is in the plural, and the possessives are *vuestro*, etc. Adjectival agreement, however, is singular: *Vos estáis muy bienvenido a esta casa.*

2. *Vos* replaces *tú* in many Latin American dialects. In some dialects, it is considered a substandard form; in other dialects, it is considered a rural form. In Argentina, it is universally used in place of *tú*. Although the morphological forms of the verb vary considerably from one dialect to another, basically affected are the present indicative, the present subjunctive, and the imperative; all other forms are usually identical with those of *tú*. (Note that a form like *dijistes* may occur with either *tú* or with *vos*.) In Argentina, the forms are almost universally regular: the *vos* form is derived from the infinitive by retaining the final syllable stress with *s* in place of the infinitive *r*: *vos hablás, vos comés, vos vivís.* Many verbs that are irregular or stem-changing with *tú* are, therefore, regular: *vos tenés, vos decís.* The imperative is completely regular with one exception, being formed by dropping the infinitive *r* and retaining final syllable stress: *hablá, comé, viví, tené, decí.* The only exception is the verb *ir*, for which the stem of *andar* is used: *andá.* If the reflexive pronoun is used, the verb stem loses the written accent: *andate.* (Note that there exists a rural and colloquial *ite* that alternates with *andate.*) Finally, although the present subjunctive may be treated the same (*hablés, comás, vivás, tengás, digás*), standard usage tends to use the customary *tú* forms and to reserve these forms for emphatic negative imperatives: *¡No digás eso, vos!* (versus the less emphatic *No digas eso, vos*). Although many native speakers of Spanish consider the *vos* forms substandard, it should be stressed that in many dialects they are completely standard and the *tú* forms are considered affected.

voseo. The use of *vos* in place of *tú*. Note that *tuteo* means to use the familiar forms, whether *tú* or *vos*, in place of *usted*. Conversely, *ustear* means to use the *usted* forms.

vosotros. In Latin America, *vosotros* is only a hyperformal or affected form, the standard plural of *tú* (and *vos*) being *ustedes*.

votar. In general, *votar por* means "to cast a vote for someone"; however, *votar a* predominates in some dialects.

vuelta. *Dar vuelta la página* alternates with the more logical *dar vuelta a la página.* Although one would expect agreement in the first construction, *vuelta* tends to remain invariable in the plural: *Dar vuelta las páginas.* It is also used with masculine nouns: *Dar vuelta los papeles.*

vuestro. Concerning the familiar and hyperformal use of this possessive in Latin America, see *usted.*

Y

y. The conjunction *y* appears as *e* before immediately following items beginning with *(h)i* (but not *hie*).

ya. *Desde ya* is considered a Latin American variant of *desde ahora; ya mismo* or *ahora mismo.*

yeísmo. The phenomenon whereby the graphemes *y* + vowel and *ll* are pronounced identically. The term is also used to refer to the semiconsonantal pronunciation typical of the Río de la Plata region, although *rehilamiento* is the more specific term. Note that, in the latter case, spellings like *hierba, hierro* are articulated with an initial semivowel or even a full vowel, while spellings like *yerba* and *yerro* are articulated with an initial semiconsonant. In non-*rehilamiento* dialects these pairs are articulated identically, either with a semiconsonant (Mexico) or with a semivowel (the Caribbean and the Andean areas).

yerno. The feminine of this noun is *nuera*, although *yerna* may be found in some dialects.

yídish. *Yídish* exists alongside *idish, yiddish,* and a number of other variants to indicate the language and culture of European Jews. The adjectival form may appear as *ídishe*, etc., especially in Yiddish phrases, *aine ídishe mame* = *una mamá judía.* The initial *yi* is pronounced always as the vowel *i.*

yo. In some usages, considered substandard and rural, *yo* may appear with prepositions that, in academic usage, take objective forms: *a yo, con yo.* The plural of *yo* as a noun is either *yos* or *yoes.*

BIBLIOGRAPHY OF SPECIAL TERMINOLOGY

For specific terminology, see the following bilingual dictionaries:

BUSINESS TERMINOLOGY

Blanes Prieto, Joaquín. *Diccionario de términos contables, inglés-español y español-inglés. Dictionary of Accounting Terms, English-Spanish and Spanish-English.* Mexico City: Compañía Editorial Continental, 1972.

Caballero, Alfredo A. *The English-Spanish Real Estate Dictionary. Diccionario español-inglés de bienes raíces.* Lanham, Del.: University Press of America, 1986.

Donaghy, P. J., comp. *Diccionario de términos usados en informes financieros: español-inglés, inglés-español. Dictionary of the Language of Financial Reports: Spanish-English, English-Spanish.* Bilbao, Spain: Deusto, 1983.

Elsevier's Dictionary of Financial and Economic Terms: Spanish-English and English-Spanish. Comp. Martha Uriona and José Daniel Kwacz. Amsterdam: Elsevier, 1996.

Fernández Collado, José Antonio. *Diccionario inglés-español, español-inglés de términos administrativos.* Mexico City: Trillas, 1980.

Garza Bores, Jaime. *Diccionario técnico de terminología comercial contable y bancaria: español-inglés, inglés-español.* Mexico City: Diana, 1964.

Goldstone, Howard. *Real Estate: A Bilingual Dictionary, Spanish-English and English-Spanish. Bienes raíces: un diccionario bilingüe, español-inglés e inglés-español.* Jefferson, N.C.: McFarland, 1986.

Kaplan, Steven M. *Wiley's English-Spanish, Spanish-English Business Dictionary.* New York: Wiley, 1996.

Lozano Irueste, José María. *Nuevo diccionario bilingüe de economía y empresa: inglés-español, español-inglés.* Madrid: Pirámide, 1993.

Routledge Spanish Dictionary of Business, Commerce and Finance. Diccionario inglés de negocios, comercio y finanzas. London: Routledge, 1998.

Salles Bergés y Chapital, Marcelo. *Diccionario del negocio inmobiliario: Guía español-inglés/inglés-español de términos de mayor uso en Norte, Centro y Sudamérica.* Chicago: Real Estate Education, 1997.

Urrutia Raola, Manuel. *Dictionary of Business: English-Spanish, Spanish-English: Accounting, Management, Finance, Economics and Marketing. Diccionario de negocios: inglés-español, español-inglés: contabilidad, administración, finanzas, economía y mercadotecnia.* Mexico City: Limusa, 1995.

LAW TERMINOLOGY

Cabanellas, Guillermo. *Butterworths Spanish/English Legal Dictionary. Diccionario jurídico español/inglés Butterworths.* 2 vols. Austin: Butterworth Legal Publishers, 1991.

Dahl, Henry S. *Dahl's Law Dictionary: Spanish to English / English to Spanish: An Annotated Legal Dictionary, Including Authoritative Definitions from Codes, Case Law, Statutes, and Legal Writing. Diccionario jurídico Dahl.* Buffalo: W. S. Hein, 1996.

Kaplan, Steven M. *Wiley's English-Spanish, Spanish-English Legal Dictionary. Diccionario jurídico inglés-español, español-inglés Wiley.* 2nd ed. New York: J. Wiley & Sons, 1997.

Vanson, George N. *Spanish-English Legal Terminology. Terminología español-inglés en el área legal.* Cincinnati: South-Western, 1982.

MEDICAL TERMINOLOGY

English and Spanish Medical Words and Phrases. Springhouse, Pa.: Springhouse, 1994.

Kelz, Rochelle K. *Delmar's English/Spanish Pocket Dictionary for Health Professionals.* Albany: Delmar, 1997.

McElroy, Onyria H. *Spanish-English, English-Spanish Medical Dictionary. Diccionario médico español-inglés, inglés-español.* 2nd ed. Boston: Little, Brown, 1996.

Pérez-Sabido, Jesús. *Spanish-English Handbook for Medical Professionals. Compendio en inglés y español para profesionales de la medicina.* 3rd ed. Oradel, N.J.: Medical Economics Books, 1989.

Rogers, Glenn T. *English-Spanish, Spanish-English Medical Dictionary.*

Diccionario médico inglés-español, español-inglés. 2nd ed. New York: McGraw-Hill, 1997.

Ruiz Torres, Francisco. *Diccionario de términos médicos: inglés-español.* Houston: Gulf, 1995.

SCIENCE AND TECHNOLOGY TERMINOLOGY

Beigbeder Atienza, Federico. *Diccionario técnico: inglés-español, español-inglés. Technical Dictionary: English-Spanish, Spanish-English.* Madrid: Díaz de Santos, 1996.

Castilla's Spanish and English Technical Dictionary. 2 vols. New York: Philosophical Library, 1958.

Collazo, Javier L. *Encyclopedic Dictionary of Technical Terms, English-Spanish, Spanish-English.* New York: McGraw-Hill, 1980.

Diccionario de química y de productos químicos, español-inglés, inglés-español. Rev. ed. by Gessner G. Hawley. Barcelona: Omega, 1975.

Draper, Grenville. *Diccionario de términos geológicos inglés/español–español/inglés. English/Spanish–Spanish/English Dictionary of Geological Terms.* Miami: Latin American and Caribbean Center, Florida International University, 1987.

García Rodríguez, Mariano. *Diccionario matemático: español-inglés, inglés-español. Mathematics Dictionary: Spanish-English, English-Spanish.* New York: Hobbs, Dorman, 1965.

Hardeo Sahai, José. *A Dictionary of Statistical, Scientific, and Technical Terms = Un diccionario de términos estadísticos, científicos y técnicos: English-Spanish, Spanish-English.* Belmont: Wadsworth, 1981.

Hartmann-Petersen, P. *Diccionario de las ciencias: Español-inglés, inglés-español.* Tr. Ana M. Rubio. Madrid: Paraninfo, 1991.

BIBLIOGRAPHICAL
REFERENCES

ABC. *Libro de estilo de ABC.* Barcelona: Ariel, 1993.

Agencia EFE. *Manual de español urgente.* Madrid: Cátedra, 1995.

———. *Vademécum de español urgente I y II.* Madrid: Fundación EFE, 1995, 1996.

Austin, J. L. *Cómo hacer cosas con palabras.* Tr. Genaro R. Carrió y Eduardo A. Rabossi. Barcelona: Paidós, 1988.

Butt, John, and Carmen Benjamin. *A New Reference Grammar of Modern Spanish.* 2nd ed. London: E. Arnold, 1994.

Casares, Julio. *Diccionario ideológico de la lengua española.* Barcelona: Gustavo Gili, 1994.

Clave (Diccionario de uso del español actual). Madrid: S. M., 1997.

Diccionario de abreviaturas y manual de uso. Sevilla: Canal Sur Televisión, 1997.

Diccionario de voces de uso actual. Madrid: Arco Libros, 1994.

Ducrot, Oswald, and Tzvetan Todorov. *Diccionario enciclopédico de las ciencias del lenguaje.* Tr. Enrique Pezzoni. Mexico City: Siglo XXI, 1974.

Fernández, David. *Diccionario de dudas e irregularidades de la lengua española.* Barcelona: Teide, 1991.

Fuchs, Catherine, and Pierre Le Goffic. *Introducción a la problemática de las corrientes lingüísticas contemporáneas.* Tr. Elvira Arnoux. Buenos Aires: Hachette, 1979.

Gómez de Silva, Guido. *Breve diccionario etimológico de la lengua española.* México: Fondo de Cultura Económica, 1995.

Labov, William. *Modelos sociolingüísticos.* Tr. José Miguel Marinas Herreras. Madrid: Cátedra, 1983.

Lavandera, Beatriz R. *Variación y significado.* Buenos Aires: Hachette, 1984.

Lázaro Carreter, Fernando. *El dardo en la palabra*. Madrid: Círculo de Lectores, 1997.

Lucas, Carmen de. *Diccionario de dudas*. Madrid: Edaf, 1994.

Lyons, John. *Lenguaje, significado y contexto*. Tr. Santiago Alcoba. Barcelona: Paidós, 1983.

Manual de estilo. Buenos Aires: Clarín/Aguilar, 1997.

Marcos Marín, Francisco. *Lingüística y lengua española: Introducción, historia y métodos*. Madrid: Cincel, 1975.

Martínez de Sousa, José. *Diccionario de usos y dudas del español actual*. Barcelona: VOX Bibliograf, 1996.

Matthews, P. H. *Gramática generativa y competencia lingüística*. Tr. Enrique Bernardez. Madrid: Espasa-Calpe, 1983.

Moliner, María. *Diccionario de uso del español*. Madrid: Gredos, 1977.

Mounin, Georges, dir. *Diccionario de lingüística*. Tr. Ricardo Pochtar. Barcelona: Labor, 1982.

El Mundo. *Libro de estilo*. Madrid: Temas de Hoy, 1996.

La Nación. *Manual de estilo y ética periodística*. Buenos Aires: Espasa, 1997.

Orr, Leonard. *Semiotic and Structuralist Analyses of Fiction: An Introduction and a Survey of Applications*. Troy, N.Y.: Whitston, 1987.

El País. *Libro de estilo*. Madrid: El País, 1996. 1st ed. 1977.

Pavis, Patrice. *Diccionario del teatro: Dramaturgia, estética, semiología*. Tr. Fernando de Toro. Barcelona: Paidós, 1983.

Ramsey, Marathon Montrose. *Textbook of Modern Spanish, as Now Written and Spoken in Castile and the Spanish American Republics*. Rev. by Robert K. Spaulding. New York: Holt, 1956.

Real Academia Española. *Diccionario de la lengua española*. 21st ed. Madrid: Espasa-Calpe, 1992.

———. *Esbozo de una nueva gramática de la lengua española*. Madrid: Espasa-Calpe, 1978.

Redfern, James. *A Glossary of Spanish Literary Composition*. New York: Harcourt Brace Jovanovich, 1973.

Searle, John. *Actos de habla: ensayo de filosofía del lenguaje*. Tr. Luis M. Valdés Villanueva. Madrid: Cátedra, 1990.

Seco, Manuel. *Diccionario de dudas y dificultades de la lengua española*. Madrid: Espasa-Calpe, 1986.

Stubbs, Michael. *Análisis del discurso: análisis sociolingüístico del lenguaje natural*. Tr. Celina González. Madrid: Alianza, 1987.

La Vanguardia. *Libro de redacción*. Barcelona: La Vanguardia, 1986.

Zorrilla, Alicia. *Diccionario de los usos correctos del español*. Buenos Aires: Estrada, 1997.

INDEX

Index does not include entries for individual items listed in the appendices and in alphabetical lists within the chapters.